STANDARD BASIC PROGRAMMING WITH QUICKBASIC

Avery Catlin

University of Virginia, Charlottesville

PRENTICE HALL, Englewood Cliffs, New Jersey, 07632

Library of Congress Cataloging-in-Publication Data

```
Catlin, Avery.
   Standard BASIC programming with QuickBASIC / Avery Catlin.
      p.   cm.
   Includes bibliographical references.
   ISBN 0-13-840828-9
   1. BASIC (Computer program language)  2. Microsoft QuickBASIC
(Computer program)   I. Title.
QA76.73.B3C379  1991
005.265--dc20                                      90-6994
                                                      CIP
```

Editorial/production supervision and
   interior design: *Kathleen Schiaparelli*
Cover design: *Ben Santora*
Cover photographer: *Reginald Wickham*
Manufacturing buyer: *Lori Bulwin*

©1991 by Prentice-Hall, Inc.
A Division of Simon & Schuster
Engelwood Cliffs, New Jersey 07632

Printed in the United States of America

10 9 8 7 6 5 4 3

ISBN 0-13-840828-9

Prentice-Hall International (UK) Limited, *London*
Prentice-Hall of Australia Pty. Limited, *Sydney*
Prentice-Hall Canada Inc., *Toronto*
Prentice-Hall Hispanoamericana, S.A., *Mexico*
Prentice-Hall of India Private Limited, *New Delhi*
Prentice-Hall of Japan, Inc., *Tokyo*
Simon & Schuster Asia Pte. Ltd., *Singapore*
Editora Prentice-Hall do Brasil, Ltda., *Rio de Janeiro*

CONTENTS

PREFACE

Standard BASIC Programming is designed to teach students how to write programs in QuickBASIC, one of the latest commercial versions of BASIC that follows the guidelines of American National Standard BASIC (ANS BASIC). Since its conception at Dartmouth College in the early 1960s, BASIC has become one of the most widely used computer languages. Unfortunately, many different versions of BASIC have been developed and they vary considerably in syntax and capabilities.

WHY STANDARD BASIC?

One of the first versions of BASIC written for the IBM Personal Computer and compatible computers was produced by Microsoft Corporation, the developers of QuickBASIC. This early version of BASIC (often called BASICA or GWBASIC) is still included in the software distributed with every IBM Personal Computer or compatible. QuickBASIC can execute most programs written in BASICA or GWBASIC.

At the same time, QuickBASIC includes much of the structured programming syntax of ANS BASIC. We use this syntax extensively in our example programs and avoid the unstructured syntax of earlier versions of BASIC.

ANS BASIC is a comprehensive language that is well suited for writing practical programs, but at the same time retains much of the simplicity and ease of use of the original BASIC language. Following adoption of the standard, most computer language developers have started to modify their own versions of BASIC to conform (at least in part) to the standard and the differences between the many versions of BASIC are gradually beginning to disappear. Thus it seems particularly appropriate to use the syntax of ANS BASIC to teach introductory programming.

There are two current versions of QuickBASIC, both of which are covered in this book. QuickBASIC 4.5 was the latest full version of the language as the book went to press. It can compile programs to memory where they can be executed immediately or it can compile programs into separate executable files. It is a complete language system and well-suited for developing large programs

QuickBASIC Interpreter is designed as an inexpensive teaching language that supports most of the statements available in QuickBASIC 4.5. It is an interpreter, as the name implies, and thus cannot compile programs into executable files. It does, however, execute BASIC programs very quickly. Differences between the two versions of QuickBASIC are noted throughout the text.

THE IMPORTANCE OF LEARNING TO WRITE PROGRAMS

This is not a book on computer literacy, but rather a book on programming. While it covers many aspects of QuickBASIC syntax, it is not meant to take the place of the QuickBASIC Language Reference manual and the on-line help system. It teaches students how to write practical programs in a modern version of standard BASIC.

Even though the subject matter is programming, most of the students who use this book will not become professional programmers. Almost all of them will, however, use personal computers in their business or professional lives. They will run application programs much of the time, but will occasionally have a need to write small programs, probably in BASIC. Thus while designed primarily to teach programming, the book is also designed to give students a better understanding of the capabilities of modern computers.

SPECIAL FEATURES OF THE BOOK

The material is suitable for a one-semester or two-quarter course in a college or school curriculum. By omitting several chapters (for example, the last two or three chapters), the book could be used in a one-quarter course. Students are expected to have completed high school algebra. While the book is written for students in all disciplines, its advanced examples are drawn mostly from the business world and are based on the everyday use of computers in business. Several areas have been given special emphasis:

• Many example programs to show how BASIC statements are used.

- An early introduction to text files because most information used by practical computer programs is read from files.
- An early introduction in Part II to modular program development through the use of independent procedure units: functions and subroutines.
- The importance of good program style, or how to write programs that are easy to read and understand and thus easy to maintain.
- Continued emphasis on program design and program testing, the latter process being often completely neglected by students.
- An early explanation of program debugging techniques.
- Examples of techniques for storing and retrieving information using data files and databases, probably the most important commercial use of computers.

A textbook is written to teach, to explain those small but difficult points that may not be understood by a student even after attending lectures. Every effort has been made to write clear and complete explanations. After years of experience teaching college students, the author has found certain ideas that students have difficulty understanding. These ideas are explained in detail here. Some points requiring special attention are the following:

- The difference between a variable name and a variable value.
- How variables store information.
- The difference between a number and a string of digits.
- The use of indexed variables, especially for students with limited mathematical experience.
- The concept of program files and data files, how they are similar, and how they differ.
- What happens when a disk file is over-written or erased.
- The concept of local variables and their scope.
- The different methods for passing information to procedures.

Programming cannot be learned just by reading. The book assumes that each student will have access to an IBM PC-compatible personal computer and will write programs. Material is presented in such a way that students can start writing programs during their first week of class. A summary of important points, a list of common errors, a dozen or so self-test questions, and several programming problems are included at the end of each chapter.

Test data for the programming problems, as well as all example programs in the book, are available on a floppy disk for IBM PC-compatible computers. This disk is packaged with each copy of the book sent to an instructor and may be freely copied by any student using this book in a course. You can also obtain a copy of the disk directly from the publisher. Information on how to use the disk is contained in a text file named README (stored on the disk) and in Appendix H of the book.

ACKNOWLEDGMENTS

This is the first book I have written where I have been responsible for all details of text formatting and for production of the final, camera-ready copy. Having done it once, I am convinced it is the best way to produce a technical textbook. The process would not have been successful, however, without the advice and support of a dedicated production editor, Kathleen Schiaparelli. My thanks to her and to my primary editor at Prentice-Hall, Marcia J. Horton. I should also add that Microsoft Word on the Macintosh made the task of formatting and preparing the final copy relatively easy.

Knowledgeable and critical reviewers are an important asset when writing a new textbook. I was fortunate to have the help of three experienced teachers who helped me turn the first draft into a much better book. My thanks to the following reviewers:

Keith B. Olson, Montana College of Mineral Science and Technology

Leonard Presby, William Patterson State College

Anthony Tiona, Broward Community College

Writing a book in one's spare time means that not enough time is left for other things. My special thanks to my wife Edie for her support and understanding during the many hours I spent in front of a computer screen and keyboard.

1

GETTING STARTED

1.1 INTRODUCTION

Before starting to write computer programs, you must decide which language to use. We explain why QuickBASIC is a good choice. When we use the term QuickBASIC, we mean either the regular QuickBASIC compiler (version 4.5 or later) or the QuickBASIC Interpreter, both developed and distributed by the Microsoft Corporation.

You must learn how to operate your computer, which we assume is an IBM Personal Computer or PC-compatible. We discuss the computer disk operating system (DOS) and the QuickBASIC environment. We also discuss how you can use this book during the learning process.

1.2 WHY LEARN BASIC?

Most people who use personal computers are not professional programmers. They use a computer as a tool to help them accomplish a particular task. They need to learn to program in order to become more familiar with the computer and to write small programs for specific tasks. Their computer language requirements are different from those of the professional programmer. QuickBASIC is an ideal language for their use, being both easy to learn and powerful enough to handle difficult jobs.

Many professional programmers and computer scientists will tell you that BASIC is not a suitable language for writing large programs. They may be correct if they refer to one of the early, limited versions of the BASIC language. But QuickBASIC, the language we will be using, is an advanced version of BASIC that combines the ease of use of simple BASIC with the structure and power of more sophisticated languages.

Here are some of the advantages of almost every version of BASIC.

- It is easy to learn.
- It is easy to use.
- It has a simple syntax.
- Its programs are easy to modify.

For these and other reasons, BASIC has become the most popular programming language for personal computers. Today more people write programs in BASIC than in any other computer language.

A simple version of BASIC has some serious disadvantages.

- It produces slow programs.
- It lacks good control statements.
- It lacks a named subprogram capability.

QuickBASIC completely eliminates these disadvantages, making it a suitable language for both casual programmers and developers of large programs.

1.3 FIRST STEPS

In this book we show you how to write programs in the QuickBASIC language. Almost all of our example programs run in both the QuickBASIC 4.5 compiler system and the QuickBASIC Interpreter system. Where this is not the case, we are careful to explain the reason. Differences between the two systems (usually features not included in the QuickBASIC Interpreter) are discussed in "QBI Notes."

Whenever we want to give an example that we know will work on a specific computer, we will use the IBM Personal Computer as our model. This designation includes not only the original models, such as the IBM/PC, IBM/XT, and IBM/AT, but also the more recent line of IBM PS/2 computers.

IBM PC-Compatibles

There are a large number of personal computers on the market that are compatible with the IBM personal computer to varying degrees. The QuickBASIC system, and thus our example programs, run equally well on almost all these machines. We used a variety of computers to write and run the example programs in this book, including an IBM PC/AT, a Compaq Portable III, an AT&T PC 6300, and a Compaq Desktop 386. **We use the term *IBM PC-compatible* to designate the entire class of IBM personal computers and compatibles.**

We concentrate on teaching programming, not on covering every detail of the language. You should supplement this textbook with the QuickBASIC Language Reference manual, published by the Microsoft Corporation, and the QuickBASIC on-line help system. The language reference manual is the final authority on correct syntax of Quick-BASIC statements and commands.

> **QBI Note:** A language manual is not normally supplied with the interpreter but it does have an excellent on-line help system. A separate language reference manual can be ordered from Microsoft, and should be available for reference use by students learning and using the QuickBASIC language.

The language reference manual is not designed to teach you how to program in BASIC; that is the objective of this book. The manual should be kept up to date because most computer languages are constantly changing and new versions are issued every year or so. You should refer to the manual or the on-line help system for detailed information that is not covered in this book, especially information on advanced or specialized uses of QuickBASIC.

We assume that you have access to a personal computer that supports the Quick-BASIC language. Computer programming can be learned only by doing, not just by reading. As you read the text, type in the example programs on your computer or load them from the example program disk. If you want an IBM PC-compatible floppy disk containing all the example programs and test data for the practice programs, contact the publisher (Prentice-Hall) or the store where you purchased this book. If you are using this textbook in a class, your instructor should already have a copy of the example program disk and you can make a copy for your own use.

Turning On Your Computer

You must learn how to turn on your computer, insert a floppy disk (if necessary), and start the QuickBASIC system. If your computer has a fixed disk (also often called a hard disk), the QuickBASIC system is probably stored on that disk. If your computer is connected to a network, you may not need to use either a floppy disk or your own fixed disk, but you will have to learn how to access the network and enter your account number and password. One of the most frustrating initial steps in learning to write computer programs is learning to use your particular computer system.

Before starting to use your personal computer, read carefully the operating instructions prepared by the computer manufacturer or by your institution. These instructions should tell you all that you need to know to get started. If you have problems, ask your instructor or another student for help. In many institutions, there are other users of the same type of computer equipment, and they will probably be glad to help you get started. Only after you become familiar with your computer equipment will you be able to concentrate on learning to write BASIC programs.

1.4 COMPUTER TERMINOLOGY

Computers, and their attached peripheral devices, are called *hardware*. Computer hardware can perform useful functions only when it is given explicit instructions by a computer program, called *software*. In this book, we learn how to design and write computer programs.

A group of hardware and software definitions are presented in the remainder of this section. We recommend that you read the definitions now, but do not try to memorize all the new terms. They should quickly become familiar with use. From time to time, you can refer back to this section for a needed definition.

Hardware Definitions

We use the term *computer system* to denote a computer and its associated peripheral equipment, as well as the programs required to make the computer operate. We start by defining some of the hardware items in a typical computer system, as shown in Fig. 1.1.

Computer. This term refers to the central processing unit (CPU) which performs actions based on software instructions and its associated electronics. The term is often used, however, to refer to the complete computer system. Most IBM PC-compatible computers use the Intel 8088, 8086, 80286, or 80386 CPU. As this book goes to press, the new and more powerful 80486 CPU is already appearing in a few advanced computers.

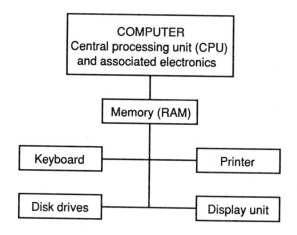

Figure 1.1   Diagram of a computer system.

Numeric coprocessor. This is an electronic device that performs arithmetic operations (multiplication, division, and so forth) in hardware rather than in software. Programs with many complicated arithmetic operations run much faster when a numeric coprocessor is present. The 8087, 80287, and 80387 are numeric coprocessors used with the 8088 (or 8086), 80286, and 80386 CPUs.

Memory. Memory consists of an array of electronic devices or chips, within the computer, where information is stored in electronic form. **You must remember that when you turn off your computer system, all information stored in memory is lost.** Memory is sometimes called RAM, short for "random-access memory."

Bit. The smallest unit of memory is a bit, which can store only one of two values, usually denoted by 0 and 1.

Byte. The byte, a common unit for specifying memory size, consists of 8 bits.

Memory location. This is the address of a place in memory where a particular item of information is stored.

Keyboard. The keyboard is a typewriterlike device with keys that you press to enter characters into a computer system. When you press most keys, a character also appears on the display unit screen.

Display unit. This unit is the televisionlike device with a screen on which characters are displayed. These characters may be sent to the screen from the keyboard or from the computer.

The current position on the screen is indicated by a bright underline character, often blinking, called a *cursor*. The cursor shows where the next typed character will appear. When editing a program, the cursor can be moved to different positions on the screen by using the four arrow keys.

Mouse. This is a small device, about the size of your hand, that can be rolled across a desk top to move an arrow or similar pointing character on the screen. A mouse has one to three buttons (usually two buttons) on its top that can be pressed to perform different functions in different programs. This device is a useful supplement to the keyboard.

Disk drive. This is a device, similar in operation to a phonograph record player, which records information on magnetic disks. The information is recorded and stored in a relatively permanent form, and any part may be quickly retrieved. Information stored on a disk is not lost when you turn off your computer system. If a disk is physically damaged, however, its stored information may be destroyed.

There are two general categories of disk drives, one for hard or *fixed* disks and one for *floppy* disks. Fixed disks are usually not removable from the drive (there is at least one well-known exception) and have large storage capacities. A typical fixed disk may store tens or hundreds of megabytes of data. Floppy disks are removable, are available in different sizes and capacities, and store a few hundred kilobytes to over a megabyte of data.

Memory is much faster than a disk (about 100 times faster), which means that it takes longer to write information on a disk than into memory, and reading from a disk is also slower. A fixed disk is about 10 times faster than a floppy disk.

Printer. This is a device connected to your computer, directly or through a computer network, that prints characters on paper as they are received from the computer. *Dot matrix* printers create characters from small printed dots, using tiny pin hammers and an inked ribbon. They are inexpensive, produce medium-quality characters, and print about one page a minute. *Laser* printers produce high-quality characters using a technology similar to that used in office copiers. They are expensive and print 5 to 10 pages per minute.

The preceding items are the customary units that make up the hardware of a computer system. Other peripheral devices, such as plotters or magnetic tape drives, may be added to meet special needs.

Software Definitions

Software is an important part of any computer system. We now define several software terms.

Program. A program consists of a sequence of instructions to the computer, telling it how to accomplish a specific task. For example, the task might be to sort a list of names and print out the sorted list on a printer. The individual instructions are called program statements. As an example, one program statement might be used to print a single name. The program itself may be stored in memory or in a file (see next definition) on a computer disk.

File. A file is a collection of characters or other information, usually stored on a computer disk. Each file is identified by name and a directory of all files is maintained on the disk. A file may contain any collection of characters, such as a computer program or a letter to a friend, and it is then called a *text file*. The contents of text files can be displayed on the screen.

On the other hand, a file may contain noncharacter information and it is then called a *binary file*. Binary files cannot be displayed on the screen. Random-access files in QuickBASIC are binary files.

QuickBASIC programs can be stored either as text files or as binary files. A text file has the advantage of being readable by any text editor. A binary file (also called QuickBASIC format) has the advantage of loading more quickly.

QBI Note: The interpreter can store files in the text format only.

Operating system. This is a special program that controls the operation of the computer. A major task of the operating system is to maintain the disk organization and supervise the reading and writing of disk files.

The most common operating system for personal computers is MS-DOS (or PC-DOS; they are essentially the same), but a new operating system named OS/2 has recently been released for IBM computers and may supplement or replace MS-DOS in the future. We use the name DOS for any version of MS-DOS or PC-DOS.

Program statements. Statements are instructions in a computer program that cause the computer to carry out a particular action. For example, the statement

```
PRINT "Hello!"
```

tells the computer to display the phrase "Hello!" (without the quotation marks) on the display unit screen. The phrase is not displayed until the statement is executed.

Compilation. This is the process of translating a computer program from its original or *source program* form into binary machine language instructions, creating an *object* *program* that is understood by the computer. QuickBASIC is different from most compilers because it compiles each line of program statements as the line is entered into the computer, rather than compiling the entire program after it has been written. This process is called *incremental compilation.*

> **QBI Note:** The interpreter does not compile or translate the entire program, but rather interprets (translates) and executes each statement every time the program is run.

Execution. Execution is the process of carrying out the machine language instructions contained in the object program. The computer carries out specific actions in compliance with program statements. The process is also called *running the program.*

Commands. Direct instructions given by the user to the computer are called commands. While a statement is an instruction that is part of a computer program, a command is an instruction that is given directly to the computer (or more accurately, to a software system such as the disk operating system or the QuickBASIC language system) by the user. For example, the QuickBASIC command Start from the Run menu tells the computer to execute the current computer program in memory.

1.5 HOW TO USE YOUR COMPUTER

In this section we tell you how to turn on your computer, start using the QuickBASIC system, and turn the computer off when you are finished. If possible, ask someone to help you the first time. Read your computer manuals and instruction books for more information. We promise you that the second time you use the computer is much easier than the first time.

We assume that you have an IBM PC-compatible computer with at least one floppy disk drive and no fixed disk. It uses the DOS operating system, version 2.0 or later. If you have two drives, you should first put a disk in the drive called drive A. On an IBM PC, this is the left drive. On an AT&T PC 6300, it is the bottom drive. On the IBM PC/AT, it is the top drive. As you can see, there is no universal agreement in the computer industry as to which floppy disk drive is drive A and which is drive B. Fortunately, there is general agreement that a fixed disk, if present, is designated drive C. You should consult your computer manual if the drives are not labeled.

Insert a disk containing both the operating system and the QuickBASIC system in drive A, close the drive door, and turn on the computer. After the computer does some checking, it may ask you for the date, which you must enter in the mm-dd-yy format. It will then ask you for the time, and you enter it in the hh:mm format. **Note that a colon is required to separate hours and minutes.** Some IBM PC-compatible computers have a built-in clock that automatically sets the date and time.

This process loads the operating system into memory, often called *booting* the computer (from the old expression "to lift oneself by one's own bootstraps"). The computer next displays the prompt A>, which indicates that drive A is the selected drive and that it is waiting for instructions. Type QB (in either uppercase or lowercase characters) and press the Enter key (often marked ↵ or Enter or Return).

QBI Note: Type QBI in response to the A> prompt to start the QuickBASIC Interpreter.

The QuickBASIC system will be loaded, and when it is ready, it displays the screen shown in Fig. 1.2. An information window may also appear and should be deleted by pressing the Esc key. This key is probably located in the upper left corner of your keyboard. You may now create a new file (see the New or New Program command in Section 1.7) and type in a BASIC computer program.

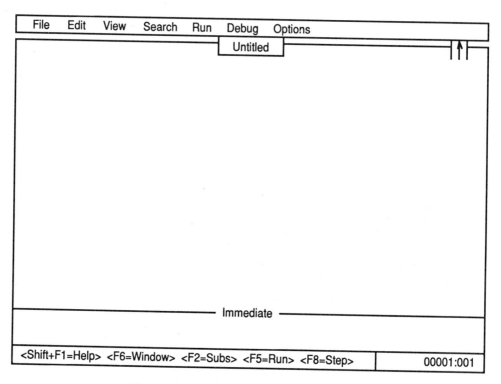

Figure 1.2   Main menu screen of QuickBASIC.

The initial screen display contains the main menu on the top line and two windows just below. The upper and larger window is called the View window. Programs are written and edited within this window. When you start QuickBASIC, the View window is the active window and contains the cursor. The lower and smaller window is called the Immediate window. This window allows the immediate execution of single program lines. We discuss its use in a later chapter.

When you are finished writing programs, you can leave the QuickBASIC system by pressing the Alt key (probably in the lower left corner of your keyboard) and then press ing the letter F key to display a menu called the File menu. Press the letter X key to invoke the Exit command. You will see the A> prompt again, and if you are through using the computer, remove your disk from the disk drive and turn off the machine.

If these instructions seem a little confusing at this point, you should not be concerned. In the next two sections we discuss the DOS operating system and the Quick-BASIC environment in more detail. We include brief instructions now because we think it is important to tell a student at the very beginning of a computer programming course how to enter the language system, and even more important, how to exit that system.

It is very possible that your computer facility has a computer network or uses computers with fixed disks. If so, our specific instructions will not apply. Be sure to ask about local instructions on how to start and operate your computers.

1.6 THE DISK OPERATING SYSTEM

As mentioned in our earlier definition, one of the main tasks of an operating system is to keep track of files stored on the computer's disks. Disk drives in the DOS system are designated by letters. On most computers, drives A and B are floppy disk drives, while drive C is a fixed disk drive.

Each disk, either floppy or fixed, contains at least one file directory. This directory, called the *root directory*, is denoted by the backslash character (\). Additional directories can be created, all under the root directory, so that different kinds of files can be stored in different directories. Fig. 1.3 shows the directory structure of a disk with multiple directories. Most floppy disks have only a root directory, while fixed disks usually have multiple directories.

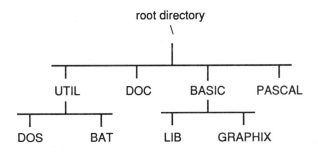

Figure 1.3   Structure of file directories on a disk.

File Names

Each file itself is identified by a *file name*. This name can be up to eight characters long and may be followed by an optional period and three-character extension. File name and extension characters can be either letters or digits. Some other characters are allowed (see the DOS reference manual), but you will be safe if you use only letters and digits. **Note carefully that a blank space is not a valid file name character.**

The extension usually describes the type of file: BAS for a QuickBASIC program file, QLB for a QuickBASIC library file, EXE or COM for an executable binary or command file, TXT for a text file, and so forth. These choices of extension names are recommended but not mandatory.

Path Names

The complete identifier for a file, called its *path name*, consists of the disk drive letter, the various directory names (separated by backslash characters), the file name, and an optional extension. There can be no blank spaces anywhere in a path name. Fig. 1.4 contains some example names.

A:\MYFILE.BAS	QuickBASIC program MYFILE.BAS in the root directory of the disk in drive A
A:MYFILE.BAS	Same as above; the backslash is not required here but recommended
C:\WEEK05\TEST.BAS	BASIC program TEST.BAS in directory WEEK05 of disk C, probably a fixed disk
C:\BIN\DOS\TYP.COM	Executable file TYP.COM in directory DOS under directory BIN of disk C
B:\QBOOK\TOC	Unspecified file TOC in directory QBOOK of the disk in drive B

Figure 1.4   Some DOS file names.

1.7 THE QUICKBASIC ENVIRONMENT

QuickBASIC is a language system that provides its own environment under DOS for writing computer programs. The relationship between operating system and language systems is shown in Fig. 1.5.

As discussed earlier, the main menu screen of QuickBASIC is shown in Figure 1.2. The main menu is a line of command menu names, positioned across the top of the screen. This menu system provides a convenient and easy-to-use format for executing QuickBASIC commands. The main menu can be selected at any time by pressing the Alt key. Fig. 1.6 summarizes the QuickBASIC commands used most often by a beginning programmer.

A command is executed by first displaying the menu containing that command and then selecting the command. The File command menu is displayed by first pressing the Alt key and then typing F (for File). Alternatively, after pressing the Alt key, use the left and right arrow keys to highlight the command menu name File and press the Enter key.

The File command menu is displayed with a vertical list of additional commands. One of the commands in the File menu can be selected by either pressing the key for the highlighted letter in the command name, or by using the up and down arrow keys to highlight the desired command and then pressing the Enter key.

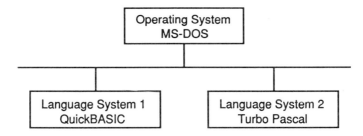

Figure 1.5   Relation between operating and language systems.

We now discuss three of the File menu commands, primarily to give you an idea of how QuickBASIC commands are implemented. Other commands will be introduced in Chapter 2 and succeeding chapters, as we learn how to write programs.

MENU	COMMANDS
File	New or New Program
	Open or Open Program
	Save As
	Print
	Exit
Run	Start
Edit	Cut
	Copy
	Paste

Figure 1.6   Selected QuickBASIC commands.

If you are using QuickBASIC 4.5, we assume that your system has been initialized to display Easy Menus, as discussed in Appendix G. The Easy Menus option displays abbreviated menus containing fewer commands than the alternate option of Full Menus. Easy Menus are designed especially for beginning programmers. Note that if Easy Menus are being used, the screen initially displays an information window which can be deleted by pressing the Esc key.

> **QBI Note:** Only one set of menus is available in the QuickBASIC Interpreter and this set is similar to the Easy Menus of QuickBASIC 4.5. Full menus are not available in the interpreter.

Using a Mouse

If your computer is equipped with a mouse (see earlier definition), you will probably want to use it when executing QuickBASIC commands. You can use the mouse in place of the arrow keys for moving the cursor about the screen. There are usually two buttons on top of the mouse. The left button performs most of the same functions as the Enter key, while the right button invokes the on-line help system.

For example, you can use the mouse to execute the Exit command from the File command menu. As you move the mouse, you should notice the mouse cursor (a large block cursor) also moving. This cursor is different in appearance from the normal cursor. Move the mouse cursor over the word File in the main menu and press the left mouse button. The File command menu is displayed. Move the mouse cursor again over the Exit command and press the left button again. The QuickBASIC system is closed and control returns to the operating system.

The NEW or NEW PROGRAM Command

The command New Program (called New in the QuickBASIC Interpreter) allows a user to create a new file. The program is not named at this point, but must be named when it is saved (see next command). After the New Program command is entered, the Quick-BASIC system goes into the editing mode, allowing you to write a new program in the View window.

> **QBI Note:** A small highlighted window appears on the screen when the New command is executed. This window allows you to specify whether you wish to write a program or a document. As you will notice, the default selection is Program mode and you should normally use this selection.
>
> The Tab key moves the highlighting between the three command buttons (enclosed in angle brackets) on the bottom line of the window. If you wish to write a new program, make sure the OK command button is highlighted and press the Enter key. Fig. 1.7 shows the New command screen.

Note that any new program is identified as Untitled. You should give it a name when you save it, as discussed in the next section. Here again are the steps to create a new program.

- Press the Alt key.
- Press the F key.
- Press the N key.

QBI Note: Two additional steps are necessary if you are using the interpreter.

- Verify that Program mode has been selected; if not, select it using the Tab key and arrow keys.
- Press the Enter key.

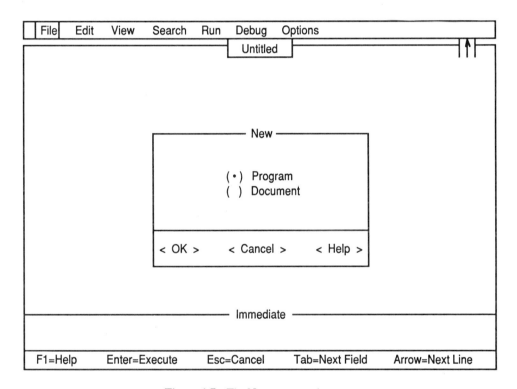

Figure 1.7 The New command screen.

The SAVE AS Command

The Save As command allows you to specify the program file name and then saves the program on disk. After writing a program, you usually want to save it as a file on disk. Remember that if a newly written program is not saved on disk, it will be lost when you exit the QuickBASIC system or when the computer is turned off. The screen produced by this command (in the QuickBASIC Interpreter) is shown in Fig. 1.8.

When you select the Save As command, a dialogue box is displayed. This box displays the path name of the disk drive and directory that you are currently using, defined as the *current drive* and *current directory*. If you have just written a new program, it has no name, so the File Name box is empty. This program is defined as the *current program.*

Type the name of your choice into the File Name box. If you specify only the file name, the file will be saved in the current directory on the current drive. You can, however, write a complete path name for your program in the File Name box.

Remember that the computer does not know where to save a program file unless you tell it explicitly. If you started QuickBASIC from a disk in drive A, it is possible that you plan to save your programs on a disk in drive B. In this case, you must place the prefix B: at the beginning of your file name. There must be no space between the prefix and the file name.

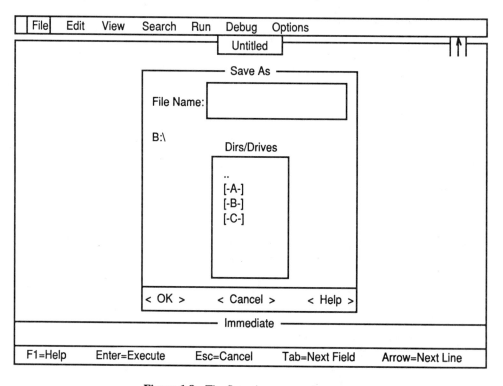

Figure 1.8 The Save As command screen.

Now check the other boxes in the dialogue window, moving from one box to the other with the Tab key. In the Dirs/Drives box you will see a list of all the directories in your current disk (if directories have been created) and all the disk drives connected to your computer. You can select one of these if you wish to write your file on a specific directory or drive. It is probably easier, however, to specify where you want the file saved by writing a complete path name in the File Name box.

In the Format selection box (not shown in Fig. 1.8), there may be a bullet in the parentheses preceding the word QuickBASIC. This symbol means that the program will be saved in QuickBASIC format. We recommend for small programs that you save your program in Text format. While a program saved as a text file takes slightly longer to execute, it uses less disk space and allows the source program to be displayed by any editor in addition to the QuickBASIC editor.

QBI Note: The Format selection box does not appear in the interpreter because all files are saved as text files. Fig. 1.8 shows the Save As screen produced by the QuickBASIC Interpreter.

If the Text format is not already selected in the Format box, move the cursor to that box with the Tab key and use the up and down arrow keys to select Text format (this action puts a bullet in the parentheses preceding the word Text). Then use the Tab key to move the cursor to the OK box (or command button) and press the Enter key to save the file. The current program now has a new name and has been saved on disk.

If you have previously saved a file, it may be that all options are properly selected. The OK box should have a double-lined or highlighted border. In this case, you can save your program file simply by pressing the Enter key.

If the OK command button does not have a highlighted border, use the Tab key to move the cursor to that button and its border will be highlighted. On the other hand, if you decide that you do not wish to save the file, use the Tab key to move the cursor to the Cancel button, notice that its border now is highlighted, and press the Enter key to cancel the Save As command.

In summary, Fig. 1.9 shows the keys used to select any command.

KEY	ACTION
Alt key	Activates the main menu
Arrow keys or highlighted letter	Selects a command menu
Arrow keys or highlighted letter	Selects a specific command in a command menu
Tab key	Moves cursor between boxes in a dialogue box
Arrow keys	Selects a specific item in a selection box
Enter key	Executes command if OK button has a highlighted border

Figure 1.9   Summary of QuickBASIC command procedures.

We repeat the steps necessary to save a new program file.

- Press the Alt key.
- Press the F key.
- Press the A key.
- Enter a file name or path name in the File Name box of the dialogue window.
- Verify that Text format and OK have been selected properly in the dialogue window (automatic in the interpreter); if not, select them using the Tab key and the arrow keys.
- Press the Enter key to create the new file on disk.

The EXIT Command

We have already introduced the Exit command, which is in the File command menu. This command turns off the QuickBASIC system and returns the user to DOS.

If the current program has been changed since it was last saved, a dialogue window appears and gives you the option of saving the modified program. One of three command buttons can be highlighted. The Yes button saves the program and then erases it from memory. The No button erases the program without saving the latest changes. The Cancel button just cancels the Exit command. Use the Tab key to select the desired button. Here are the steps for exiting the QuickBASIC system.

- Press the Alt key.
- Press the F key.
- Press the X key.
- If a dialogue window appears, verify that the proper command button has been chosen and press the Enter key.

1.8 HOW TO USE THIS BOOK

The first six chapters of the book constitute Part I and should be read in sequence. They give you enough knowledge of the BASIC language to write many programs. The last five chapters are Part II and cover several important advanced topics in BASIC programming, as well as useful programming techniques.

We have included examples of QuickBASIC statements and example programs written in QuickBASIC throughout each chapter. As mentioned earlier, these example programs are available on a floppy disk for IBM PC-compatible computers. If this disk is in drive B, enter the command TYPE B:README from DOS to receive instructions on how to read the programs. These same instructions are printed in Appendix H. We urge you to run all the example programs, typing them in from the book if you do not have them on disk. Do not be afraid to modify a program; even if you make mistakes, you will learn more about programming. Several programming assignments are listed at the end of all chapters except this first chapter. These assignments can and should be used for further practice and to help you evaluate your progress.

Summary of Important Points

- We use the term *IBM PC-compatible* to designate the entire class of IBM personal computers and compatibles.
- You must remember that when you turn off your computer system, all information stored in memory is lost.
- A colon is required to separate hours and minutes when entering the current time into the computer.
- A blank space is not a valid DOS file name character. There can be no blank spaces anywhere in a path name.

Common Errors

- Confusing the terms *bit* and *byte*.
- Failing to distinguish between DOS commands and QuickBASIC commands.
- Trying to start the computer system by inserting the startup disk in drive B.
- Trying to start the computer system by inserting a disk in drive A that is not a system disk.
- Including a space in a path name, especially between the colon after the drive letter and the first letter of the file name.
- Failing to save a program on disk before turning off the computer.

Self-Test Questions

1. Where can you find additional information on the QuickBASIC language beyond that included in this book?
2. What operating system is normally used by IBM PC-compatible computers?
3. What is the meaning of the following hardware terms?
   (a) numeric coprocessor
   (b) memory location
4. What is the meaning of the following software terms?
   (a) program compilation
   (b) program execution
5. Should the startup disk used to boot the system be inserted in drive A or drive B?
6. What is the correct format for entering the date when requested by the operating system?
7. What is the correct format for entering the time?

8.   If the prompt B> is displayed on the screen, which disk drive is the current or selected drive?

9.   What command is entered to start the QuickBASIC system?

10. Should QuickBASIC commands be entered in uppercase or lowercase characters?

11. What is a disk file?

12. Is information stored on a floppy disk lost when the computer is turned off?

13. Is information stored in memory lost when the computer is turned off?

14. Are the following DOS path names valid?

    (a) A:SALE.BAS

    (b) A:\SALE.BAS

    (c) A:OLD SALE.BAS

    (d) A:\PROG\NEWSALE.BAS

    (e) A:SALESRECORD.BAS

15. Which key is used to access the main menu in QuickBASIC?

16. Which key moves the cursor from box to box in a dialogue window?

17. What is the current program?

2

WRITING AND EDITING SIMPLE PROGRAMS

2.1 INTRODUCTION

We first show you how to write a simple computer program in QuickBASIC and how to make the computer execute the program instructions (run the program). We introduce program statements that accept information typed on the keyboard and then display this information on the screen. We discuss the QuickBASIC language system in some detail, including its editing facilities for writing computer programs and its on-line help facilities. We also discuss the disk operating system (DOS) and explain several DOS commands that are used to manage disk files and directories.

2.2 A SIMPLE PROGRAM WITH OUTPUT

Here is our first QuickBASIC program, containing three statements. As you might expect, this program displays the message Hello! on the screen.

```
REM   Example Program 2-1
PRINT "Hello!"
END
```

We present the example first so that you can see what a simple program looks like, and then we discuss it in detail in the remainder of this section.

Entering a New Program

As we discussed in Chapter 1, when you enter the QuickBASIC system, the computer is ready to accept a new program typed in from the keyboard. If for some reason the editor already contains an old program, use the New or New Program command in the File menu of QuickBASIC to erase the old program and allow you to write a new program.

Any new program that you write is originally untitled. You can associate a file name with the program when you save it using the Save As command in the File menu. As you probably remember, we discussed both the New Program and Save As commands in Section 1.7. A program consists of one or more statements that may be written in either uppercase or lowercase letters. You can insert a blank line at any point in a QuickBASIC program to make the program easier to read.

No Line Numbers

Many versions of BASIC require that you write a numeric label, called a *line number*, at the beginning of each statement. **Line numbers are not required in QuickBASIC and** we will not use them in this book.

The Enter Key

You type in each line of your program by pressing the appropriate keys on the keyboard. The cursor shows where the next character will be displayed. You must end each line by pressing the Enter or Return key on your keyboard. On many IBM PC-compatible keyboards, the Enter key is marked with a broken arrow symbol (↵) .

We will call this key the Enter key. It is similar in action to the familiar typewriter carriage-return key, although on a display unit it moves the cursor to the left margin of the screen.

Its function when writing a program is to tell the computer that you have finished typing a statement line. The computer then examines the statement and immediately compiles it (in QuickBASIC 4.5) or accepts it (in the QuickBASIC Interpreter). The cursor moves to the beginning of the next line, indicating that the computer is ready for you to type in another statement.

When you press the Enter key, you generate a nonprinting character called a *carriage return* and the cursor moves to the left edge of the screen. When the computer receives a carriage return, it compiles or accepts the statement line, and if the process is successful, generates another nonprinting character called a *line feed.* The cursor then moves to the next line. This pair of characters, the carriage return and line feed, mark the end of each program line.

All this explanation can be condensed into one simple instruction: **Always press the Enter key when you have finished typing a BASIC statement line or command.**

Multiple Statements per Line

It is possible to write two or more QuickBASIC statements, separated from each other by colons (:), on a single program line. Thus it is more accurate to say that when you have finished entering a program line containing one or more program statements, press the Enter key.

Reserved Words in QuickBASIC

A *reserved word* or keyword is a word that has a special meaning in any QuickBASIC statement. When a statement is successfully compiled or accepted, all reserved words are changed to uppercase if they were entered in lowercase. Appendix A contains a complete list of QuickBASIC reserved words.

If there is an error in the statement line, compilation or acceptance cannot occur and the change to uppercase letters does not take place. If the specific error can be determined by the QuickBASIC system, use the arrow keys (see Fig. 2.1) to move to the point of error and correct the line. Section 2.4 explains how to edit program statements. If you cannot see or understand the error, it will be highlighted when you attempt to run the program, and you can correct the line at that time.

The Comment or REM Statement

Here is our first program again.

```
REM   Example Program 2-1
PRINT "Hello!"
END
```

The first line contains a REM statement. This is a comment or remark that is placed in a program for the convenience of the programmer and anyone else who reads the program. The reserved word REM and any words that follow it are ignored by the computer. A single quotation character (') can be used instead of the word REM and most of our example programs use that character. Note that the single quotation character must be the acute accent, appearing on most keyboards on the same keytop as the double quotation mark ("). Most keyboards also have the grave accent ('), a completely different character that cannot be used to denote a remark. The grave accent often appears on the same keytop as the tilde (~).

The PRINT and END Statements

The purpose of the PRINT statement is to display the characters within quotation marks on the display unit screen. In computer terminology, this set of characters is called a *string constant* and must be enclosed in double quotation marks. The END statement is used to indicate the end of the program. It is required in all QuickBASIC programs.

The RUN Command

To run or execute this program after you have finished writing the statements, you must access the Run menu. This menu is another important menu that is entered from the main menu. Remember that to activate a command menu, you first press the Alt key and then press a letter key to select the desired command menu. When the Run menu appears, select the command Start to execute the current program in memory.

As soon as program execution starts, the screen display reverts to the normal DOS screen and the results of the program are displayed on that screen. In our example, the word "Hello!" (without quotation marks) is displayed. A message near the bottom of the screen, "Press any key to continue", means that after you have finished observing program output, you can press any key to return the display to the QuickBASIC screen.

There is a shortcut method for executing a program. Pressing Shift-F5 (hold down the Shift key and simultaneously press the F5 key) at any time when a program is displayed causes that program to be executed. In actual practice, the F5 key works just as well. The F5 key causes the program to continue execution. If the program has not started, however, continuing execution and starting execution are the same action.

Here is another, but similar, example program. Use the New or New Program command from the File command menu to erase the current program and then type in the following new program.

```
' Example Program 2-2
PRINT 22.5   ' print a number
END
```

This program displays the number 22.5 on the screen.

The value displayed is called a *numeric constant* and is never enclosed in quotation marks. Spaces are not required in QuickBASIC statements to separate words and numbers, but we recommend that they be used, just as they are in ordinary sentences. Normal spacing makes a program statement easier to read. Extra spaces between words and numbers usually cause no harm.

We write a comment, beginning with the single quotation mark, after the PRINT statement. Remarks may be included in programs as separate lines or as comments at the end of program statement lines. In the latter case, you must use a single quotation mark rather than the keyword REM, or separate the remark statement from the preceding statement with a colon, as shown in the next example program.

```
' Example Program 2-3
PRINT 22.5 : REM print a number
END
```

Remember that we normally use a single quotation mark rather than the keyword REM in our example programs.

Example Program 2-3 shows how two or more program statements can be included on a single line. **We advise you to use this capability sparingly because lines with multiple statements can be difficult to read and make a program harder to understand.**

2.3 ANOTHER PROGRAM WITH KEYBOARD INPUT

We now write another, slightly longer program. Before writing a new program, you should erase the old program from the screen and from memory, using the New or New Program command. If you do not, you may get a program consisting of a mixture of old program statements and new program statements.

The INPUT Statement

The following example program asks a user to type in his or her name and the computer displays that name on the screen.

```
' Example Program 2-4
' Prompts the user for a name
' and displays it on the screen.

INPUT "Type in your name: ", Name$
PRINT Name$
END
```

Note that we have included several comment lines in this example program. The fourth line of the program (after the comments) is a blank line that is created just by pressing the Enter key. It makes the program a little easier to read.

The fifth line introduces a new statement, the INPUT statement with a prompt string. This statement does two things; it displays on the screen the words within quotation marks (the prompt string) and then waits on the same line for the user to type a reply of one or more characters, followed by pressing the Enter key. All characters typed in before the Enter key is pressed are associated with the word Name$, which is called a *variable*.

We will discuss variables at some length in the next chapter, but for the time being, you can think of Name$ as the name of a mailbox (actually, a memory location) where a string or sequence of characters can be stored. This string of characters is called the value of the variable Name$. We say that the characters typed in from the keyboard are stored in the variable Name$. The PRINT statement in the fifth line then displays this stored value on the screen.

Here is a sample display produced by this program. Characters entered by the user are identified by bold-face style, although the user does not specify bold-face style when typing characters.

```
Type in your name: John Wilson
John Wilson
```

The character in the INPUT statement after the prompt string can be either a comma (as in the preceding example program) or a semicolon. The comma adds no characters to the prompt, while the semicolon adds a question mark followed by a space to the end of the prompt string. Here is a similar program that uses the INPUT statement with a semicolon following the prompt.

```
' Example Program 2-5
' Prompts the user for a name
' and displays it on the screen.

INPUT "Your name"; Name$
PRINT Name$
END
```

It produces the following display.

```
Your name? John Wilson
John Wilson
```

Note the question mark and space at the end of the prompt.

Printing Multiple Values

We have used the PRINT statement to display only a single constant or variable value. It is possible, however, to include several constants or variables in one PRINT statement. These constants or variables should be separated by semicolons. For example, the last statement in Example Program 2-5 can be written with a string constant and a variable to make the output a little more understandable.

```
' Example Program 2-6
' Prompts the user for a name
' and displays it on the screen.

INPUT "Your name"; Name$
PRINT "Your name is "; Name$
END
```

This program displays the following output.

```
Your name? John Wilson
Your name is John Wilson
```

Note that if a space is desired between the word "is" and the word "John," it must be included explicitly in the string constant.

INPUT Statement without Prompt

An INPUT statement can be used without the optional prompt string in quotation marks. In this case a single question mark and a space are displayed on the screen to indicate that input is expected. Most programs are easier to use and understand if a prompt string is included in each INPUT statement. If an INPUT statement does not include a prompt string, a separate PRINT statement can be used to tell the user what to enter. Here is an example.

```
' Example Program 2-7
' Use of an input statement without a prompt,
' and use of multiple values in a print statement.

PRINT "Type in your name after the question mark."
INPUT Name$
PRINT "You entered the name "; Name$
END
```

It produces the following interactive dialogue.

```
Type in your name after the question mark.
? Mary Simpson
You entered the name Mary Simpson
```

Once again, bold-face style is used to identify characters entered by the user.

2.4 EDITING PROGRAMS

To edit a program means to change it, most often by modifying or deleting existing statements or by inserting new statements. QuickBASIC allows you to edit the current program.

Cursor Movement Keys

Several special keys on the IBM PC-compatible keyboard are used for editing. These keys are in the keypad on the right side of the keyboard. We begin by listing, in Fig. 2.1, several keys for moving the cursor. If these keys produce numbers instead of the actions listed here, press the Num Lock key to deactivate the numeric keypad and allow the cursor movement functions to work.

The latest IBM keyboard has both a numeric keypad and separate editing keys. When using this keyboard, the numeric keypad is normally used for entering numbers (Num Lock on) and the editing keys for editing. If you are more comfortable with the original IBM keyboard design, however, you can turn off Num Lock and still use the numeric keypad keys for editing.

KEY	ACTION
left arrow	Moves cursor one character left
right arrow	Moves cursor one character right
up arrow	Moves cursor up one line
down arrow	Moves cursor down one line
Home	Moves cursor to start of line
End	Moves cursor to end of line
Ctrl-Home	Moves cursor to start of program
Ctrl-End	Moves cursor to end of program
PgDn	Displays next page of program
PgUp	Displays previous page of program
Ctrl-PgDn	Displays end of statement line
Ctrl-PgUp	Displays beginning of statement line

Figure 2.1   Cursor movement keys in the QuickBASIC editor.

The designation *left arrow* means to press the key marked with a left arrow. This statement may be confusing because there are several such keys close together on the keyboard; we mean the keypad key, which is also marked with the digit 4. The designation *Ctrl-Home* means to hold down the control key (often marked Ctrl) and press the Home key at the same time.

The INSERT Key

A more detailed explanation is required to explain the use of the Ins or Insert key. This key switches or changes the mode of typing from insert mode to overwrite mode.

When you first start QuickBASIC, if you move the cursor to some point in your program and press a character key, that character is inserted in the text at the position of the cursor. The character above the cursor and all characters to the right are moved one position to the right. You are in the insert mode and the cursor symbol is an underline beneath the character.

Pressing Ins switches typing to overwrite mode. You will notice that the cursor has changed to a rectangle or box that overlays the character. Now when you press a character key, the character under the cursor is replaced by the new character. The Ins key acts like a toggle switch; each time you press it, you change from one mode to the other.

You may want to insert a new line rather than insert new characters in an existing line. If you place the cursor under the first character in a line when in insert mode and press the Enter key, a new blank line will be inserted in your program just above the cursor. You can then type in a new program statement.

How to Print a Blank Line

For example, you might insert the statement PRINT on a line by itself, just above the statement PRINT Name$ in Example Program 2-4. The program will then read as follows.

```
' Example Program 2-8
' Prompts the user for a name
' and displays it on the screen.

INPUT "Type in your name: ", Name$
PRINT
PRINT "Your name is "; Name$
END
```

It produces the following output.

```
Type in your name: John Wilson

Your name is John Wilson
```

The PRINT statement, used by itself, produces a blank line in the program output. If you want to produce two blank lines, include two PRINT statements in your program, each statement on a separate line or both on the same line separated by a colon.

The DELETE Key

The Del or Delete key deletes the character specified by the cursor. If you want to delete several characters, hold the key down and it will repeat automatically. Use this technique carefully because if you hold the Del key down too long, you may delete more characters than you had planned. The Del key can also be used to delete a block of marked text, as discussed in a later section.

There are many times when you want to delete a single line in a computer program. The key combination Ctrl-Y performs this task. Ctrl-Y means to hold down the Ctrl or control key and press the letter Y key. You can think of Ctrl-Y as meaning yank, as in the phrase "yank out this line." Move the cursor to any point on the line to be deleted and press Ctrl-Y to delete the line.

Blocks of Text and the Clipboard

It is often convenient to be able to edit blocks of text rather than single characters. When editing computer programs, these blocks usually consist of one or more program statement lines. Fig. 2.2 is a summary of the various block commands.

KEY	ACTION
Shift-up arrow or Shift-down arrow	Marks block of program lines
Shift-Del	Deletes marked text and moves it to the Clipboard
Ctrl-Ins	Copies marked text and moves it to the Clipboard
Shift-Ins	Inserts marked text from the Clipboard at the cursor
Del	Deletes marked text without moving it to the Clipboard

Figure 2.2   Keys for manipulating marked blocks of text.

Shift-up arrow and Shift-down arrow are useful key combinations for marking program statements. Shift-down arrow means to hold down the Shift key and press the down arrow key. As you press these key combinations, you will notice that one or more program statement lines are highlighted. When you have marked the block of statements that you wish to move or delete, press Shift-Del. The marked text is deleted from the screen and placed in a memory location called the Clipboard. **Any previous contents of the Clipboard are overwritten and thus erased.** Pressing the Shift-Del key combination is the same as invoking the Cut command from the Edit menu.

Pressing Ctrl-Ins copies marked text from the program to the Clipboard without deleting the text. This action produces the same results as the Copy command from the Edit menu.

If you want to insert a block of text contained in the Clipboard into another part of your program, move the cursor to the desired position and press Shift-Ins. The block of text currently saved in the Clipboard is inserted just ahead of the line containing the cursor. Pressing the Shift-Ins key is the same as invoking the Paste command from the Edit menu. Note that the contents of the Clipboard are not altered or destroyed, and the same block can be inserted at another point in your program. The Shift-Del and Shift-Ins keys are especially useful for rearranging program statements in a program.

Pressing the Del key by itself deletes any marked block of text without placing it in the Clipboard. This is the same as the Clear command from the Edit menu.

If you have a mouse, you will find that it is a convenient tool for marking a group of program statements. Move the mouse cursor any place on top of the first statement, hold down the left button, and drag the highlighted area down over as many statements as you wish to mark. When you have highlighted the desired statements, release the mouse button. If you mark the wrong area, move the mouse cursor completely off the program statements and press the left button. All highlighting is removed and you can now try again to mark the correct statements. A marked block can be cut or copied as explained previously.

2.5 THE ON-LINE HELP SYSTEM

QuickBASIC provides a comprehensive on-line help system. This system gives general help, specific help on any command, and detailed help on all QuickBASIC reserved words. You can escape from the help system at any time by pressing the Esc key.

General Help

General help is provided when Shift-F1 is pressed. A new window called the Help window is opened and a menu line of words is presented, as shown in Fig. 2.3.

Figure 2.3   General help menu.

These words, each displayed with a highlighted triangle at the beginning and the end, are called *hyperlinks*. A hyperlink is a branch point or node in a linked chain of information about QuickBASIC. The cursor can be moved from one hyperlink to another by pressing the Tab key. When the cursor is under any part of a hyperlink, pressing the Enter key displays the information connected with that word.

The hyperlink Help on Help explains how the QuickBASIC help system works. The PgUp and PgDn keys can be used to scroll from one help screen to another.

The hyperlink Contents displays a table of contents of the entire help system. Each item in the table of contents is itself a hyperlink (denoted by highlighted triangles) and can be accessed with the Tab key. You can also use the arrow keys to move the cursor to any hyperlink. Remember that pressing the Enter key, when the cursor is on a hyperlink, displays the information associated with that hyperlink word.

You can follow a chain of hyperlinks, revealing more and more information on a particular subject. You can also back up one or more levels in the chain by pressing Alt-F1. Remember that the Esc key can be used to escape back to your previous position in the QuickBASIC system from any level of the help system.

The hyperlink Index displays a list of all QuickBASIC reserved words. Each of these words is also a hyperlink and can be selected and have its meaning displayed. In QuickBASIC 4.5, there is a fourth hyperlink in the general Help menu, named Product Support, that gives information on how to obtain product support from Microsoft, the manufacturers of QuickBASIC.

Help on Commands

Any time one of the QuickBASIC commands is highlighted, you can obtain help on that command by pressing F1. A small, overlaying window is displayed, containing an explanation of how the command works. In some cases there is more than one screen of text and you can scroll from one to the other with the PgUp and PgDn keys. When you are finished, use the Esc key to return to the command menu.

Help on Program Statements

One of the most useful features of the on-line help system is its ability to provide assistance while you are writing a program. Place the cursor on any reserved word or keyword in your program and press F1. A Help window is created and a short description of the selected keyword is displayed.

If you have a mouse, place the mouse cursor over the keyword and press the right button. You can continue to get more help by moving the mouse cursor over hyperlinks and pressing the right button.

Note that the cursor is normally in the View window, making that window the current window. If you are using the keyboard and desire more help, move the cursor to the Help window by pressing the F6 key twice.

Once in the Help window, you can obtain more information by selecting another hyperlink (identified by the highlighted triangles) with the cursor and pressing the Enter key. The hyperlink named Details displays one or more screens of detailed usage information. The hyperlink named Example shows one or more examples of how the keyword is used in program statements. In addition, keywords of a similar nature are displayed as hyperlinks for possible further information.

Remember that you can always back up to the previous hyperlink by pressing Alt-F1. At any time, you can delete the Help window and return to the View window by pressing the Esc key. A table summarizing the various Help keys is shown in Fig. 2.4.

2.6 COMMANDS

Commands are direct instructions to the computer telling it to do something immediately. Some commands are entered from the QuickBASIC system, others from DOS. Even though we show commands in uppercase characters, either lowercase or uppercase characters can be used.

KEY	ACTION
Shift-F1	Gets general help on QuickBASIC
Tab	Moves cursor from one hyperlink to another
F1	Gets help on a specific command when that command is highlighted
F1	Gets help on a specific keyword when the cursor is on that word
F6	Moves cursor from one window to another (press twice to move from the View window to the Help window)
Alt-F1	Backs up to the previous hyperlink
Esc	Exits the on-line help system

Figure 2.4   Special keys used in the help system.

We have already introduced several QuickBASIC commands from the File, Run, and Edit menus. This selection of commands is listed in Fig. 1.6 of Chapter 1.

The OPEN or OPEN PROGRAM Command

We continue our discussion of important QuickBASIC commands by introducing the Open Program command (called Open in the QuickBASIC Interpreter). This command is used to load a program that has been saved previously on disk, and make it the current program. A dialogue window is used, similar to that used by the Save As command but containing slightly different information, as shown in Fig. 2.5.

The File Name box contains the file name *.BAS as a default value. We define the asterisk as a *wildcard* that represents any legal file name. The name of the desired file (or its path name) can be entered in the File Name box in place of the wildcard file name. Note that the current directory name is shown in the window, as well as a list of all files in that directory with the extension BAS, as specified by the file name *.BAS.

You can either type in a specific file name or use the Tab key to move the cursor to the Files directory box. If you move to the Files box, use the up and down arrow keys to highlight the desired file name, and press the Enter key. The file name you have chosen will appear in the File Name box and that file will be loaded as the current program. Note that the existing current program is erased before a new program is loaded from disk.

It is also possible to change the current disk and directory within the Open Program command window. Instead of entering a file name in the File Name box, enter a path name with the wildcard file name *.BAS (for example, the wildcard path name B:\CH02*.BAS). The disk drive and directory specified in this path name then become the current drive and directory. The names of all BASIC program files in the new current directory are displayed in the Directory box. For more information on wildcards in file names, consult the DOS operating manual.

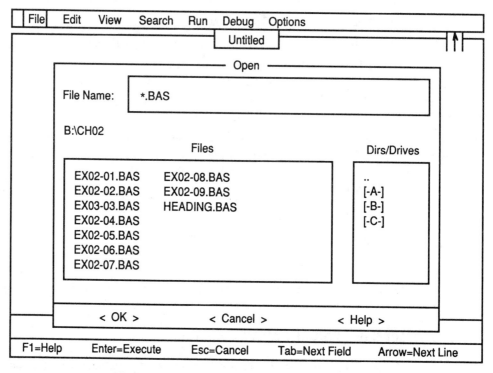

Figure 2.5   Dialogue window of the Open command.

Here is a technique you might use to examine and possibly modify a group of QuickBASIC programs, such as the example programs for Chapter 2 of this book. These programs are stored in directory CH02 on the example program disk. If you have a system with two floppy disk drives, place the example program disk in drive B and the QuickBASIC system disk in drive A.

Change your current drive to B by entering the DOS command B: and change the current directory to B:\CH02 by entering the DOS command CD CH02 (meaning Change Directory to CH02). Start the QuickBASIC system from the current directory by entering the command A:\QB or A:\QBI.

Now use the directory display in the Open or Open Program command window to select an example program. Edit this program if desired, and run it one or more times. When you have finished with the program, use the Open command again to examine another program in the same directory.

There are many more commands that you will gradually find yourself using as you write computer programs. We assume that you have started using QuickBASIC with Easy Menus selected. After you become more familiar with the system, and especially when you start to write multimodule programs, you will want to select Full Menus from the Options command menu. This selection provides access to a larger choice of commands. A complete list of all QuickBASIC commands is given in Appendix C.

> **QBI Note:** Only one set of menus, similar to Easy Menus, is available in the interpreter.

DOS Commands

These commands are not part of the QuickBASIC environment but are operating system commands entered in response to the A> or B> prompt. We do not list all possible commands at this time but rather discuss five of the most useful commands. Remember that we have already introduced the CD command (in the preceding paragraphs) for changing the directory. You should consult your DOS manual for further information.

DIR. This command lists the contents of the current file directory. If the A drive is the current drive, the command DIR lists all files on the disk in drive A. The command

```
DIR  B:\HWORK
```

lists all files in the root directory on the disk in drive B. The command (DIR) must be separated from the path name (B:\HWORK) by at least one space (we use two spaces in the book for clarity). There is no space between the colon (:) and the backslash (\).

COPY. This command copies a file from one disk or directory to another disk or directory. For example, the command

```
COPY  B:\HWORK\HW02.BAS  A:\
```

copies the program file HW02.BAS from directory HWORK on the disk in drive B to the root directory of the disk in drive A. Spaces are used again to separate the command name and the two path names. **Note that when we copy a file, we do not erase the original version, so we end up with two files having the same file name and contents.** In this example, each file is on a different disk.

DEL. This command deletes a file from the disk. Assuming that drive A is the current drive and its root directory is the current directory, the command

```
DEL  FIRST.BAS
```

deletes the file FIRST.BAS in the root directory of the disk in drive A. It is better practice to use the command

```
DEL  A:\FIRST.BAS
```

where the disk and directory are stated explicitly. **Once a file has been deleted from a disk, it cannot be recovered by any simple method.** If you should delete a file by mistake, remove the disk from your computer and write nothing else on it. Your instructor or another computer expert may be able to help you recover the information in the deleted file.

REN. This command changes the name of a disk file. For example, the command

```
REN  A:\FIRST.BAS  A:\FIRST.BAK
```

renames a QuickBASIC program file named FIRST.BAS and makes it a backup file named FIRST.BAK. Note that a new file is not created.

TYPE. This command lists the contents of a file. For example, the command

```
TYPE  B:\BOOK\CH12.TXT
```

displays the contents of the specified text file on the screen. **Note that QuickBASIC program files saved in the QuickBASIC format are not ordinary text files, and thus cannot be displayed with this command.** One of the reasons we recommend saving programs in the Text format is so that they can be displayed with a command such as TYPE.

> **QBI Note:** Program files are always saved in the Text format.

These commands are just a few of the many commands available in DOS. Additional commands are listed in your operating system manual.

The Interrupt Key

You may want to stop the execution of a program before it reaches its normal end. An interrupt or break key, the Ctrl-Break key, is provided in QuickBASIC. Hold down the Ctrl key and simultaneously press the Break key in the upper right-hand corner of the keyboard. Program execution stops and the main menu screen is displayed.

2.7 GOOD PROGRAMMING TECHNIQUES

As you learn to write computer programs, there are certain procedures or habits of good programming that you should develop. We discuss a few of these procedures in this section.

Saving Your Program during Development

We urge you to develop the habit of saving your program on disk as soon as you have spent 15 minutes or so entering new program statements. Use the Save As command in the File menu. If anything happens to halt your computer, such as a power failure or a mistake on your part that locks up the operating system, everything you have written will not be lost. Programs on disk are relatively safe, whereas programs in memory can easily be lost. Just a slight flicker in the power supply may cause a computer to restart, erasing the contents of its memory. As you continue writing a new program, or as you modify an existing program, use the Save As command often to save the latest version on disk.

Backing Up Your Disk

Another good habit is to keep backup copies of all important programs on a second floppy disk. You can use the DOS COPY command to transfer programs to the backup disk. Remember that floppy disks are easily damaged and wear out. Sooner or later, you will be unable to access a program stored on your program disk. It is not a question of if this event will occur, just when it will occur. A backup disk becomes invaluable at that moment.

DEVELOP THE BACKUP HABIT NOW

Saving the Screen Image: The PRINT Command

The Print command produces a paper copy of all or part of the current program, provided that a printer is attached to your computer. There are several choices for printing, although you probably want to select the Current Module in QuickBASIC 4.5, meaning the current program. Select the OK box and press the Enter key to start printing.

> **QBI Note:** The Print command screen displayed by the interpreter is somewhat different than that displayed by QuickBASIC 4.5. The most common choice when using the interpreter is the Entire Program selection, as shown in Fig. 2.6.

Printing can occur only if the printer is attached to your computer and turned on. If this is not the case, you will see the error message "Waiting for printer" appear on the screen. If the printer is turned off, you now have time to turn it on before printing starts. If the printer is not attached or does not exist, the computer waits for several minutes and then displays a Device Timeout error window. Sometimes that wait seems very long! Pressing the Enter key with the OK box selected cancels the Print command.

It is not as easy, however, to produce a paper record of the execution of your program. If all the information you want to capture on paper is displayed on a single screen, use the Shift-PrtSc key to transfer an image of the screen to your printer. Hold down the Shift key and press the PrtSc key. On extended keyboards with a separate Print Screen key, all you need to do is press that key.

If the information you want to capture fills many screens, there is really no completely satisfactory way to print program output.

QBI Note: One method works only with the QuickBASIC Interpreter and with printers attached to the parallel port. You must exit the QuickBASIC system and restart it with the DOS command QBI >LPT1:, where the colon after LPT1 is required. Input prompts and output text do not appear on the screen but are printed on the printer. User input is also printed. This method is not very satisfactory when your program has many prompts because you can easily lose track of which question you are answering.

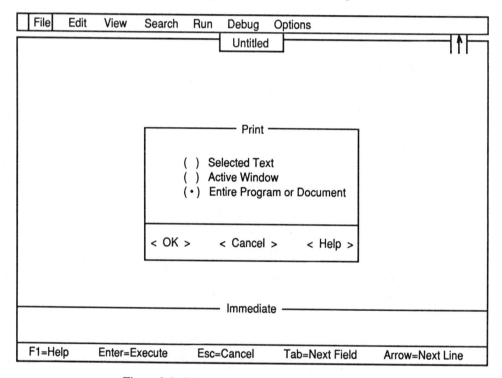

Figure 2.6 Dialogue window of the Print command.

A method of capturing some computer output on paper is to change all PRINT statements in your program to LPRINT statements. The LPRINT statement sends output to the printer rather than to the screen. Unfortunately, prompts in INPUT statements and information entered by the user are not printed. If a printer is not attached to your computer and turned on, a program containing one or more LPRINT statements refuses to run. A Device Timeout error window should appear after a wait of several minutes. If you get tired of waiting, you can reboot the computer by pressing the Ctrl, Alt, and Del keys simultaneously and then turn on the printer. Remember that you will lose any program statements that have not been previously saved. Here is another version of Example Program 2-6 with LPRINT statements replacing PRINT statements.

```
' Example Program 2-9
' Prompts the user for a name
```

```
' and prints it on a printer.

INPUT "Type in your name: ", Name$
LPRINT
LPRINT Name$
END
```

If no printer is attached to your computer, but it is connected to a network that includes printers, see local computer experts for specific printing instructions.

Writing Program Outlines

You cannot write a program to solve a problem until you fully understand the problem. This is an obvious statement, but a lot of people start programming before they understand clearly what the program must do. Keep asking questions or investigate further until you do understand the problem.

A common mistake made by beginning programmers is to start writing their programs too soon. This doesn't mean to do nothing until just before the program is due, but it does mean to do a lot of thinking and planning before writing your first program statement. There are two steps you should take.

First, you must decide how you will solve the problem. The method of solution is called an *algorithm*. You want an efficient algorithm that will solve the problem accurately and quickly. You learn algorithms by reading books and articles, by looking at other programs, and by discussing methods of solution with experienced programmers. Second, you must write an outline of your program. An outline can be written as one or more descriptive paragraphs, or in the more traditional outline form. Try to divide your problem solution into separate tasks and then outline a solution for each task. When you learn about the procedure capabilities of QuickBASIC in Chapter 7, you will be able to write each task as a separate procedure. The more detailed your outline, the easier it will be to write the computer program. Only when you have taken these two steps are you ready to start writing the program itself.

It is always difficult to convince beginning programmers that they should write outlines for short and simple programs. Programs like the ones in this chapter are so short that written outlines hardly seem necessary. If you wait until the programs are large and difficult, however, you may develop the bad habit of not writing outlines. We often see students just sitting down at a computer console and writing code, without sufficient previous thought or formal organization of their ideas. The result is likely to be a disorganized program that contains logical errors, does not run properly, and is almost impossible to correct.

Even though the first programs you write will be short and simple, **we still recommend that you get in the habit of planning and outlining your program before you type the first line of code.** Your motto as a computer programmer should be the following phrase:

PLAN FIRST, PROGRAM LATER

Summary of Important Points

- Line numbers are not required with QuickBASIC statements.
- Always press the Enter key when you finish typing a BASIC statement line or command.
- We advise you to use lines with multiple statements sparingly, because such lines can be difficult to read and make a program harder to understand.
- When a new block of text is sent to the Clipboard, any previous contents are overwritten and thus erased.
- One of the most useful features of the on-line help system is its ability to provide assistance while you are writing a program.
- When a file is copied using the COPY command of DOS, the original version is not erased.
- Once a file has been deleted from the disk, it cannot be recovered by any simple method.
- QuickBASIC program files saved in the QuickBASIC format are not ordinary text files and thus cannot be displayed with the TYPE command.
- Develop the habit of frequently saving your current program.
- Keep backup copies of all important programs on a separate disk.
- You cannot write a program to solve a problem until you fully understand the problem.
- Plan and write an outline of your program before writing the first line of code.

Common Errors

- Using the grave accent (`) instead of the acute accent (') to denote a comment.
- Failing to enclose a string constant in quotation marks.
- Forgetting to write an END statement as the last statement in a program.
- Using a semicolon after an INPUT statement prompt and also including a question mark in the prompt string, thus displaying two question marks.
- Cutting two items in succession from your program and moving them to the Clipboard, thus overwriting and deleting the first item.
- Copying a new version of a file on top of an old version of the same file and then deciding that you prefer the old version. Always change the name of the old version with the REN command before saving the new version, or save the new version under a new name.
- Failing to save your program on disk during two hours of difficult programming, only to have the lights flicker and hear the computer rebooting, deleting all the program code that you had stored in memory.
- Starting to write program statements before you fully understand the problem and have written a program outline, resulting in a program that will not run, that you cannot fix, and that must be completely rewritten.
- Deleting a file by mistake from your disk and then immediately writing a new file on the disk, thus eliminating almost any possibility of recovering the deleted file.

Self-Test Questions

1. Is information stored on a floppy disk lost when the computer is turned off?
2. Is information stored in memory lost when the computer is turned off?
3. Are line numbers at the beginning of program statement lines required in QuickBASIC?
4. After you type the letters of a DOS command, which key do you press to tell the computer to execute the command?
5. Which character or characters are used to denote the beginning of a remark statement?
6. What statement is required in every QuickBASIC program?
7. What program statement is used to accept characters typed in from the keyboard?
8. How do you indicate to the computer that you are finished typing information in response to a prompt?
9. When you first start entering program statements in QuickBASIC, are you in the insert mode or the overwrite mode?
10. Which mode are you in, insert mode or overwrite mode, when the cursor is a flashing underline character?
11. What action results when a statement consisting of the single word PRINT is executed?
12. How do you delete an entire line of your program?
13. Which function key do you press to get help?
14. When you enter the New or New Program command, what happens to your current program?
15. What process is used to load the program file HW3.BAS from the disk in drive B as the current program?
16. Which key or keys do you press to stop a program that is already executing?
17. What process is used to save a new version of the current program file?
18. You are working in QuickBASIC and have just saved a new program file named PROJECT.BAS on the disk in drive B. Explain how you would save a backup copy of this program file on another disk.
19. What happens when you hold down one of the shift keys and press the key marked PrtSc?

Practice Programs and Exercises

Write a QuickBASIC program for each of the following problems.

1. Display the following lines on the screen.

    Microsoft Corporation
    16011 NE 36th Way
    Redmond, WA 98073

2. Display your full name, local address, and telephone number on the screen, placing each item on a separate line.

3. Ask a user (the person who runs the program) to enter his or her name and then display that name again on the screen. Test your program using the name William P. Blank. Use an appropriate prompt and an appropriate label for the displayed name.

4. Ask a user to enter three numbers in response to three prompts and assign these values to three variables. Without reassigning values to the variables, display these numbers again on the screen, one above the other, in reverse order (the opposite order from entry). Test your program using the numbers -7, 2, and 13. Use the phrases "First number", "Second number", and "Third number" for prompts and labels, and the words First, Second, and Third for variables.

5. Display the names of four of your friends on the screen. Display these names in double-spaced format (names separated by blank lines). Test your program using the following list of names.

> Mary F. Jones
> Hannah G. Forbes
> Bill Bradley
> Peter C. Johnson

The following exercises are designed to give you practice using some of the QuickBASIC and DOS commands.

6. Use the QuickBASIC editor to write or edit a sequence of remark statements like those in the file HEADING.BAS on the example program disk or as specified by your instructor. Name this sequence of statements HEADING.BAS and save it on your program disk in place of the original file. Complete one of the following sections, (a) or (b), depending on the Quick-BASIC system in use.

 (a) If you are using the QuickBASIC Interpreter, write a short program following the heading and save the modified program (heading and program together) on disk under a different name. If a printer is available, list the modified program on paper.

 (b) If you are using QuickBASIC 4.5, change from Easy Menus to Full Menus. Use the Open command to open an existing program, making it your current program. Use the Merge command to insert HEADING.BAS at the beginning of this current program. Save the modified program on disk and if a printer is available, list it on paper.

7. Copy a QuickBASIC program from your program disk to a separate backup disk. Use the COPY command with the verify option to make the copies. If your program disk is in drive B and your backup disk is in drive A, the command

```
COPY  B:HW01.BAS  A:
```

can be used to backup file HW01.BAS.

8. Use the COPY command to make a copy of one of the program files on your program disk. Give the copy a different name from the original program. Use the DIR command to display the directory of files saved on your program disk.

3

ASSIGNING VALUES TO VARIABLES

3.1 INTRODUCTION

QuickBASIC uses labeled mailboxes (memory locations) called variables to store information that can be accessed from a program. We discuss two types of variables, those that store numbers (numeric variables) and those that store characters (string variables). We explain how to assign values to variables and how to manipulate variables. We also introduce named constants whose values do not change once assigned.

Information can be stored in a reserved section of memory by DATA statements. We show how to read this information and use it in a program. We discuss the concept of loops in computer programs, and introduce our first program control statement, the FOR statement. This statement is used in several example programs. We enhance our ability to display information by introducing new syntax and statements that provide more control over the format of screen displays.

3.2 THE ASSIGNMENT STATEMENT

A *variable name* in a computer program is the name of a memory location where information is stored. You might think of a variable name as the label of a mailbox used for information storage. This mailbox itself is really just a small area of memory. A typical variable for storing a number might be named Cost. The rules for forming variable names are discussed in the next section.

Assigning Numeric Values

The information stored in a variable is called its value. Thus you can assign the value 29 to the variable Cost or store the value 29 in the mailbox whose label is Cost. Quick-BASIC allows you to use the variable name Cost for only one memory location or mailbox; this name should not be used for any other purpose in your program.

An *assignment statement* or LET statement is used to assign a value to a variable. In our example, this statement would be

```
LET Cost = 29
```

Note that the equal sign (=) is used here as a symbol for an assignment operation, not as an equality symbol. The distinction will become clear later. **The keyword LET is optional in QuickBASIC** and we shall omit it in most of our example programs.

Our mailbox or variable has certain unusual properties that you must learn and understand. When another value is placed in the mailbox (or a new value is assigned to the variable), the original value is overwritten and destroyed. It cannot be recovered. A variable can contain only one value at a time. Thus the statement

```
Cost = 86
```

replaces the original value of 29 with the new value of 86. The value 29 is erased.

We said that the equal sign is not an equality symbol when used in this manner. Look at the following example statement.

```
Cost = Cost + 10
```

This statement tells the computer to find the mailbox Cost, take out the current value (this value is presently 86), add 10 to it, and place the resulting sum value back in the mailbox. The variable Cost now has a value of 96. As you consider this example, you realize that an assignment statement is obviously not a mathematical equality.

Please read over this section again if you have any questions about the difference between a variable and its value. There are two important points to remember.

- **A variable can have only one value at a time.**
- **Assigning a new value to a variable destroys the old value.**

Here is a simple program that uses the assignment statements just discussed.

```
' Example Program 3-1
' Use of assignment statements.

Cost = 29
PRINT Cost
Cost = 86
PRINT Cost
Cost = Cost + 10
PRINT Cost
Cost = Cost - 25
PRINT Cost
END
```

This program displays the following numbers.

```
29
86
96
71
```

Note that the variable Cost is called a *numeric variable* because it is used to store a numeric value.

Initial Values

What happens if you execute a program statement like

```
PRINT Cost
```

and you have not yet assigned a value to Cost? QuickBASIC assigns an initial value of zero to a numeric variable and thus a zero will be printed.

```
' Example Program 3-2
' Display the initial values
' of two numeric variables.

PRINT First    ' These two variables have
PRINT Second   ' not been initialized.
END
```

The results displayed are as follows.

```
0
0
```

It is good programming practice, however, always to assign an initial value yourself to a program variable before it is displayed or used in calculations, even though Quick-BASIC does not require this step.

3.3 VARIABLE NAMES

A variable name must begin with a letter of the alphabet. It may contain up to 40 characters. While certain punctuation characters are allowed in a variable name, we recommend that you use only letter and digit characters. **A space or blank character is not allowed in variable names.** One of the five special characters, %, &, !,#, or $, can be used as a suffix to denote a specific variable type, as discussed in later sections.

In variable names, lowercase and uppercase versions of a letter are treated as the same character. Our usual practice is to use an uppercase letter for the first character and lowercase letters for the other characters. If a variable name consists of two English words, such as MyFile, we capitalize each word. A QuickBASIC reserved word (such as PRINT; see Appendix A for a list of reserved words) cannot be used as a variable name.

The QuickBASIC editor keeps track of all variable names. If you enter a previously entered name with a different combination of uppercase and lowercase letters, all prior occurrences of that name throughout the program are changed to the latest version. For example, if you had used the variable name MyFile and later entered the name Myfile, both occurrences are changed to Myfile. **Be careful to be consistent in the capitaliza-tion of variable names.**

You should choose appropriate variable names that describe the physical entities that they reference. For example, a variable used to hold the sum of several numbers might be named Sum, while a variable used to hold the balance in a bank account might be named Balance. An even better choice for the latter variable would be the name Bank-Balance.

Numeric Variables

QuickBASIC has two general types of simple variables. The example variable name we have been using, Cost, is the name of a numeric variable because it has no special character suffix. This type of variable can have only numeric values, such as 29 or -109.23 or 1300 or 0.000025. As we shall see in the next section, there are several subdivisions within the general type of numeric variable.

String Variables

The other type of variable is the *string variable.* A string variable name differs from a numeric variable name by having a dollar sign ($) as its last character or suffix. The maximum length of a string variable name is still 40 characters, including the dollar sign.

Remember that a string is any sequence of characters (even a sequence of digits) and this sequence of characters is the value of the string variable. When a string value or constant is assigned to a variable, it must be enclosed in quotation marks.

```
Phrase$ = "a test string"
```

The initial value of a string variable in QuickBASIC is the null string, meaning that it contains no characters. Thus a string variable may have a value of "covered boxes" or "abc" or "12345" or even a null value denoted by the symbol"", an empty pair of quotation marks.

Here is an example program that may help to illustrate the differences between numeric and string values.

```
' Example Program 3-3
' Display the values of a numeric
' and a string variable.

Cost = 225.75
Cost$ = "225.75"
PRINT Cost
PRINT Cost$
END
```

The following values are displayed.

```
 225.75
225.75
```

In the first assignment statement, the variable Cost is of numeric type and its value can be used in arithmetic calculations. This value is stored in the computer as a single binary number. In the second assignment statement, the variable Cost$ is of string type and its value consists of six characters, five digits, and a decimal point. It is stored in the computer as six encoded characters and cannot be used in calculations.

Note especially that these two variables, Cost and Cost$, are not the same and are not equal to each other, even though their values look similar. In fact, the only difference in the appearance of the two displayed values is the extra space before the numeric value. **A numeric variable is never equal to a string variable**, although it is possible to use special functions to convert from one to the other.

3.4 NUMBERS

We look first at the various kinds of numeric variables and see how their values are displayed.

Numeric Types

QuickBASIC defines four different types of numbers, as shown in Fig. 3.1. They are distinguished from one another by different suffix characters.

Integers and long integers are whole numbers, while single-precision and double-precision real numbers are decimal numbers. For example, Count% is an integer variable, Zip& is a long integer, Cost! is a single-precision real number, and AstroDistance# is a double-precision real number. If no suffix is used, the variable name (for example, Cost) denotes a single-precision real number.

TYPE	SUFFIX	RANGE	MEMORY
integer number	%	-32,768 to +32,767	2 bytes
long integer number	&	-2,147,483,648 to +2,147,483,647	4 bytes
single-precision real number	!	-3.4E+38 to -1.4E-45; +1.4E-45 to +3.4E+38	4 bytes
double-precision real number	#	-1.8D+308 to -5.0D-324; +5.0D-324 to +1.8D+308	8 bytes

Figure 3.1   Numeric types in QuickBASIC.

Some programs have no need for decimal numbers and use only integers. A group of program statements allows the default value of some or all numeric variables without suffixes to be changed from single-precision to another type. An example statement is

```
DEFINT A-Z
```

which changes all numeric variables in a program (any variable name beginning with A through Z, uppercase or lowercase) to the integer type.

One benefit derived from making this change is that an integer variable occupies half as much memory storage space as does a single-precision real variable (see Fig. 3.1). A second benefit is that arithmetic operations (see Section 3.5) with integers take much less computer time than operations with real numbers. A third reason for using integers is to avoid inaccuracies in calculations. Integer variable values are stored as exact values in memory while real variable values are stored as approximate values. We discuss this subject in greater detail in Chapter 8.

Other statements similar to DEFINT (such as DEFDBL to define double-precision real numbers) are listed in the language reference manual. We show a typical use of the DEFINT statement in Example Program 3-12. Note that if a special suffix (as described in the preceding paragraphs) is added to a numeric variable name, the DEFINT statement is ignored for that variable and its type is determined by the suffix.

Decimal and Exponential Notation

Real numbers can be written or displayed in decimal format, like 13.375, or in exponential format. The latter format is especially useful for very large or very small numbers. For example, the number 1,475,000,000,000 is displayed as 1.475E+12 if it is a single-precision value. This format is shorthand notation for 1.475 multiplied by 10 raised to the twelfth power (or 1.475 multiplied by a number consisting of a 1 followed by 12 zeros). When entering numbers, the plus sign is optional; the number can be written as 1.475E12. Small numbers can be represented in a similar fashion, the number 0.0000228 being written as 2.28E-5, which is 2.28 divided by 10 raised to the fifth power.

Double-precision real number values are written and displayed with the letter D instead of the letter E. Thus if the number 2,955,000,000 is a double-precision value, it is displayed as 2.955D+09 in exponential form.

Characters in Numbers

Sometimes when you write large numbers in documents or reports, you insert a comma between every three digits, like 2,125,000,000. **This format cannot be used when you enter a number into a computer program; the commas are not allowed.** Other common numeric formats, such as $19.95 and 75%, are also not allowed when entering numeric values (the dollar sign and percent sign are not valid characters in numeric values).

When you use a number in a program, as a constant or as the value of a variable, you can write it in either decimal or exponential format. A user can enter a number in response to the INPUT statement in either format.

Displaying Numeric Values

Depending on the size of a real number, QuickBASIC will make an automatic decision to display the number in either decimal or exponential format. If a PRINT statement can represent a single-precision number with seven or fewer digits, it displays the number in decimal (fixed-point) format. Otherwise, the number is displayed in exponential (floating-point) format.

In a similar manner, if a PRINT statement can represent a double-precision number with 16 or fewer digits, it displays the number in decimal format. Otherwise, the number is displayed in exponential format. Here is an example program that shows both display formats.

```
' Example Program 3-4
' Format for displaying single-precision numbers.
```

```
Large! = 1000
PRINT "The value of variable Large! is"; Large!
Larger! = -1000000
PRINT Larger!; "is a larger negative number"
Largest! = 1000000000
PRINT Largest!; "is displayed in exponential notation"
END
```

The following results are displayed.

```
The value of Large! is 1000
-1000000 is a larger negative number
 1E+09 is displayed in exponential notation
```

Note that the PRINT statement puts a space at the beginning of a positive number and a space at the end of all numbers. It puts a minus sign instead of a space at the beginning of a negative number.

3.5 ARITHMETIC OPERATIONS

Arithmetic expressions are used in BASIC to make numeric calculations. These expressions may contain arithmetic operators, numeric constants, and numeric variables. Here are the arithmetic operators and their symbols.

+	addition
–	subtraction
*	multiplication
/	division
\	integer division, quotient
MOD	integer division, remainder
^	exponentiation

The symbols for addition and subtraction are familiar. Some examples follow.

```
Sum = Sum + 1
N1 = N2 - N3
Ans = A - (B - C)
```

The symbol for multiplication is an asterisk (*) and must always be used. While the expression 2X in mathematics means 2 times X, in BASIC it must be written 2*X (or 2 * X, the spaces are optional). The symbol for ordinary division is the forward slash (/). In some cases it is necessary to perform integer division, and the symbol for calculating the quotient is the reverse slash (\). The operator MOD calculates the remainder. Here is an example program.

```
' Example Program 3-5
' Use of arithmetic operators.

PRINT "Let the variable X equal 3"
X = 3
PRINT "Divide the expression ((X * 7) - 2) by 5"
Result = ((X * 7) - 2) / 5
PRINT "Result of regular (/) division is"; Result
Result = ((X * 7) - 2) \ 5
PRINT "Result of integer (\) division, quotient is";
Result
Result = ((X * 7) - 2) MOD 5
PRINT "Result of integer (\) division, remainder is";
Result
END
```

It displays the following results.

```
Let the variable X equal 3
Divide the expression ((X * 7) - 2) by 5
Result of regular (/) division is 3.8.
Result of integer (\) division, quotient is 3
Result of integer (\) division, remainder is 4
```

Note that the second and third expressions use integer division and thus the values assigned to Result are integers.

As another example, we calculate the total cost of an item that has both a sales tax and a handling charge.

```
' Example Program 3-6
' Calculate the total price of an item
' using simple arithmetic operations.

Price = 13.90
TaxRate = .1   ' 10 percent
Handling = 1.00
Total = Price + (TaxRate * Price) + Handling
PRINT "Total price is $"; Total
END
```

This program displays the following output.

```
Total price is $ 16.29
```

Note the extra space between the dollar sign and the numeric value. This space is displayed because the PRINT statement puts a space at the beginning of a positive number. We show how to avoid displaying this space when we introduce the PRINT USING statement in Section 3.8.

Exponentiation means raising to a power. The variable X multiplied by itself is called X squared and is written X^2. Here is an example program.

```
' Example Program 3-7
' Use of the exponentiation operator.

X = 5
PRINT "The value of"; X; "cubed is"; X^3
END
```

It displays this line of output.

```
The value of 5 cubed is 125
```

The CONST Statement

A similar program can be used to calculate the area of a circle. In this program we introduce the concept of a symbolic constant. Just as we have named variables, we can have named constants. **The value of a named constant cannot be changed during the execution of the program.**

Named constants offer the advantage of making a program easier to read and understand. The constant name PI has more meaning for the average reader than the constant value 3.14159. The keyword CONST defines one or more constant definitions, separated by commas. The syntax is

```
CONST NAME1 = value1, NAME2 = value2,...
```

where NAME1 and NAME2 are constant names. We usually write constant names in all uppercase characters to distinguish them from variable names. A constant and a variable cannot have the same name. Here is an example program.

```
' Example Program 3-8
' Calculate the area of a circle
' using a named constant for pi.

CONST PI = 3.14159
Radius = 12.2
```

```
Area = PI * (Radius ^ 2)
PRINT "A circle of radius"; Radius;
PRINT "has an area of"; Area
END
```

It displays this result.

```
A circle of radius 12.2 has an area of 467.5943
```

Order of Precedence

There is a rule called the order of precedence for arithmetic operators. It says that operators within an expression (without parentheses) are evaluated from left to right, first
exponentiation, then division and multiplication, then addition and subtraction. Parts of
an expression within parentheses are always evaluated first, starting with the innermost
pairs of parentheses. By using this rule, we can determine just how QuickBASIC will
evaluate an expression.

For example, in the statement

```
X = 2 * 5 + (9 / 3) ^ 2 - 7
```

the first scan evaluates the expression in parentheses (9 / 3) and produces a value of 3,
resulting in the equivalent statement

```
X = 2 * 5 + 3 ^ 2 - 7
```

The second scan performs the exponentiation (the highest precedence operation), raising
3 to the 2 power and producing a value of 9. The equivalent statement then becomes

```
X = 2 * 5 + 9 - 7
```

The third scan multiplies 2 by 5 (the next highest precedence), giving a result of 10 and
an equivalent statement of

```
X = 10 + 9 - 7
```

The last scan performs the addition and subtraction and assigns a value of 12 to X.

An alternative way to write arithmetic expressions is to use lots of parentheses. For
example, we could have written our original statement as

```
X = (2 * 5) + ((9 / 3) ^ 2) - 7
```

We then follow the rule of evaluating the contents of inner parentheses first and quickly
calculate the value of the expression. **If you use lots of parentheses** (as we do in our
example programs), **you seldom need to worry about the order of precedence.**

As an example of how parentheses can change the value of an expression, look at the following program.

```
' Example Program 3-9
' Use of parentheses in expressions.

PRINT "Let A equal 5 and B equal 7"
A = 5
B = 7
PRINT
PRINT "A - 2 / B + 3 is"; A - 2 / B + 3
PRINT "(A - 2)/(B + 3) is"; (A - 2)/(B + 3)
PRINT "A - (2/B) + 3 is"; A - (2/B) + 3
PRINT "A - (2/(B + 3)) is"; A - (2/(B + 3))
END
```

This program displays these results.

```
Let A equal 5 and B equal 7

A - 2 / B + 3 is 7.714286
(A - 2)/(B + 3) is .3
A - (2/B) + 3 is 7.714286
A - (2/(B + 3)) is 4.8
```

As you can see, placing parentheses at different locations produces quite different arithmetic results.

QuickBASIC arithmetic expressions can be used with numbers having a wide range of sizes, depending on the type of numeric variables and constants. If a number is too large in absolute size (greater than 3.4E+38 or less than -3.4E+38 for single-precision real numbers), an Overflow error window is displayed when the program is executed. Pressing the Enter key with the OK box highlighted erases the error window. If a number is too small (closer to zero than 1.4E-45 or -1.4E-45 for single-precision real numbers), Quick-BASIC will substitute zero for the number. Double-precision variables allow much larger and smaller values to be used.

3.6 READING VALUES FROM MEMORY

The programs we have discussed so far require string or numeric values to be entered from the keyboard. An alternative form of input is to read values from a section of computer memory where they have been stored. We sometimes call this information stored in memory a *memory data file.*

The DATA Statement

DATA statements are used to store string or numeric constants in a memory data file. String constants must be enclosed in quotation marks if they contain commas, colons or significant leading or trailing blanks. Individual constants are separated from each other by commas. Here are some typical DATA statements.

```
DATA 10, 15, 25
DATA 8, Chair, 2, "Table, 3 ft. by 8 ft."
```

In the second DATA statement, note that the last constant (containing the word Table) is enclosed in parentheses because it contains a comma. DATA statements may be placed anywhere in a program before the END statement. When you run the program, one of the first actions that the computer takes is to scan the DATA statements and store their constants in memory.

The READ Statement

One or more READ statements are used to read these stored constant values from the memory data file and assign them to variables. The variables in a READ statement are separated from each other by commas. For example, the following READ statement can be used with the first of the preceding DATA statements.

```
READ Depth1, Depth2, Depth3
```

The computer keeps track automatically of which constants have been read and which is the next constant to read. We sometimes say there is an imaginary *data pointer* pointing to the location of the next data constant to be read. Reading starts with the first constant in the first DATA statement.

In the foregoing examples, when the first DATA statement is read, the first constant (10) is assigned to the first variable (Depth1), the second constant (15) to the variable (Depth2), and so forth.

The single READ statement with three variables can be replaced by three READ statements, each with one variable, and the results are identical. For example, the three statements

```
READ Depth1
READ Depth2
READ Depth3
```

are equivalent to the previous single READ statement.

Nonnumeric constants or values must be read into string variables. The statement

```
READ Quantity1, Name1$, Quantity2, Name2$
```

might be used to read the second DATA statement. If you try to assign a nonnumeric string to a numeric variable, you will get an error message. You can, of course, assign digit characters to a string variable, but you must remember that these digits represent a string value, not a numeric value.

If the number of variables in a program's READ statements is greater than the number of constants in its DATA statements, you will get an error when you try to read a constant that does not exist. No error occurs if the number of constants is greater than the number of variables, although the extra constant values will not be read.

Here is an example program that reads three numbers from a DATA statement, calculates their sum, and prints it on the screen.

```
' Example Program 3-10
' Use of the READ and DATA statements.

PRINT "Read three numbers from a DATA statement"
READ First, Second, Third
Sum = First + Second + Third            .
PRINT "The sum of the three numbers is"; Sum

DATA 15.3, -181.7, 225
END
```

This program displays the following output.

```
Read three numbers from a DATA statement
The sum of the three numbers is 58.6
```

READ and DATA statements are often used with the READ statement in a loop, as discussed in the next section.

3.7 A SIMPLE LOOP

Statements are executed sequentially, one after another, in a simple BASIC program. In the example program that follows, first a PRINT statement is executed, then three INPUT statements, then another PRINT statement, and finally an END statement. The result of the program is to print the sum of three numbers entered from the keyboard.

```
' Example Program 3-11
' Use three INPUT statements to enter
' three numbers and display their sum.

PRINT "Enter a number when prompted by '?'"
INPUT A
INPUT B
```

```
INPUT C
PRINT "The sum is"; A + B + C
END
```

This program produces the following results.

```
Enter a number when prompted by '?'
? 1.5
? 3
? 5
The sum is 9.5
```

Writing the program as a sequential structure becomes cumbersome and unsatisfactory if you want to find the sum of many numbers. Computer programs often need to repeat the same statement or sequence of statements over and over again. The technique used to accomplish this repetition is called *looping*, and we now introduce a simple loop structure called the FOR loop.

The FOR and NEXT Statements

There are many occasions when you wish to repeat one or more statements a fixed number of times. Two companion statements, the FOR statement and the NEXT statement, are used to create a loop for this purpose. For example, you might write the following program to sum the integers from 1 through 10.

```
' Example Program 3-12
' Calculate the sum of the first ten digits
' using a FOR loop.

DEFINT A-Z
Sum = 0
FOR Count = 1 TO 10
   Sum = Sum + Count
NEXT Count
PRINT "The sum of the first ten digits is"; Sum
END
```

It produces this line of output.

```
The sum of the first ten digits is 55
```

The variable Count is called a *control variable*. At the top of the loop, it is given the *initial limit value* of 1. After this value has been added to the variable Sum, the NEXT statement returns control to the top of the loop The FOR statement). The control variable

Count is automatically incremented by one to a value of 2 and looping continues. When Count reaches the value of 11, the FOR statement notes that this value exceeds the *final limit value* of 10 and looping stops, with control transferring to the statement following the NEXT statement.

Note that the variable Sum is initialized to a value of zero. Even though Quick-BASIC automatically initializes every variable, it is good programming practice to initialize variables that are used for this or similar purposes. Imagine the inaccuracy that would result if Sum had an initial value different from zero. It is clear to anyone reading the program that the value of Sum has been set initially to zero.

We indent the statement Sum = Sum + Count that makes up the body of the loop. Our custom is to indent all statements in the body of a loop; we think an indented format makes a program more readable.

Finally, note that because all variables in this program are numeric variables and have integer values, we designate all variables as integer variables. The DEFINT statement, introduced in Section 3.4, is used for that purpose. Integer definition of variables saves memory space and results in a faster-running program.

The STEP Modifier

The foregoing example is a simple FOR loop and illustrates the most common use of FOR and NEXT statements. The general FOR statement is defined as

```
FOR I = A TO B STEP C
```

where the initial and final limits, A and B, may be numeric variables, constants, or expressions. The step C may also be a numeric variable, constant, or expression and may be positive or negative. As demonstrated in Example Program 3-12, if no step is specified, a step of +1 is assumed.

After you have executed a FOR loop, the value of the control variable (see variable Count% in the next example program) **will often be different from the value of the final limit.** You should not use this control variable value for subsequent calculations or decisions because its value may vary depending on the limit values and step value used in the FOR loop.

```
' Example Program 3-13
' A FOR loop with the step greater than one
' and with two statements in the loop body.

Sum = 0
Product = 1
First% = 1
FOR Count% = First% TO 10 STEP 4
    Sum = Sum + Count%
    Product = Product * Count%
```

```
NEXT Count%
PRINT "Sum ="; Sum
PRINT "Product ="; Product
PRINT
PRINT "Last value of control variable is"; Count%
END
```

The preceding program produces the following output.

```
Sum = 15
Product = 45

Last value of control variable is 13
```

This time we denote integer variable names with a percent sign (%) suffix rather than using a DEFINT statement. The variable Count% takes on the successive values of 1, 5, and 9. The next value of Count% is 13 and because this value exceeds the final limit, the loop is terminated. Thus the final value of Sum is 15 and the final value of Product is 45. Go through the example yourself and verify these numbers.

We initialize the value of Product to one rather than zero to avoid multiplication by zero. Note that this example program has two statements in the body of the loop.

It is customary to use an integer variable for the counter variable. The initial limit variable First% should then also be an integer variable. The variables Sum and Product are designated as real variables (by default) because their values can become very large if the value of the final limit is increased.

If the step is positive and the initial limit is greater than the final limit, the loop is never executed and the control variable retains the value of the initial limit. Look at this variation of our previous example.

```
' Example Program 3-14
' A FOR loop with the initial value
' greater than the final value.

Sum = 0
Product = 1
First% = 11
FOR Count% = First% TO 10 STEP 4
   Sum = Sum + Count%
   Product = Product * Count%
NEXT Count%
PRINT "Sum ="; Sum
PRINT "Product ="; Product
PRINT
PRINT "Last value of control variable is"; Count%
END
```

The modified program produces this output.

```
Sum = 0
Product = 1

Last value of control variable is 11
```

Note that the variables Sum and Product keep their initial values.

Looping with a Negative Step

Another example program contains a loop with a negative step.

```
' Example Program 3-15
' FOR loop with a step variable
' having a negative value.

DEFINT A-Z
Total = 0
Jump = -2
FOR Count = 4 TO -4 STEP Jump
   Total = Total + Count
NEXT Count
PRINT "Total ="; Total
END
```

It generates the following output.

```
Total = 0
```

Note that the initial limit (4) must be greater than the final limit (-4) for the loop to work properly with a negative step (-2). We use the value of the variable Jump as the step.

3.8 MORE ON PRINTING

We have used the PRINT statement in several examples either to display a single value or to display several values separated by semicolons. Now we introduce other ways to control the format of PRINT statement displays.

The Comma Separator

Commas are used to separate the variables First, Second, and Third in the next example program. These separators tell the PRINT statement to display the three values in separate *print zones*, where a print zone is a subdivision of the screen width. The width of a print zone in QuickBASIC is 14 columns and each variable value is displayed at the beginning of a zone. Remember that an extra space is left in front of nonnegative numbers.

```
' Example Program 3-16
' Display of numeric values in print zones.

First = 5
Second = 10
Third = -20
PRINT First, Second, Third
END
```

Program output has the following format.

```
5                10             -20
```

Print zones provide a quick and easy way to format the output of a program, although they allow the programmer little flexibility.

Trailing Semicolons and Commas

A semicolon at the end of a PRINT statement, often called a *trailing semicolon,* has a special meaning: It suppresses the carriage return and line feed that normally follow a PRINT statement. A trailing comma does the same thing, but also advances to the beginning of the next print zone. For example, Fig. 3.2 shows the results produced by a pair of PRINT statements: one pair with a trailing semicolon, one with a trailing comma, and the third without trailing punctuation.

STATEMENTS	DISPLAY	
PRINT "A"; PRINT "B"	AB	
PRINT "A", PRINT "B"	A	B
PRINT "A" PRINT "B"	A B	

Figure 3.2 PRINT statement with trailing semicolon or comma.

You can use a PRINT statement with a trailing semicolon in place of the prompt in an INPUT statement, as shown in the next example program. This technique is often used with a long prompt string that if used in an INPUT statement would create a statement longer than the screen width. Here is a program that uses a PRINT statement with trailing semicolon as a prompt.

```
' Example Program 3-17
' Another version of Example Program 2-6
' but using a PRINT statement for a prompt.

PRINT "Enter your name, including first and last names";
INPUT Name$
PRINT
PRINT "Your name is "; Name$
END
```

The following results are produced.

```
Enter your name, including first and last names? Jo Kim

Your name is Jo Kim
```

Nested FOR Loops

We now consider a program that displays a rectangle of asterisks on the screen. It prints five rows of ten asterisks per row.

```
' Example Program 3-18
' Display five rows of ten asterisks on the screen,
' using a single FOR loop.

DEFINT A-Z
FOR Count = 1 TO 5
    PRINT "**********"
NEXT Count
END
```

The following display is produced.

```
**********
**********
**********
**********
**********
```

Remember that a FOR loop can contain one or more statements in the loop body. There is no reason that another FOR statement cannot be one of these statements. We can write a more general program to accomplish the same task by using a second FOR loop to produce each row of asterisks. This technique is called *nesting* FOR loops.

```
' Example Program 3-19
' Display five rows of ten asterisks on the screen,
' using nested FOR loops.

DEFINT A-Z
FOR Row = 1 TO 5
   FOR Column = 1 TO 10
      PRINT "*";    ' put a single asterisk in the row
   NEXT Column
   PRINT           ' start a new row after inner loop
NEXT Row
END
```

While control variable Row has a value of 1, the inner loop displays 10 asterisks on a single row. Control variable Column runs through the values from 1 to 10. Note the trailing semicolon after the PRINT statement inside the loop. This semicolon suppresses line feeds and keeps all asterisks on the same row. After a complete row of asterisks is displayed, another PRINT statement (without an argument) positions new output at the beginning of the next row.

The outer loop is controlled by the control variable Row, which is now assigned a value of 2. Control variable Column again runs through its range of values, displaying the second row. This process continues until all five rows have been displayed, producing the same output as Example Program 3-18.

Simple PRINT USING Statement

Another way to control the format of information displayed on the screen is to use a special PRINT statement called the PRINT USING statement. We introduce a simple form of that statement for use with numeric variables, values, and expressions. We refer you to the language reference manual or the on-line help system for information on additional forms and capabilities.

The PRINT USING statement uses a format string to control the appearance of items displayed on the screen. The format string is a string constant or variable, usually consisting of a sequence of numeric format characters (the # character) and an optional decimal point. The number of format characters included in the string must be large enough to accommodate the longest numeric value that will be displayed.

The number of format characters after the decimal point specifies the number of decimal digits that will be displayed. The numeric value is right-justified in the format string field and if necessary, padded with zeros on the right. The value is rounded if it contains too many decimal digits. If the field specified by the format string is too short, an error character, the percent sign (%), is displayed in front of the number.

Here is an example program showing how the PRINT USING statement works.

```
' Example Program 3-20
' Use of the PRINT USING statement
' with numeric constants and variables.

Number = 7
PRINT USING "####"; 125
PRINT USING "####"; Number, Number, Number
PRINT USING "####"; 1285.9
PRINT USING "####"; 34562
PRINT
PRINT USING "###.##"; 12.5, 25
PRINT USING "###.##"; -12.521
PRINT USING "###.##"; -133.33
END
```

This program produces the following display.

```
 125
   7   7   7
1286
%34562

 12.50 25.00
-12.52
%-133.33
```

Note that the displays of the third and sixth numbers are error displays because in each case, the format string did not provide a wide-enough field for the specified number.

A limitation of the PRINT USING statement is that the format string must be written with enough numeric format characters to accommodate the largest displayed number. The result is that smaller numbers are often displayed with leading blanks (see the second line of the preceding program's output). We discuss a more complicated way to solve this problem in Chapter 6.

Two other format characters are commonly used in numeric format strings. A pair of dollar signs ($$) can be used to replace the first numeric format (#) character in the format string. Any numbers formatted by this modified string are displayed with a dollar sign just before the first digit.

A comma can be placed directly in front of the decimal point in a format string, causing a comma to be displayed before every third digit left of the decimal point. The comma specifies another character position. Be sure that the number of format characters is greater than or equal to the number of characters to be displayed, including the dollar sign and each comma .

Ordinary text and spaces can also be included in a format string. You must be careful to avoid the other special format characters (!, \, -, +, *, ^, _, and %) that are listed and explained in the language reference manual and the on-line help system.

The next example program shows how the dollar sign and comma format characters can be used.

```
' Example Program 3-21
' Use of the PRINT USING statement
' with dollar amounts.

PRINT USING "$$#######,.##"; 1275.5
PRINT USING "$$#######,.##"; 52.95
PRINT USING "$$#######,.##"; 7531275
END
```

The following values are displayed.

```
    $1,275.50
       $52.95
$7,531,275.00
```

As explained previously, the two dollar signs create the leading dollar sign in the output. The comma before the decimal point creates any commas needed for separating thousands. Count carefully and note that ten format characters before the decimal point are needed to accommodate the third and largest numeric value.

Summary of Important Points

- The keyword LET is optional in QuickBASIC.
- A variable can have only one value at a time.
- Assigning a new value to a variable destroys the old value.
- A space or blank character is not allowed in variable names.
- Be consistent in the capitalization of variable names.
- A numeric variable is never equal to a string variable.
- Commas and dollar signs are not allowed in numbers or numeric constants entered by the user.
- The value of a named constant cannot be changed during the execution of a program.
- If you use lots of parentheses in an expression, you seldom need to worry about the order of precedence of arithmetic operators.
- After you have executed a FOR loop, the value of the control variable will often be different than the value of the final limit.

Common Errors

- Assigning a string value to a numeric variable.
- Including a blank or space character in a variable name.
- Using a QuickBASIC reserved word as a variable name.
- Changing the capitalization of a variable name and thus inadvertently changing all occurrences of that name throughout the program.
- Trying to use a string variable in an arithmetic statement.
- Entering a numeric value, containing commas or a dollar sign, from the keyboard.
- Confusing the forward slash (/) for conventional long division with the reverse slash (\) for integer division.
- Failing to put enough parentheses in a complicated arithmetic expression and then getting the wrong answer because the correct operator precedence was not recognized.
- Trying to READ more values than are stored in the program's DATA statements.
- Making the final limit value greater than the initial limit value in a FOR statement with a negative step.
- Assuming that the value of the control variable is equal to the final limit value after leaving a FOR loop.
- Improperly nesting FOR loops so that the NEXT statements are in the wrong order. Here is an example of this error.

      ```
      FOR I = 1 TO N
      FOR J = 1 TO N
      PRINT "*"
      NEXT I
      PRINT
      NEXT J
      ```

  The error is most likely to occur when loops are improperly indented, as they are in this example.
- Including too few formatting characters in the format string of a PRINT USING statement.

Self-Test Questions

1. What is the assignment operator in QuickBASIC?
2. Is the reserved word LET required in an assignment statement?
3. How does a program differentiate between a numeric variable name and a string variable name?
4. Is the statement B = B + 2 a valid QuickBASIC statement? Explain your answer.
5. What happens to the old value stored in a variable when a new value is assigned to the variable?

6. What is the initial value of
    (a) a numeric variable;
    (b) a string variable?

7. Can a space be included as part of a variable name?

8. How many characters are allowed in a variable name?

9. Which of the following expressions are valid variable names?
    (a) Ending
    (b) 2ndEnding
    (c) Spare Tire
    (d) NoSuchLuck

10. If the variable Value$ is assigned a value of 12, can you evaluate the expression Value$ - 2? Explain your answer.

11. What, if anything, is wrong with each of the following statements?
    (a) Value = 1,230,000
    (b) Value = 1.23E6
    (c) Value = 1.23D6
    (d) Value = 15%
    (e) Value = $12.95

12. Evaluate the following expressions.
    (a) $X = 1 - 2 / 2$
    (b) $X = 2 ^ 3 \ 1 / 2$
    (c) $X = 1 + 2 - 3 * 4 / 2$
    (d) $X = 2 + 2 / 2 + 2$

13. Can a DATA statement be
    (a) the first statement in a program;
    (b) the last statement in a program?

14. If the first READ statement in a program is `READ Number` and the first DATA statement is `DATA 3, -2, 7` what value is assigned to the variable Number?

15. If a program has one READ statement and one DATA statement, what happens if the number of variables in the READ statement is greater than the number of values in the DATA statement?

16. If a step value is not specified in a FOR statement,
    (a) what step size is assumed;
    (b) is it positive or negative?

17. If the step size is positive, how many times does a FOR loop execute if the initial limit
    (a) is equal to the final limit;
    (b) is greater than the final limit?

18. Given the FOR loop

```
FOR I = 1 TO 5 STEP 3
NEXT I
```

what is the value of variable I after the loop has finished executing?

19. How many times will the following FOR loop execute?

```
FOR Count = 1 TO 5 STEP -1
NEXT Count
```

20. What is the effect of a trailing semicolon at the end of a PRINT statement?

21. What display is produced by the statement

```
PRINT USING "##.##": Number
```

when Number has
(a) a value of 17.2;
(b) a value of -17.2?

Practice Programs

1. Assign the value 10259 to the variable A and the value 137321 to the variable B. Display the sum of these two variables on the screen.

2. A DATA statement contains three numeric values. Display the average of these three values on the screen. Test your program using the following DATA statement.

```
DATA 1001, 12.3, -2.59
```

3. Ask a user to enter his or her first name, middle initial, and last name, all on separate lines. Store these values in three separate variables. Then display the complete name on the screen, with a single space between names and initial, and a period and space after the initial. Test your program by entering the following three string values.

```
"Constance"
"W"
"Green"
```

4. Ask a user to enter a number and then display the cube of the number on the screen. Your screen should look like this (entered number is in bold-face type).

```
Number? 3
Cube of 3 is 27
```

Test your program using the numbers 3 and -7.

5. A DATA statement contains five string values, each consisting of a single character. Assign these characters to variables and display them on the screen in the following pattern.

```
M  O  V  I  E
O
V
I
E
```

Note that the first data value is displayed only once. Test your program using the following DATA statement.

```
DATA M, O, V, I, E
```

6. Ask a user to enter three numbers and store them in variables A, B, and C. Calculate and display the value of the expression $B^2 - 4AC$. Test your program using the values A = 4, B = 7, and C = 3.

7. A farmer has a 14-foot-diameter silo that is 60 feet high. Ask a user to enter the depth of silage that has been stored in this silo. Display the number of tons of silage in storage. Assume corn silage that has an average density of 45 pounds per cubic foot. Test your program using a silage depth of 46 feet.

8. Use the FOR statement with a negative step to display the integers from 10 down to 1 in a single horizontal line.

9. Ask a user to enter two numbers and then display their sum and difference on the screen. The screen display should look like this.

```
Enter two numbers: 13.2, 7.5
Sum is 20.7  Difference is 5.7
```

Test your program using the following number pairs.

```
13.2, 7.5
128.3, 301.7
56, 7
```

10. A temperature in degrees Fahrenheit (F) can be converted to a temperature in degrees Celsius (C) by using the following equation:

$$C = \frac{5 \times (F - 32)}{9}$$

Ask a user to enter a temperature in degrees Fahrenheit and display the corresponding temperature in degrees Celsius. The screen should look as follows.

```
Fahrenheit temperature? 59
Celsius temperature is 15 degrees
```

Test your program using Fahrenheit temperature values of 59, 32, and 212 degrees.

11. The total resistance of several resistors in parallel can be calculated using the expression

$$R = \frac{1}{\dfrac{1}{R_1} + \dfrac{1}{R_2} + ... + \dfrac{1}{R_n}}$$

where R_1, R_2, and so forth are the individual resistances in ohms and R is the total resistance. Calculate the total resistance of 10 resistors, each with a resistance value of 2 megohms (2.0E+06 ohms), that are connected in parallel. Display your result with an appropriate label.

12. Ask a user to enter the size of a room (width and length, in feet) and the price of carpet per square yard. Add a charge of $2.50 per square yard for delivery and installation. Display the total cost of carpeting the room. Use the PRINT USING statement to display dollar amounts rounded to the nearest cent. The screen should look as follows.

```
Length of room in feet? 18
Width of room in feet? 12
Price of carpet per square yard? 12.50
Cost of installed carpeting is 348.00
```

Test your program using the following data.

LENGTH	WIDTH	PRICE
18	12	$12.50
11	11	$14.35
10	8	$9.75

13. The present value (P) of an amount (A) produced by compounding interest annually for N years at a percentage interest rate of I is given by the equation

$$P = \frac{A}{\left(1 + \dfrac{I}{100}\right)^N}$$

Ask a user to enter the amount of money in dollars, the interest rate in percent, and the number of years. Display the present value of this amount. The screen should look like the following display. As before, use the PRINT USING statement to display output.

```
Amount? 10000
Interest in percent? 11.5
Number of years? 12
Present value is 2708.33
```

Test your program using the following data.

AMOUNT	INTEREST	YEARS
10,000	11.5%	12
5,000	8.3%	9

14. Ask a user to enter the amount of an initial deposit in a savings account. Assuming an interest rate of 8 percent, compounded annually, calculate and display the amount of money in the account at the end of 10 years. Test your program using initial deposits of $100, $1,200, and $5,000.

4

PROGRAM CONTROL STATEMENTS

4.1 INTRODUCTION

Computer programs become more powerful and useful when they are capable of repeating actions (looping) and making decisions (branching). We discuss both concepts and explain how to use specific looping and branching statements. **Any computer program can be written using only three program structures: sequential, loop, and branch.**

Before discussing loops and branches, we introduce relational operators and logical expressions, fundamental concepts in any discussion of program control statements. We then examine the DO loop and the IF branch. We introduce a multibranch structure using the SELECT CASE statement.

Having introduced strings in Chapter 2, we now discuss string variables and operations in greater detail. We examine further the use of DATA statements in a program. We show two common examples of computer programs; one to count and sum a sequence of numbers, the other to identify the largest and smallest numbers in a sequence.

4.2 RELATIONAL OPERATORS

The operation of many looping and branching statements depends on the value of an expression that may be either true or false. This expression is called a *logical expression.*

Simple Logical Expressions

A *simple* logical expression consists of two variables or values connected by a *relational operator*. For example, the phrase Sum = 7 is a logical expression, where Sum is a numeric variable, the equal sign is a relational operator, and 7 is a constant. **This is not an assignment statement, even though it has the same syntax and uses the same symbol** (the equal sign) **as an assignment statement.**

You can always distinguish between an assignment statement and a logical expression by the context in which the statement or expression is used. Note that the equal sign, when used as a relational operator, has a different meaning than the same symbol used as an assignment operator (see Chapter 3).

The logical expression Sum = 7 is true if the variable Sum has a value of seven. We can also say that the logical expression itself has a value of true. If Sum has a value other than seven, then the logical expression is false (or has a value of false).

We have previously introduced the idea of a variable having a value. **Now we introduce the idea of a logical expression having a value of true or false; it cannot have any other value.** Thus the expression Sum = 7 has a value of true if Sum has a value of seven.

The six relational operators are listed below.

=	equal
<>	not equal
<	less than
<=	less than or equal
>	greater than
>=	greater than or equal

We look next at some examples of logical expressions, such as Limit >= 0, which has a value of true if Limit has a zero or positive value. Another logical expression containing a string variable is Ans$ <> "OK", where, as before, the string constant must be enclosed in quotation marks. The logical expression is true if Ans$ has a value other than "OK".

Most string comparisons involve the equal or not-equal operator. It is possible to use the other relational operators with string variables and constants, but an explanation of how these comparisons are made is deferred until Chapter 10.

Compound Logical Expressions

So far we have discussed simple logical expressions with only a single relational operator. It is possible to join together two or more simple logical expressions by using the reserved word AND or the reserved word OR. The result is called a *compound* logical expression.

For example, the expression (A = 5) AND (B = 7) is a compound logical expression. Parentheses are not required but are added for clarification. This expression has a value of true only if the variable A has a value of five and the variable B has a value of seven. The reserved word AND requires that both simple logical expressions be true for the compound expression to be true. If either simple logical expression is false, or if both are false, then the compound expression is false.

As another example, look at the expression (A < 2) OR (A > 9), which is true if A is less than two or if A is greater than nine. The reserved word OR requires that either one or the other simple logical expression be true (or that both be true) for the compound expression to be true. If both simple logical expressions are false, then the compound expression is false.

Here is an example program that uses these compound logical expressions.

```
' Example Program 4-1
' Display the values of two logical expressions,
' where value -1 means true and 0 means false.

A = 5
B = 7
PRINT "A equals 5 and B equals 7"
PRINT
PRINT "The value of (A = 5) AND (B - 7) is ";
PRINT (A = 5) AND (B - 7)
PRINT "The value of (A < 2) OR (A > 9) is ";
PRINT (A < 2) OR (B > 9)
END
```

It produces the following display.

```
A equals 5 and B equals 7

The value of (A = 5) AND (B = 7) is -1
The value of (A < 2) OR (A > 9) is  0
```

Note that instead of displaying the words "true" or "false", QuickBASIC displays a numeric value of -1 for true and a value of 0 for false.

A Truth Table

The properties of compound logical expressions are shown in Fig. 4.1, in a format sometimes called a truth table. X and Y are any two logical expressions, while T means true and F means false. For example, if X is false and Y is true, then the expression X AND Y is false, while the expression X OR Y is true.

It is possible to combine more than two simple logical expressions into a compound expression. Such complicated compound expressions are seldom needed in QuickBASIC because of the availability of the SELECT CASE statement (see Section 4.5).

It is also possible to reverse the value of any logical expression by preceding it with the reserved word NOT. For example, if the expression X = 3 is true, then the expression NOT (X = 3) is false. Note that the latter expression is identical in value to the expression X <> 3.

X	Y	X AND Y	X OR Y
T	T	T	T
T	F	F	T
F	T	F	T
F	F	F	F

Figure 4.1   A logical truth table.

4.3 CONTROL OF PROGRAM FLOW: THE DO LOOP

We have already discussed the value of a program structure that repeats the same statement or sequence of statements over and over again. In Chapter 3 we introduced one type of loop, the FOR loop, where the number of repetitions is determined when the program is written. A more general type of loop structure should allow the number of repetitions to be varied by input from the user or by a decision of the program itself.

A General Looping Structure

A general looping structure requires two kinds of actions, one to tell the program to repeat a block or group of adjoining statements, and the other to tell it when to stop repeating. Look at the following example program.

```
' Example Program 4-2
' Display the sum of positive numbers
' entered from the keyboard.

Sum = 0
PRINT "Display the sum of several positive numbers."
PRINT "Enter a positive number at each question mark."
PRINT "Enter a nonpositive number to stop."
INPUT Number
```

```
DO WHILE Number >= 0
   Sum = Sum + Number
   INPUT Number
LOOP
PRINT "The sum is"; Sum
END
```

User interaction is very similar to that in Example Program 3-11.

```
Display the sum of several positive numbers.
Enter a positive number at each question mark.
Enter a nonpositive number to stop.
? 1.5
? 3
? 5
? -1
The sum is 9.5
```

The DO and LOOP Statements

We have introduced two new statements, DO and LOOP. These statements enclose an indented block of statements called the *loop body* that is executed over and over again. Whenever the LOOP statement is reached, control is transferred back to the DO statement. At this point in the program (the DO statement), a check is made to determine whether the value of Number is positive or not. While the value is positive, the loop continues. If the value becomes nonpositive, control is transferred out of the loop and the statement following the LOOP statement (the last PRINT statement) is executed.

The first INPUT statement (outside the loop) accepts the first number entered by the user. If this number is nonpositive, no sum is calculated. The INPUT statement inside the loop is used for subsequent entries. Indentation is used to set off the block of statements in the body of the loop.

In the example of user interaction, when a value of -1 is entered for Number, the DO statement transfers control to the statement after the LOOP statement and the sum is printed. Note that the variable Sum contains the sum of only the positive numbers entered, and does not include the negative number (-1).

The DO loop provides the most general looping structure in QuickBASIC. **Either the DO statement or the LOOP statement may be modified to control the duration of the loop. The test phrase used to modify DO or LOOP may contain either the reserved word WHILE or the reserved word UNTIL,** and whichever word is used, it must be followed by a logical expression.

The WHILE and UNTIL Tests

A DO WHILE or LOOP WHILE statement causes the loop to repeat as long as the logical expression following WHILE is true. One example loop structure is

```
DO WHILE Sum < 10
LOOP
```

and another example is

```
DO
LOOP WHILE Flag = 0
```

A DO UNTIL or LOOP UNTIL statement causes the loop to repeat until the logical expression following the reserved word UNTIL is true. Here are two more example loop structures.

```
DO UNTIL Sum >= 10
LOOP

DO
LOOP UNTIL Count = 7
```

Our next example program uses a DO loop with an UNTIL test at the end of the loop. The value of Line$ is displayed at least once before the value of More$ is checked at the bottom of the loop.

```
' Example Program 4-3
' Display a line of text and repeat
' if requested by the user.
' This is Version 1 of the program.

Line$ = "This is a sample line of text."
DO
    PRINT Line$
    INPUT "Display again (Y/N)? ", More$
LOOP UNTIL More$ = "N"
END
```

Typical user interaction with the program is as follows.

```
This is a sample line of text.
Display again (Y/N)? y
This is a sample line of text.
Display again (Y/N)? n
This is a sample line of text.
Display again (Y/N)? N
```

Note that the logical expression More$ = "N" is case sensitive. The expression is false if either a lowercase "y" or "n" is entered and so the loop continues. If the character "N" is entered, the expression becomes true and the loop stops.

A DO WHILE or DO UNTIL statement checks the logical expression at the top of the loop before it is executed the first time and each subsequent time. A LOOP WHILE or LOOP UNTIL statement checks the expression at the bottom of the loop before the loop is repeated.

QuickBASIC supports DO loops with a test phrase (containing WHILE or UNTIL) either at the top of the loop after the DO statement or at the bottom of the loop after the LOOP statement, but not at both places. This practice conforms with the principle that there should be only one exit point from a loop.

Here are three more example programs that accomplish essentially the same task as Example Program 4-3 but use different programming structures and logical expressions. The next program uses a WHILE test instead of an UNTIL test. It also allows the user to enter either uppercase or lowercase characters for "Y" and "N".

```
' Example Program 4-4
' Display a line of text and repeat
' if requested by the user.
' This is Version 2 of the program.

Line$ = "This is a sample line of text."
DO
    PRINT Line$
    INPUT "Display again (Y/N)? ", More$
LOOP WHILE More$ = "Y" OR More$ = "y"
END
```

Typical user interaction might look as follows.

```
This is a sample.line of text.
Display again (Y/N)? y
This is a sample line of text.
Display again (Y/N)? n
```

In this example, entering any value except "Y" or "y" makes the logical expression false and the loop stops. We will discuss in Chapter 5 how the UCASE$ function can be used to accomplish the same result as this compound logical expression. The ability to accept either lowercase or uppercase input is important because it reduces errors made by inexperienced users.

Here is another version of the same program, using an UNTIL test after the DO statement.

```
' Example Program 4-5
' Display a line of text and repeat
' if requested by the user.
' This is Version 3 of the program.
```

```
Line$ = "This is a sample line of text."
INPUT "Display line (Y/N)? ", More$
DO UNTIL More$ = "N" OR More$ = "n"
    PRINT Line$
    INPUT "Display again (Y/N)? ", More$
LOOP
END
```

In this example, the first request for input is placed outside the loop and the value of More$ is checked at the beginning of the loop. If the value is "N" or "n", the value of Line$ will never be displayed. If the value is "Y" (or any other character), the line is displayed and another request for input is executed inside the loop. This is the only version of the program that can prevent the line of text from being displayed at least once, as shown by the following program output.

```
Display line (Y/N)? N
```

The EXIT DO Statement

Our final example in this series of programs provides a direct exit from inside the loop using the EXIT DO statement but does so at the risk of making the program more difficult to understand. We do not recommend the use of this statement.

```
' Example Program 4-6
' Display a line of text and repeat
' if requested by the user.
' This is Version 4 of the program

Line$ = "This is a sample line of text."
DO
    PRINT Line$
    INPUT "Display again (Y/N)? ", More$
    IF More$ = "N" OR More$ = "n" THEN EXIT DO
LOOP
END
```

As before, we show a sample of user interaction.

```
This is a sample line of text.
Display again (Y/N)? N
```

This program introduces a simple version of the IF statement, which we will discuss in more detail in the next section. In the present program, however, it is used to test the compound logical expression (More$ = "N" OR More$ = "n"). If the expression is true, the EXIT DO statement exits the loop, meaning that it transfers control to the statement following the LOOP statement.

In general, the EXIT DO statement does not produce as readable and easily understood a program as does the WHILE or UNTIL test. The reason for this lack of clarity is that a loop exit occurs in the middle of the loop, whereas we normally look for a loop exit at the beginning or the end of a loop. In small loops like those in our example programs, the difference is not apparent. But if the loop is large, maybe covering two or three pages, it is often difficult to find a separate loop exit that is not part of either the DO or LOOP statement. **We recommend that you use the EXIT DO statement only as an emergency exit from a loop where the normal WHILE or UNTIL tests cannot be used conveniently.**

The EXIT FOR Statement

Another, similar statement is the EXIT FOR statement. There may be times when you want to stop a FOR loop before the counter variable has reached the final limit. This statement is available for that purpose.

We hesitate to introduce the EXIT FOR statement because it should be used only in extreme cases when no other reasonable solution can be found. A FOR loop is designed to execute a fixed number of times. If you stop it before the counter variable reaches its final limit, you stand the risk of confusing anyone who is reading and trying to understand your program.

The following program asks a user to enter three numbers, one at a time, and displays the inverse of each number after it has been entered. The number zero is not a valid entry because you cannot divide by zero. If a zero (whose inverse is infinite) is entered, the EXIT FOR statement causes the program to stop. Again note our use of a simple IF statement.

```
' Example Program 4-7
' Enter three numbers and display their inverse
' values. Stop the program if any number is zero.

FOR Count% = 1 to 3
    INPUT "Number? ", Number
    IF Number = 0 THEN EXIT FOR
    PRINT "Inverse is"; 1 / Number
NEXT Count%
END
```

The program produces these results.

```
Number? 0.5
Inverse is 2
Number? 0
```

Think of the EXIT FOR statement as providing an emergency exit from a FOR loop that would normally be expected to go to completion. It should never be used for normal termination of a FOR loop. In fact, the EXIT FOR statement is seldom necessary, as shown by Example Program 4-10, which provides a better solution to this particular problem.

Infinite Loops

Sometimes a programming mistake is made and a loop repeats itself over and over. The program never stops; the loop just keeps repeating. This type of loop is called an *infinite loop*. If you suspect that your program is caught in an infinite loop, you can interrupt it by pressing the Interrupt key (the Ctrl-Break key).

4.4 CONTROL OF PROGRAM FLOW: THE IF BRANCH

As we have seen in the previous example programs, it is often necessary for a computer program to make decisions. The IF statement is used by a computer program to decide which of two blocks of statements to execute. This process is called *branching*.

The IF, ELSE, and END IF Statements

The most common branching structure in QuickBASIC is the IF branch. The syntax of this structure is as follows.

```
IF logical expression THEN
    first block of statements
ELSE
    second block of statements
END IF
```

Each block of statements consists of one or more statement lines. The logical expression can be either a simple expression or a compound expression. The first block is executed if the logical expression is true, and control then transfers to the statement following the END IF statement. The ELSE statement and its associated block of statements (the second block) is executed if the logical expression is false. The ELSE statement and its block of statements are optional.

The structure we have described is called the block IF structure. The ELSE and END IF statements must be on separate lines by themselves. **Note that END IF must be two words; the space is significant.**

The following syntax is used when the ELSE statement is omitted. An END IF statement is always required with the block IF structure, even if there is no ELSE block.

```
IF logical expression THEN
   block of one or more statements
END IF
```

Here is a simple program that illustrates the use of the block IF structure. This type of program would normally be part of a larger program and used to determine whether a user's answer to a question is Y or N (for yes or no).

```
' Example Program 4-8
' Use the block IF structure
' to select an answer.

INPUT "Answer Y or N: ", Reply$
IF Reply$ = "Y" OR Reply$ = "y" THEN
   PRINT "Your answer is YES"
ELSE
   PRINT "Your answer is NO"
END IF
END
```

The following output is produced in two runs of the program.

```
Answer Y or N: N
Your answer is NO

Answer Y or N: Y
Your answer is YES
```

The combination of IF and ELSE statements allows the choice of one of two blocks of statements. If the value of Reply$ is "Y" or "y", the logical expression in the IF statement is true and the first block of statements (just a single PRINT statement in this case) is executed. If Reply$ has any other value, the second block (another PRINT statement) is executed. An END IF statement is used to indicate the end of the block IF structure. A more accurate version of this program is Example Program 4-12.

Here is another example using a compound logical expression. The parentheses around the simple expressions A = 0 and B = 0 are not necessary but may make the program a little easier to read.

```
' Example Program 4-9
' A two-way branch using a compound
' logical expression.

INPUT "Value of A? ", A
INPUT "Value of B? ", B
```

```
IF (A = 0) OR (B = 0) THEN
    PRINT "Either A or B is zero."
ELSE
    PRINT "The value of A/B is"; A / B
    PRINT "The value of B/A is"; B / A
END IF
END
```

If either equality in the logical expression is true, one of the divisions (A/B or B/A) is not defined. This program traps the error (A = 0 or B = 0) and displays an error message. Here are two sample runs.

```
Value of A? 6
Value of B? 0
Either A or B is zero

Value of A? 6
Value of B? 3
The value of A/B is 2
The value of B/A is .5
```

Note that the block of statements following ELSE contains two statements

A third example of the block IF structure is a program, similar to Example Program 4-7, that avoids the use of the EXIT FOR statement. We think it is a better program structure.

```
' Example Program 4-10
' Enter three numbers and display their inverse values.
' Display an error message if any number is zero.

FOR Count% = 1 to 3
    INPUT "Number? ", Number
    IF Number = 0 THEN
        PRINT "You cannot take the inverse of zero."
    ELSE
        PRINT "Inverse is"; 1 / Number
    END IF
NEXT Count%
END
```

These results are produced.

```
Number? 0.5
Inverse is 2
```

```
Number? 0
You cannot take the inverse of zero
Number? 0.1
Inverse is 10
```

This program illustrates our belief that there is seldom a need for the EXIT FOR statement and we urge you not to use it in the programs that you write.

The Single-Line IF Statement

A simple variation of the IF structure is the single-line IF statement.

```
IF Ans = 17 THEN PRINT "Correct" ELSE PRINT "Wrong"
```

When using this IF statement, the entire statement must be written on a single line. As
before, the ELSE clause is optional. Here is another example without that clause.

```
IF Reply$ = "Y" THEN PRINT Value
```

Note that an END IF statement is not required and not allowed. We used this IF
structure in Example Programs 4-6 and 4-7.

The ELSEIF Statement

There is an extended version of the block IF structure that uses the ELSEIF statement to
support multiple branching. Each ELSEIF statement creates a separate branch that may
contain its own block of statements. The ELSEIF statement has a syntax similar to that of
the IF statement.

In the next example, a menu is displayed and the user is asked to choose one of
three options. Depending on the choice, a different line of characters is displayed. If a
number is entered that does not appear in the menu, the user is told that the choice is
invalid.

```
' Example Program 4-11
' A menu-driven program that uses the ELSEIF
' statement in a multibranch structure.

DEFINT A-Z
PRINT "       Command Menu"
PRINT
PRINT "1...display line of stars"
PRINT "2...display line of periods"
PRINT "3...display line of pluses"
```

```
PRINT
INPUT "Your choice? ", Choice
PRINT
IF Choice = 1 THEN
    FOR I = 1 to 50
        PRINT "*";
    NEXT I
    PRINT
ELSEIF Choice = 2 THEN
    FOR I = 1 to 50
        PRINT ".";
    NEXT I
    PRINT
ELSEIF Choice = 3 THEN
    FOR I = 1 to 50
        PRINT "+";
    NEXT I
    PRINT
ELSE
    PRINT "You must enter 1, 2, or 3."
END IF
END
```

We use a FOR loop in each branch to display a line of characters. Note the use of trailing semicolons in the statements that print these characters, keeping all characters on the same line. Also note the final PRINT statement that prints a carriage return and line feed at the end of each line of characters.

An IF statement and two ELSEIF statements are used to select one of three valid choices. The ELSE statement displays an error message if the user enters a number other than 1, 2, or 3. The error message is positive, not negative, telling the user what numbers can be entered. Here is a sample of program output.

```
        Command Menu

1...display line of stars
2...display line of periods
3...display line of pluses

Your choice? 3

++++++++++++++++++++++++++++++++++++++++++++++++++++
```

Now that we have introduced the ELSEIF statement, we show a better but slightly more complicated version of Example Program 4-8 that checks both positive and negative answers.

```
' Example Program 4-12
' Check both the YES and NO answers.

INPUT "Answer Y or N: ", Reply$
IF Reply$ = "Y" OR Reply$ = "y" THEN
   PRINT "Your answer is YES"
ELSEIF Reply$ = "N" OR Reply$ = "n" THEN
   PRINT "Your answer is NO"
ELSE
   PRINT "You must answer Y or N"
END IF
END
```

This program produces the following output in two runs.

```
Answer Y or N: Q
You must answer Y or N

Answer Y or N: N
Your answer is NO
```

This is a better program because it forces the user to enter an answer (either Y or N) anticipated by the programmer.

4.5 CONTROL OF PROGRAM FLOW: THE SELECT CASE BRANCH

Another variation of the branching structure is provided by the multibranch SELECT CASE statement. This structure allows one of several branches or actions to be selected. The basis of selection can be broader than the simple true or false condition of the IF structure.

The SELECT CASE Statement

The general form of the SELECT CASE structure is as follows.

```
SELECT CASE case expression
CASE test1, test2
   first block of statements
CASE test3
   second block of statements
CASE test4, test5, test6
   third block of statements
CASE ELSE
   another block of statements
END SELECT
```

The *case expression* in the first line may be any expression or variable, string or numeric. If the case expression is of type string, all the tests must be string tests; if numeric, all tests must be numeric. If a test is satisfied, the block of statements associated with that test is executed and control transfers to the statement after END SELECT. If no test is satisfied, the block of statements after CASE ELSE is executed.

The CASE ELSE statement and its block of statements is optional. You will get a run-time error, however, if none of the tests is satisfied and there is no CASE ELSE statement. **We recommend that you always include a CASE ELSE statement in a SELECT CASE structure.**

Here is the previous example, written using this new structure.

```
' Example Program 4-13
' A menu-driven program that uses the SELECT
' CASE statement in a multibranch structure.

DEFINT A-Z
PRINT "        Command Menu"
PRINT
PRINT "1...display line of stars"
PRINT "2...display line of periods"
PRINT "3...display line of pluses"
PRINT
INPUT "Your choice? ", Choice
PRINT
SELECT CASE Choice
CASE 1
   FOR I = 1 TO 50
      PRINT "*";
   NEXT I
   PRINT
CASE 2
   FOR I = 1 TO 50
      PRINT ".";
   NEXT I
   PRINT
CASE 3
   FOR I = 1 TO 50
      PRINT"+";
   NEXT I
   PRINT
CASE ELSE
   PRINT "You must enter 1, 2, or 3."
END SELECT
END
```

This program produces the same output as Example Program 4-11. The form of these two programs is very similar.

The CASE Tests

The real power of the SELECT CASE structure lies in the variety of case tests that are available. These tests can be any combination of three different types of tests, using constant values or constant expressions.

One type of test specifies a constant value, either string or numeric, that the case expression must match. If the case expression is a numeric variable named Choice, a CASE statement with two tests might be CASE -7, 10 / 2 and is satisfied if Choice has a value of -7 or 5 (the value of the expression 10 / 2). Here is the CASE structure for these tests.

```
SELECT CASE Choice
CASE -7, 10 / 2
   PRINT "Choice has value of -7 or 5."
END SELECT
```

Another type of test specifies a range of values, in the format low value TO high value, that the case expression must match. Using the same case expression as before, a CASE statement might be CASE 14 TO 21 and is satisfied if Choice has a value between 14 and 21 inclusive. Here is a revised CASE structure that includes both the preceding tests.

```
SELECT CASE Choice
CASE -7, 10 / 2
   PRINT "Choice has value of -7 or 5."
CASE 14 TO 21
   PRINT "Choice has value between 14 and 21."
END SELECT
```

The preceding CASE structure could also have been written in the following form.

```
SELECT CASE Choice
CASE -7, 10 / 2, 14 TO 21
   PRINT "Choice has value of -7 or 5 ";
   PRINT "or between 14 and 21."
END SELECT
```

A third type of test specifies a logical comparison, in the form IS OP value, that the case expression must satisfy. The symbol OP means one of the logical operators. Again using the variable Choice, a CASE statement might be CASE IS > 175 and is satisfied if Choice has a value greater than 175. The CASE structure for all three test types now looks as follows.

```
SELECT CASE Choice
CASE -7, 10 / 2
    PRINT "Choice has value of -7 or 5."
CASE 14 TO 21
    PRINT "Choice has value between 14 and 21."
CASE IS > 175
    PRINT "Choice has value greater than 175."
END SELECT
```

Note that variables and variable expressions cannot be used in a CASE test; only constant values and constant expressions are allowed. These tests are more comprehensive than the simple tests of the IF structure.

Here is another example program using the SELECT CASE structure.

```
' Example Program 4-14
' Display the result of reading the
' body temperature of a patient.

INPUT "Temperature reading? ", Temperature
SELECT CASE Temperature
CASE 80 TO 98.5
    PRINT "Temperature is subnormal"
CASE 98.5 TO 98.7
    PRINT "Normal temperature"
CASE IS > 98.7
    PRINT "The patient has a fever"
CASE ELSE
    PRINT "That reading is much too low. Be sure to"
    PRINT "enter a reading in degrees Fahrenheit."
END SELECT
END
```

It produces the following output in two different runs.

```
Temperature reading? 98.6
Normal temperature

Temperature reading? 100.5
The patient has a fever
```

Finally, we look at an example program, similar to Example Program 4-8, that uses a string expression for the case expression. This program has two new features. First, it defines the constant FALSE as being equal to zero and the constant TRUE as being equal to NOT FALSE (any nonzero value). Second, it uses the numeric variable ValidAnswer as a flag variable to determine if a valid answer was given. A *flag variable* is usually an integer variable that has a value of either true (nonzero) or false (zero). It is often used in a program to determine the next action to be taken. In this case the DO loop continues until flag variable ValidAnswer is true.

```
' Example Program 4-15
' Define constants TRUE and FALSE. Ask a question and
' determine if the answer is Y or N. Keep asking the
' question until an acceptable answer is given.
' Use variable ValidAnswer as a flag variable.

DEFINT A-Z
CONST FALSE = 0, TRUE = NOT FALSE
DO
    INPUT "Your answer? ", Ans$
    SELECT CASE Ans$
    CASE "Y", "y"
       PRINT "The answer is YES"
       ValidAnswer = TRUE
    CASE "N", "n"
       PRINT "The answer is NO"
       ValidAnswer = TRUE
    CASE ELSE
       PRINT "Please enter Y or N"
       ValidAnswer = FALSE
    END SELECT
LOOP UNTIL ValidAnswer = TRUE
END
```

This program produces the following output

```
Your answer? q
Please enter Y or N
Your answer? y
The answer is YES
```

The tests in a SELECT CASE structure must be written in such a manner that the case expression can choose only one block of statements. If tests in two different CASE statements satisfy the case expression, the program will become confused. You may be able to use the block IF structure instead of the SELECT CASE structure if this situation occurs in one of your programs.

4.6 MORE ABOUT STRINGS

As explained earlier, string variable names always end with a dollar sign character. These variables contain string values, character sequences of varying length. The maximum length of a string in QuickBASIC is about 32,000 characters. In normal usage, you have no need to be concerned about exceeding this maximum length.

In addition to its maximum length, every string has a current or dynamic length, the actual number of characters currently stored in the string variable. Information on dynamic length is also stored in the string variable and can be accessed with a standard QuickBASIC function (the LEN function, described in Chapter 5).

Quotation Marks in String Constants

It is not possible in QuickBASIC to include quotation marks within a string because these punctuation marks are used as string delimiters. One solution is to use single quotation marks (acute accent or grave accent or one of each) as a substitute for regular double quotation marks. For example, the example program

```
' Example Program 4-16
' Display a word in quotation marks,

Phrase$ = "He said 'Hello' and smiled."
PRINT Phrase$
END
```

displays the sentence

```
He said 'Hello' and smiled.
```

The Null String

We have already mentioned and used the null string, but define it now as a string with a dynamic length of zero. It can be created by the statement

```
Example$ = ""
```

where no character (not even a space) is enclosed between the two quotation marks.

Note that the null string is not the same as a string containing a single blank or space character, like the string created by the following statement.

```
Example$ = " "
```

Every string variable is set initially to a null string by the QuickBASIC system. It is **still a good idea, however, to initialize all variables, string and numeric, before use.**

Concatenation of Strings

A useful operation with strings, similar to the addition operation with numbers, is *concatenation*. This means adding one string of characters to the end of another string of characters. The plus sign (+) is used to denote string concatenation in QuickBASIC. The following example program concatenates three strings and creates a new, single string.

```
' Example Program 4-17
' Concatenate three strings together
' and display the result.

FirstName$ = "Mary"
LastName$ = "White"
Name$ = FirstName$ + " " + LastName$
PRINT Name$
END
```

A one-character string, consisting of a single blank, is placed between the strings First-Name$ and LastName$ to form the string Name$. The resulting full name is displayed.

```
Mary White
```

Note that the results of the previous example program could have been achieved by writing the following statement.

```
PRINT FirstName$; " "; LastName$
```

One of the advantages of using concatenation is that a new string containing the full name is created, whereas a new string is not created in the preceding PRINT statement.

Another example program uses string concatenation to create the names of a list of books. All books in the list have similar titles, but the specific subject matter of each book is read from DATA statements.

```
' Example Program 4-18
' Read a sequence of names from DATA statements
' and display a list of book titles.

FOR Count =1 TO 5
   READ SubjectName$
   BookName$ = "The Case of the " + SubjectName$
   PRINT BookName$
NEXT Count

DATA Howling Dog, Dizzy Blonde, Hungry Horse
DATA Timid Preacher, Purple Dress
END
```

This program produces the following list of book names.

```
The Case of the Howling Dog
The Case of the Dizzy Blonde
The Case of the Hungry Horse
The Case of the Timid Preacher
The Case of the Purple Dress
```

The same output strings could have been displayed by using PRINT statements with multiple string parameters. Concatenation, however, produces a single string variable containing the desired characters. This difference can be important in some programs where the resulting string must be tested or manipulated further. Here is an example.

```
' Example Program 4-19
' Ask the user to enter the name of a book
' and check if that book is in stock.

DEFINT A-Z
CONST FALSE = 0, TRUE = NOT FALSE
Count = 0
Found = FALSE
INPUT "Name of book? ", SearchName$
DO UNTIL Count >= 5 OR Found = TRUE
    Count = Count + 1
    READ SubjectName$
    BookName$ = "The Case of the " + SubjectName$
    IF SearchName$ = BookName$ THEN Found = TRUE
LOOP
IF Found = TRUE THEN
    PRINT "This book is in stock."
ELSE
    PRINT "This book must be ordered."
END IF

DATA Howling Dog, Dizzy Blonde, Hungry Horse
DATA Timid Preacher, Purple Dress
END
```

This program produces the following output.

```
Name of book? The Case of the Purple Dress
This book is in stock.
```

We use a DO loop in this program rather than the FOR loop of the preceding program. The loop stops either when all data values are exhausted or when the entered book name is found. Note that the first IF statement (within the DO loop) is a single-line IF statement and does not require a matching END IF statement. The second IF statement, however, starts a block IF structure that must end with END IF.

Entering Multiple String Values

If you use the INPUT statement to enter a string value from the keyboard, a comma cannot be one of the characters that you type in. An INPUT statement interprets a comma as the end of input and accepts no more characters. The general form of the INPUT statement is

```
INPUT Var1, Var2, Var3,...
```

where the variables may be either numeric or string. A user must use commas to separate the several values that are entered from the keyboard and assigned to variables. The following program uses multiple variables in INPUT statements.

```
' Example Program 4-20
' Entering multiple values with INPUT statements.

PRINT "Enter names of two employees:"
INPUT Name1$, Name2$
INPUT "Enter both salaries: ", Salary1, Salary2
PRINT
PRINT "EMPLOYEE"; TAB(20); "SALARY"
PRINT
PRINT Name1$; TAB(20); Salary1
PRINT Name2$; TAB(20); Salary2
END
```

The preceding example program produces the following interaction between user and program, and displays a table of employee names and salaries.

```
Enter names of two employees:
John H. Smith, Mary Johnson
Enter both salaries: 25000, 35000

EMPLOYEE                SALARY

John H. Smith           25000
Mary Johnson            35000
```

In general, we discourage the use of an INPUT statement with more than one variable. If two or more values must be entered by a user in response to a prompt, the user should be informed of that fact before the values are typed in. There still exists a good possibility that a data entry error will occur because the user may not understand that entered values on the same line must be separated by commas. **We recommend that you write programs with only one variable in each INPUT statement.**

The LINE INPUT Statement

If you need to enter a string of characters containing one or more commas, you must either enclose the entire string in quotation marks or use the LINE INPUT statement. **The latter statement can be used only with a single string variable.** A prompt can be included in the LINE INPUT statement, using almost the same format as the INPUT statement.

```
' Example Program 4-21
' Demonstrate use of the LINE INPUT statement
' when entering a string containing a comma.

LINE INPUT "Description and size of item? "; Name$
PRINT
PRINT "You entered: "; Name$
END
```

Here is a sample of program dialogue.

```
Description and size of item? blue rug, 3 by 5 ft

You entered: blue rug, 3 by 5 ft
```

Note that a semicolon should be used to separate the prompt and the variable, rather than the comma that is usually used with the INPUT statement. In practice, however, there seems to be no difference between a comma and a semicolon. A semicolon separator does not display a question mark as it does with the INPUT statement.

The LINE INPUT statement has another useful property: It accepts a null string value (the user just presses the Enter key) and assigns that value to a string variable. This type of entry is often used in programs to signal a particular user response. Remember that the regular INPUT statement will not accept a null string value from the keyboard.

4.7 MORE ON READING DATA VALUES

We introduced the READ and DATA statements in Chapter 3. At that time, we explained that if you tried to read more values than were available in the DATA statements, your program would stop and display an error message. We can now discuss how to determine if there are any more valid data values.

Testing for More Data

A dummy data value must be used to determine whether unread but valid data values remain in DATA statements. This dummy value is usually called a *sentinel value*. It must be a value that can never be mistaken for a valid data value. Here is an example program.

```
' Example Program 4-22
' List all valid names in the DATA statements.
' Stop when the sentinel value ZZZZZ is read.

PRINT "LIST OF NAMES"
PRINT
READ Name$
DO UNTIL Name$ = "ZZZZZ"
    PRINT "    "; Name$
    READ Name$
LOOP

DATA John, Betty, Mary
DATA Tom, Penelope, ZZZZZ
END
```

This program reads values, one by one, from the DATA statement. It assumes that the name ZZZZZ is not a valid person's name and so uses it as the sentinel value. A test at the top of the DO loop stops the loop when the sentinel value is read. Note that the first READ statement is outside the loop, so if the first or only value in the first DATA statement is the sentinel value, no names are displayed.

Valid names are read from the DATA statements and displayed on the screen. Reading stops when the sentinel value is read. This program produces the following list.

```
LIST OF NAMES

    John
    Betty
    Mary
    Tom
    Penelope
```

The RESTORE Statement

Sometimes a set of data values in a program must be read more than once. The RESTORE statement resets the system so the next item read by a READ statement is the first value in a specified DATA statement. The syntax is

```
RESTORE label
```

where the label is an identifier, similar to a variable name, that must start with a letter and end with a colon. This label must precede the specified DATA statement and may be on the same or a separate line. The syntax is

```
label DATA Item1, Item2, Item3,...
```

If no label is included in the RESTORE statement, the specified DATA statement is the first DATA statement.

In order to understand how DATA statements are read, we imagine that there is a data pointer that points to or indicates the next data value to be read. The effect of RESTORE is to reposition this pointer at the first item in the specified DATA statement.

We illustrate this process in an example program that displays the appropriate zip code when the name of a city is entered. A table of city names and zip codes is placed into DATA statements. The user is asked to type in a city name.

The program searches through the data in memory for the city name. If the name is found, it is displayed. A dummy city name ZZZZZ is the last city name in the table. If the search reaches that name, a message tells the user that the search was not successful.

The process of entering a name and searching the table is placed in a loop. At the beginning of the search, the RESTORE statement sets the data pointer to the beginning of the first DATA statement after the label If the user presses the Enter key in response to a request for a city name, the program stops.

```
' Example Program 4-23
' Demonstrate a use of the RESTORE statement by finding
' and displaying the zip code for a given city name.

PRINT "Capitalize the first letter of the city name."
PRINT "Press the Enter key to stop."
PRINT
LINE INPUT "City name? ": Name$
DO UNTIL Name$ = ""
   RESTORE CityZipData:
   READ City$, Zip$
   DO UNTIL City$ = Name$ OR City$ = "ZZZZZ"
      READ City$, Zip$
   LOOP
   IF City$ = "ZZZZZ" THEN
      PRINT "This city name is not in the list."
   ELSE
      PRINT "Zip code for "; Name$; " is "; Zip$
   END IF
   LINE INPUT "City name? "; Name$   ' try again
LOOP

CityZipData:   ' this is the data label
DATA Churchville, 21028, Claiborne, 21624
DATA Clarksburg, 20734, Clear Spring, 21722
DATA Clements, 20624, Clinton, 20735, ZZZZZ, 0
END
```

Here is what happens if the user enters a city name of Clarksburg.

```
Capitalize the first letter of the city name.
Press the Enter key to stop
City name? Clarksburg
Zip code for Clarksburg is 20734
City name? Clarksville
This city name is not in the list.
City Name?
```

The program ends when only the Enter key is pressed in response to the prompt; no visible character is displayed on the screen. Note that a RESTORE statement without a label could have been used because the data pointer is restored to the beginning of the first DATA statement. If this program was designed for practical use, it would have many more DATA statements containing a much larger table of city names.

Counting and Summing Numbers

Another example program computes the average value of a sequence of positive numbers read from DATA statements. A check is made at the beginning of the loop to see if the value just read was the sentinel value (a negative number). When the sentinel value is read, the loop stops.

The variable Sum is used to accumulate the sum of all data values. Within the loop, a counting variable named Count% is incremented each time a new data value is read and this value is added to the variable Sum.

```
' Example Program 4-24
' Average the numbers in a DATA statement.
' Use a negative number as the sentinel value.

Count% = 0   ' initialize counter
Sum = 0      ' and accumulator
READ Number
DO UNTIL Number < 0
   Sum = Sum + Number
   Count% = Count% + 1
   READ Number
LOOP
PRINT "The average of"; Count%;
PRINT "numbers is"; Sum / Count%

DATA 1,5,3,4,2,3,7,8,9,2,5,1,9, 1
END
```

Note that both Count% and Sum are initialized before the loop starts. After the loop ends, an average value is computed, dividing Sum by Count%. This program displays the following answer.

```
The average of 13 numbers is 4.538462
```

Finding Minimum and Maximum Values

Another useful program selects the smallest and largest values from a sequence of DATA statement values. We shall use numeric values and define the largest value as the most positive number; the smallest value as the most negative number. We choose zero as our sentinel value, which means that zero cannot be a valid data value.

```
' Example Program 4-25
' Find the largest and smallest values in a list
' of numbers. Use zero as the sentinel value.

CONST MAXNUM = 3.4E+38
Largest = -MAXNUM    ' set initial values of the
Smallest = MAXNUM    ' largest and smallest values
READ Number
DO UNTIL Number = 0
   IF Number > Largest THEN Largest = Number
   IF Number < Smallest THEN Smallest = Number
   READ Number
LOOP
PRINT "Largest value is"; Largest
PRINT "Smallest value is "; Smallest

DATA 12,-3,231,-5,-505,223,147,199,58,0
END
```

The constant MAXNUM is defined as the largest single-precision real number value in QuickBASIC. The variable Largest is set initially to the smallest possible number (negative MAXNUM). After a number has been read, its value is compared with the current value of Largest. If this new number is larger than Largest, it is assigned to Largest and replaces the current value. By starting off with the smallest possible number in Largest, we ensure that any larger number read from a DATA statement is assigned to the variable Largest. Similarly, the variable Smallest is set initially to the largest possible number. If a number is read that is smaller than Smallest, it is assigned to Smallest and replaces the current value.

This choice of initial values for Largest and Smallest ensures that the largest and smallest values will be found. The program displays the following output.

```
Largest value is 231
Smallest value is -505
```

Summary of Important Points

- Any computer program can be written using only three program structures: sequential, loop, and branch.
- A logical equality statement is not an assignment statement, even though both statements have the same syntax and use the same symbol. You can determine the type of statement from the way it is used.
- We introduce the idea of a logical expression having a value of true or false; it cannot have any other value.
- Either the DO statement or the LOOP statement may be modified by a WHILE test or an UNTIL test to control the duration of the loop.
- QuickBASIC supports DO loops with a test phrase (such as WHILE or UNTIL) either at the top of the loop after the DO statement or at the bottom of the loop after the LOOP statement, but not at both places.
- Avoid using the EXIT DO statement to exit a loop if a WHILE or UNTIL phrase can be used instead.
- Think of the EXIT FOR statement as providing an emergency exit from a FOR loop that would normally be expected to go to completion.
- Use the Ctrl-Break key to interrupt an infinite loop.
- The END IF statement must be two words; the space is significant.
- An END IF statement is not required and not allowed in a single-line IF statement.
- All variables, string and numeric, should be initialized before use.
- We recommend that you always include the CASE ELSE statement in a SELECT CASE structure.
- Variables and variable expressions cannot be used in a CASE test; only constant values and constant expressions are allowed.
- We recommend that you use only one variable in each INPUT statement.
- The LINE INPUT statement can be used with only a single string variable.

Common Errors

- Using the conjunction AND in a compound logical expression when you mean OR, and vice versa.
- Using the keyword NOT incorrectly in a logical expression, as in the incorrect statement X NOT = 3, when you should write NOT (X = 3).
- Forgetting to change a DO loop control variable within the loop body, thus creating an infinite loop.

- Appending an UNTIL or WHILE test to both the DO and LOOP statements of a loop.
- Failing to test for both lowercase and uppercase input when a character reply is expected. This is an example of poor program design, not a syntax error.
- Using the EXIT DO or EXIT FOR statement when it is not absolutely necessary— another example of bad program design.
- Not recognizing the difference between the block IF structure and the single-line IF statement.
- Failing to include an END IF statement in a block IF structure. This statement is not needed (nor allowed) with a single-line IF statement.
- Forgetting to include a CASE ELSE statement in a SELECT CASE structure. This is not illegal but can cause the program to abort or crash.
- Writing a SELECT CASE structure so that it is possible to satisfy more than one CASE test.
- Using double quotation marks to enclose a quoted phrase in a string constant.
- Entering a null string as the value of a string variable in response to an INPUT statement.
- Designing a program that requires multiple numbers or strings to be entered in response to a single INPUT statement. This is poor design but not illegal.
- Using a LINE INPUT statement with a numeric variable.
- Choosing a sentinel value for a DATA statement that is a valid data value.
- Failing to initialize the counter and accumulator variables when calculating the average value of a list of numbers. QuickBASIC may initialize properly for you, but it is poor programming practice not to initialize yourself.
- Setting an initial large value for the variable that is designed to hold the largest value in a sequence of values.
- Setting an initial small value for the variable that is designed to hold the smallest value in a sequence of values.

Self-Test Questions

1. Which reserved word is used to mark
   (a) the beginning of a loop;
   (b) the end of a loop?

2. In a program containing an IF statement with two branches, which keyword is used to mark
   (a) the beginning of the first branch;
   (b) the beginning of the second branch?

3. What are the values (true or false) of the following logical expressions?
   (a) $1 = 1$
   (b) $2 > 7$
   (c) "AA" <> "AB"
   (d) $2 < 7$

4. If $X = 1$ and $Y = 2$, what are the values of the following logical expressions?
   (a) $X + 1 = Y$
   (b) $X = Y + 1$

(c) Y <> 2 * X
(d) NOT (X = Y)
(e) (X = 3) OR (Y > 1)
(f) (X <> Y + 1) AND (X + 1 = Y)

5. Does the statement LOOP UNTIL X = 0 check for further looping at
    (a) the top of the loop;
    (b) the bottom of the loop?

6. If you have a choice of writing a loop using the DO WHILE statement or the EXIT DO statement as a test for exiting the loop, which statement is preferable?

7. How do you stop a program that is executing an infinite loop?

8. Is the ELSE statement always required in a block IF structure?

9. Are both END IF and ENDIF valid statements?

10. What letter is displayed by the following program if a user presses the Enter key in response to the prompt?

```
LINE INPUT "Your choice? ", Reply$
IF Reply$ = "" THEN
    PRINT "A"
ELSE
    PRINT "B"
END IF
END
```

11. Can a string variable named Long$ be assigned a string value containing 500 characters?

12. If Prefix$ has a value of "lady" and Suffix$ has a value of "bird", what is the value of
    (a) the expression Prefix$ + Suffix$;
    (b) the expression Suffix$ + " " + Prefix?

13. What letter is displayed by the following program if a user presses the letter A key and then the Enter key in response to the prompt?

```
LINE INPUT "Your choice? ", Reply$
IF Reply$ = "" THEN PRINT "A" ELSE PRINT "B"
END
```

14. A CASE structure starts with the statement SELECT CASE Result. If Result has a value of 5, what is the logical value (true or false) of the following CASE tests?
    (a) CASE 1, 3, 6
    (b) CASE 1 TO 6
    (c) CASE IS > 1
    (d) CASE IS < 5

15. Is the statement LINE INPUT Value a valid QuickBASIC statement? Explain your answer.

16. A program reads a sequence of numbers from DATA statements. What information does it have to calculate and store to compute the average value of the numbers in the sequence?

17. A variable Store is used to hold the largest number in a sequence. What initial value should be assigned to Store at the beginning of the program?

18. If variable Store is used to hold the smallest number in a sequence, what initial value should be assigned to it?

19. What is the syntax of a label?

20. What does the RESTORE statement do when it has
(a) no parameters;
(b) a label parameter?

Practice Programs

1. Use a loop statement to display all the even integers between 1 and 20 on a single line.

2. Ask a user to enter 15 numbers from the keyboard and then display the largest number and the smallest number with appropriate labels. Test your program using the sequence of numbers 2, 7, -13, 8, 19, 5, -3, 15, -6, 21, -2, 0, 13, 4, 9.

3. Ask a user to enter a sequence of positive numbers from the keyboard. Enter a negative number to stop the data entry process. Display the average value of the positive numbers. Test your program using the sequence of numbers 2, 15, 6, 13, 26, 78, 4, 125, -1.

4. Repeat Practice Program 3 but read all the numbers from one or more DATA statements. A negative number is used as a sentinel value. Test your program using the following statement.

```
DATA 35,76,180,2,99,54,39,62,101,3,45, -1
```

5. Ask a user to enter a number between 1 and 9. If the number is not in this range, display the message "Your number must be between 1 and 9", loop back, and let the user try again. Otherwise, display the message "Successful entry" and halt the program. Test your program using the numbers 0, 1, 9, and -9.

6. Display a string of 50 asterisks and then the prompt "More (Y/N)?" on a separate line. Wait for the user to enter a character. Your program should be insensitive to letter case. If the character is "N" or "n", halt the program. Otherwise, display the stars again on a new line and then display the prompt once more. Test your program using the characters "Y", "y", "N", and "n".

7. Rewrite Practice Program 6 with more careful checking of input. Allow a user to enter only one of the characters "Y", "y", "N", or "n". If any other character is entered, display an error message and ask the user to try again. Test your program using the characters "Y", "y", "z", "n", and "N".

8. The Fibonacci series is a mathematical number series. In this series, the next term is the sum of the previous two terms in the series. For example, if the first term is 1 and the second term is 1, then the third term is (1 + 1) or 2 and the fourth term is (1 + 2) or 3.

Assume a value of 1 for each of the first two terms in a series. Ask a user to enter the number of terms (or numbers) in the series and then display the values of all the terms. Test your program using a Fibonacci series of 2, 5, and 13 terms.

9. Ask a user to enter a number from the keyboard. If the number is zero, display the word ZERO; if it is positive, display the word POSITIVE; if it is negative, display the word NEGATIVE. Test your program using the numbers 12, -2, 0, and 199.

10. The examination grades for a class are stored in one or more DATA statements, using a negative number as the sentinel value. Calculate and display the two highest grades in the class. Test your program using the following DATA statement.

```
DATA 70,63,92,100,80,92,85,91,78,88,82,90,-1
```

11.   A shipping department is preparing an order of transistor radios for shipment. Their large packing cases hold 100 radios, medium cases hold 20 radios, small cases hold 5 radios, and single cases hold 1 radio. Ask a user to enter the number of radios to be shipped and display a table showing how many cases of each size are needed. The following table shows sample output for shipping 1257 radios.

```
CASE              NUMBER

large               12
medium               2
small                3
single               2
```

Test your program using input values of 1257, 356, and 5 radios.

12.   DATA statements contain the selling prices of used cars sold during the week by an automobile dealership. These prices include the sales tax. Assume a sales tax of 3 percent on the first $1,000 of the price and 2 percent on everything over $1,000. Calculate and display the total sales tax liability for the week. Test your program when it contains the two following DATA statements. As before, a negative number is used as a sentinel value.

```
DATA 6434,1985,7910,12163,785,4350
DATA 4750,2335,1890,3995,1030,1017,-1
```

5

TEXT FILES AND
STANDARD FUNCTIONS

5.1 INTRODUCTION

Disk files provide a way to store information in a computer system in a relatively permanent form. We discuss how to name and open text files from QuickBASIC programs, how to write information on files, and how to read information from files. We examine some of the limitations of text files.

QuickBASIC contains many standard or built-in functions that can be used in both arithmetic and string expressions. We discuss a few of these functions in this chapter and continue the discussion in Chapter 6. A complete list of all standard functions is given in Appendix E. In the final section we introduce two simple debugging tools that are available in QuickBASIC and are a great help in finding program errors.

5.2 TEXT FILES

You may remember that we defined a file in Chapter 1 as a collection of characters or other information, usually stored on a computer disk. We have talked about saving programs in files on disk. In QuickBASIC, these program files may or may not be text files, depending on how they were saved.

There is no reason, however, to restrict text files to BASIC programs. Any kind of textual information may be placed in a text file. You are familiar with the concept of entering characters from the keyboard and displaying characters on the screen. In a similar manner, we can write characters on a disk file and read characters from a disk file.

In this chapter we discuss only files containing characters. These files are called *text files*. They are further identified as *sequential* text files, meaning that the information they contain can only be read sequentially, from beginning to end. We start with a short discussion of binary notation, needed to explain the ASCII character set used in text files.

Binary Notation

At the most fundamental level, information is stored in a computer as binary number values: sequences of binary bits. Integer numbers, for example, are converted from decimal form to binary form and stored in 16 bits or 2 bytes. This amount of storage space is what limits the size of an integer to 32,767. Characters must be encoded as numbers and the numbers converted to binary form before they can be stored in a computer.

The ASCII Character Set

The usual choice of a character coding scheme is ASCII, short for "American Standard Code for Information Interchange." The standard ASCII character set contains 128 characters, including digits, uppercase and lowercase letters, and punctuation marks, with numeric codes from 0 to 127. Most IBM PC-compatible computers have an additional 128 characters in their character set, with numeric codes from 128 to 255. These latter characters consist of foreign letters, mathematical symbols, musical notes, and so forth.

Here are some examples of ASCII character codes.

ASCII value of "A" is 65

ASCII value of "+" is 43

ASCII value of a space is 32

Appendix B contains a complete table of the standard ASCII set of 128 characters with their numeric codes.

Text characters are usually stored in a computer as ASCII code numbers. Any such number, when converted to binary form, occupies a space of 8 bits or 1 byte.

Sequential Text Files

A sequential file of text characters stores its information as a sequence of data items, each data item consisting of a separate line of text characters. Two nonprinting characters, the carriage return (ASCII value 13) and the line feed (ASCII value 10), are used together to separate one data item from another. This pair of characters, carriage return and line feed, is called a line delimiter or *end-of-line marker*.

In summary, our type of simple, sequential text file has lines of information consisting of ASCII characters, these lines are stored sequentially, and they are separated from one another by end-of-line markers. A line may contain digits and other numeric characters and represent a numeric value or it may contain any sequence of characters and represent a string value.

There is no other structure inherent in the file itself; it is nothing more than a sequence of lines of text (ASCII) characters. Here is a list showing the contents of a short text file containing names.

Mark C. Kitchin
Judy Wright
G. Helen Lee
Frederic Taylor
J. Andrew Koontz
Mary G. Sandridge
H. B. Napier
Roger Shingle
William A. Sampson III
Joseph P. Smith

Here is another list showing the contents of a text file containing numbers.

22903
22945
22932
24521
23607
22932
22931
22191
23230
24219

A BASIC program can write information on a sequential file or it can read information from the file. Writing on an existing or newly created file usually starts at the beginning of the file, overwriting and erasing any existing information. Writing can also start at the end of an existing file, adding new information to that which already exists. Reading from a file always starts at the beginning and continues as long as requested by the program or until the end of file is reached.

These descriptions of writing and reading may seem obvious, but they are crucial to understanding the nature of sequential text files. **You cannot start reading somewhere** in the middle of a sequential file, only at the beginning. **You cannot go to the middle of an existing sequential file and write new information.**

We now examine the writing process in more detail. It is useful to imagine a *file pointer* that indicates or points to the position in the file where the next character will be written. If you have opened the file for writing but have not yet written anything on it, the pointer points to the beginning of the file. When you write one character on the file, the pointer moves to a position immediately after that character, pointing to the position where the next character will be written. At the same time, this position is denoted as the current end of file. When you write the next character, the pointer moves ahead again and its new position now becomes the current end of file.

File Names

Files are identified by their names. We discussed DOS file names in Chapter 1 and learned that they can be only eight characters long. They can have an optional extension consisting of a period and three characters. The characters in file names are usually letters and digits, although certain other characters are allowed. **We recommend that you use only letter or digit characters, remembering that spaces or blank characters are not allowed.** Here are some examples of valid file names.

CHAPT5.DOC might be a document file.

PAYROLL.DAT might be a data file.

WHITTLE.LTR might be a letter file.

The computer does not care whether the information stored in a file is a document or data or a letter. The user, however, does need to distinguish files containing one type of information from files containing another type, and file name extensions that indicate the file contents can be helpful for this purpose.

As discussed previously, a disk may be subdivided into more than one file directory with each directory containing several files. In this case, you must specify the path name when accessing a file. For example, the file named TEST.DAT, located in directory CH09 on the disk in drive B, is designated by the path name B:\CH09\TEST.DAT. Note that backslash (\) characters are used to denote the root directory (the first backslash) and to separate the directory name (CH09) from the file name (TEST.DAT).

If a disk has only one directory, it is not necessary to specify a directory name. The backslash separator between the disk drive name and the file name, denoting the root directory, may be omitted. If the disk in our preceding example contained only a single directory, a correct path name for file TEST.DAT is B:TEST.DAT. More information about disk directories can be found in the DOS manual.

5.3 OPENING AND CLOSING TEXT FILES

Before using a file in a BASIC program, it must be opened. After the program has finished using the file, it may be closed.

Opening a File

The process of opening a file associates a file number with the DOS file name and specifies how the file is to be used. A BASIC program can neither write information on a file nor read information from a file until the file has been opened.

Every file used in a BASIC program must be identified by a file number. There are three variations of the OPEN statement for sequential text files.

```
OPEN Pathname$ FOR OUTPUT AS #N
OPEN Pathname$ FOR APPEND AS #N
OPEN Pathname$ FOR INPUT AS #N
```

Variable N is a numeric variable or constant representing the file number and variable Pathname$ is a string variable, expression, or constant representing the path name. In many cases, the path name is just the file name. Once a file has been opened, it is known from then on in the program by its file number, not by its file name.

The File Number

The file number must be an integer between 1 and 255. If N has a noninteger value, it is rounded to the nearest integer. You can use a numeric constant like 2 or a numeric expression like N + 1 instead of a numeric variable. We usually open the first file in a program as file #1, the second as file #2, and so forth, but actually any number up to 255 is allowed.

The Access Mode

The OPEN statement also specifies how the file will be accessed. The statement

```
OPEN Pathname$ FOR OUTPUT AS #N
```

opens the specified file for output; that is, for writing information at the beginning of a new or an existing file. The statement

```
OPEN Pathname$ FOR APPEND AS #N
```

opens the file for appending; that is, for writing additional information at the end of an existing file. The statement

```
OPEN Pathname$ FOR INPUT AS #N
```

opens the file for input; that is, for reading information from an existing file.

As these statements imply, a text file in QuickBASIC can be opened for either writing (output) or reading (input), but not for both actions at the same time. As an example, assume that you wish to write information on a file and then read that information. You must first open the file for output (or append), write the information on the file, then close the file (see subsequent discussion) and open it again for input.

Here are some other examples of statements that open text files for reading or writing.

```
OPEN "B:MYFILE.DAT" FOR INPUT AS #1

OPEN Reply$ FOR OUTPUT AS Num%
   (assuming Num% = 2 and Reply$ = "HW1.DAT")

OPEN Fname$ FOR APPEND AS #3
   (assuming Fname$ = "A:\WILCOX\RESUME.DOC")
```

Closing a File

After you have finished writing on a file, you can release the specific file name from the assigned file number by closing the file. The statement CLOSE #1 is used to close file #1. The syntax for closing three files is

```
CLOSE #N1, #N2, #N3
```

While it is not strictly necessary to close a file unless you plan to use the file number with another file name or change mode of access (say from output to input), it is good programming practice to do so. Closing a file makes certain that all information you have written on the file has actually been transferred to the disk from a section of memory called a *file buffer*.

The disk operating system allows only a limited number of files (usually five files) to be open in your program at any one time. The maximum number of open files can be increased through the FILES statement in the CONFIG.SYS file of DOS (see your DOS manual for details). Closing a file that is no longer needed allows you to open another file in your program without exceeding the maximum number. It does no harm and produces no error message to close a file that is already closed. **We suggest that you develop the habit of closing each file when you are through using it.**

5.4 WRITING ON A TEXT FILE

A modified form of the PRINT statement is used to write information on a file. The syntax is

```
PRINT #N, Item
```

where the identifier Item represents a variable, expression, or constant, either string or numeric. Note that if Item is numeric, the digits and other characters in the number are still written on the file as individual ASCII characters.

You may choose to have more than one identifier in your PRINT statement, and if so, the identifiers should be separated by commas or semicolons, as in the following statement.

```
PRINT #1, Item1, Item2, Item3
```

Values represented by the Item identifiers are formatted on the file in the same way they are formatted on the display screen. This means that several blanks may be stored on the disk between item values, especially if commas are used as separators.

We recommend that you use the PRINT statement with only a single variable, expression, or constant. Using a single item produces a simpler file structure with each item value on a separate line, and makes the file easier to read. Adjoining values are separated from each other by an end-of-line marker (a carriage return and a line feed). This method may even save space on the disk by eliminating the blanks between items. The following example program writes text characters on file EXAMPLE.TXT with the format shown in Fig. 5.1.

```
' Example Program 5-1
' Write three line of text on text file
' EXAMPLE.TXT in the current directory.

OPEN "EXAMPLE.TXT" FOR OUTPUT AS #1
First$ = "First line"
PRINT #1, First$
PRINT #1, "Second line"
PRINT #1, "Third line"
CLOSE #1
PRINT
PRINT "File EXAMPLE.TXT has been written."
END
```

Fig. 5.1 allows you to visualize how this example program writes text on a file. The symbol (CRLF) represents an end-of-line marker and (EOF) represents an end-of-file marker.

```
First line(CRLF)Second line(CRLF)Third line(CRLF)(EOF)
```

Figure 5.1 Format diagram of part of a disk track.

You might think of the format diagram as depicting a section of magnetic disk track, showing how the characters and delimiters have been written on that part of the track. This program produces only the following line of output on the screen.

```
File EXAMPLE.TXT has been written.
```

It is good programming practice to tell the user that a file has been written, otherwise there is no indication of what the program has done.

Programs to Write Files

We look first at a simple and fundamental program to accept information from the keyboard and write it on a text file. This type of program is part of every application program that manipulates text, such as a text editor or word processor. We write on a file named TEST.DOC in the current directory.

Our program writes one line of text at a time. We select a character (in this case, a period) that would not normally appear as the first and only character on a line of text, and use that character to signal the end of text entry.

```
' Example Program 5-2
' Write a new sequential text file.
' Assume the current directory contains file TEST.DOC

OPEN "TEST.DOC" FOR OUTPUT AS #1
PRINT "Type a line of text after each question mark."
PRINT "Enter a single period to stop the program."
LINE INPUT "? ", Reply$
DO UNTIL Reply$ = "."
    PRINT #1, Reply$
    LINE INPUT "? ", Reply$
LOOP
CLOSE #1
PRINT "File TEST.DOC has been written."
END
```

A file named TEST.DOC is created in the current disk directory and opened for writing. The DO loop then prints string values on the file until a single period causes the program to exit the loop. If the file TEST.DOC already exists, its contents are overwritten. After exiting the loop, the file is closed and the program ends. User interaction might appear as follows:

```
Type a line of text after each question mark.
Enter a single period to stop the program.
? This is the first line of text.
? This is the second line of text.
? .
File TEST.DOC has been written.
```

File TEST.DOC contains the following lines after the program has run.

```
This is the first line of text.
This is the second line of text.
```

Remember that you can use the QuickBASIC editor to view any text file. The command Open or Open Program from the File command menu can be used to display the contents of TEST.DOC.

A slight modification of Example Program 5-2 allows additional information to be written on an existing text file. In the following program, we ask the user to specify a file name.

```
' Example Program 5-3
' Append to an existing text file.
' Assume the named file is in the current directory.

INPUT "Name of file? ", FileName$
PRINT
OPEN FileName$ FOR APPEND AS #1
PRINT "Type a line of text after each question mark."
PRINT "Enter a single period to stop the program."
LINE INPUT "? ", Reply$
DO UNTIL Reply$ = "."
    PRINT #1, Reply$
    LINE INPUT "? ", Reply$
LOOP
CLOSE #1
PRINT "File "; FileName$; " has been written."
END
```

The user is prompted to enter a file name that is assigned to the variable File-Name$. The file is assumed to exist and entered lines are appended to it. If it does not exist, a new file is created and entered lines are written on the new file. Note how the file name entered by the user is included in the final message.

If the file TEST.DOC is specified and a single line is appended to the file created by Example Program 5-2, the following dialogue is produced.

```
Name of file? TEST.DOC

Type a line of text after each question mark.
Enter a single period to stop the program.
? This is an appended line of text.
? .
File TEST.DOC has been written.
```

The resulting text file would look as follows.

```
This is the first line of text.
This is the second line of text.
This is an appended line of text.
```

Here is Example Program 5-2 again, modified to write numbers rather than strings on a text file named NUMBERS.DAT.

```
' Example Program 5-4
' Write a new text file containing numbers.
' Assume file NUMBERS.DAT is in the current directory.

OPEN "NUMBERS.DAT" FOR OUTPUT AS #1
PRINT "Enter a number after each question mark."
PRINT "Enter a value of zero to stop the program."
INPUT Number
DO UNTIL Number = 0
    PRINT #1, Number
    INPUT Number
LOOP
CLOSE #1
PRINT "File NUMBERS.DAT has been written."
END
```

The variable Number is a numeric variable, but its value can still be written on a text file as a sequence of digits. A value of zero is used to stop the program and thus cannot be one of the values written on the file. Note that we must use an INPUT statement rather than a LINE INPUT statement because the latter statement can only be used with string variables.

Here is how a typical user interaction might be displayed on the screen if three numbers are entered.

```
Enter a number after each question mark.
Enter a value of zero to stop the program.
? 121.00
? 3.75
? 10.50
? 0
File NUMBERS.DAT has been written.
```

The file NUMBERS.DAT contains the following lines of characters.

```
121
3.75
10.5
```

Note that the numbers are written on the file in a format that is somewhat different from the way they were entered from the keyboard. Formatting of numbers on a file is controlled by QuickBASIC, just as it is for numbers displayed on the screen. If you want further control over the format, use the PRINT USING statement instead of the PRINT statement, as shown in the following program.

```
' Example Program 5-5
' Write a new text file containing formatted numbers.
' Assume file NUMBERS.DAT is in the current directory.

OPEN "NUMBERS.DAT" FOR OUTPUT AS #1
PRINT "Enter a number after each question mark."
PRINT "Enter a value of zero to stop the program."
INPUT Number
DO UNTIL Number = 0
    PRINT #1, USING "###.##"; Number
    INPUT Number
LOOP
CLOSE #1
PRINT "File NUMBERS.DAT has been written."
END
```

User interaction is the same as before. File NUMBERS.DAT now contains the following formatted lines of characters.

```
121.00
  3.75
 10.50
```

5.5 READING FROM A TEXT FILE

Statements for reading information from sequential text files are similar to those for writing. The file must first be opened for reading.

Opening a File for Reading

The following OPEN statement must be executed if file FileName$ is to be used for reading as file #1.

```
OPEN FileName$ FOR INPUT AS #1
```

A file opened in this manner may not be used for writing, only for reading. It must already exist and have information stored in it. You will receive an error message if the named file does not exist.

When a file is opened for reading, the file pointer is placed at the beginning of the file. **This is the only place where you can start reading a sequential text file.**

Reading from a File

Modified forms of the INPUT and LINE INPUT statements are used to read information from a file. For example, the statement

```
LINE INPUT #1, Line$
```

reads a complete line of text from file #1. **When reading string values from a text file, we recommend the use of the LINE INPUT statement** because it will read all characters, including commas, up to the end of the line. The variable Line$ must be a string variable. After reading a line of text, the file pointer moves to the beginning of the next line.

You can also use the LINE INPUT statement with two or more variables. As usual, we assume that the file was written with a single string value on each line. The values of sequential lines in the file will be assigned to the variables in the LINE INPUT statement, one line per variable. For example, the statement

```
LINE INPUT #1, Line1$, Line2$
```

assigns the value of the first line to variable Line1$ and the value of the second line to Line2$.

If a line in your file contains characters representing a number, you can read the line as a string and convert it to a number with the VAL function (see Chapter 6). **You can also use the INPUT statement (not LINE INPUT) with a numeric variable,** as shown in Example Program 5-7. A fatal error occurs if one of the characters you are converting or reading is not allowed in a numeric expression.

Closing a file is not necessary when you have finished reading it unless you want to assign the same file number to another file. It does no harm, however, to close a file that is either open or already closed and we usually close every file that we are through using.

Programs to Read Files

Another fundamental program reads text information from a file specified by the user and displays it on the screen. This type of program is also part of every application program that manipulates text. We start reading at the beginning of the file and continue until we reach the end of the file.

```
' Example Program 5-6
' Read a sequential text file and
' display its contents on the screen.
```

```
INPUT "Name of file? ", FileName$
PRINT
OPEN FileName$ FOR INPUT AS #1
DO UNTIL EOF(1)
    LINE INPUT #1, Line$
    PRINT Line$
LOOP
CLOSE #1
END
```

The user is asked to name an existing file and it is opened. If the file does not exist, an error message is displayed. A new logical function, EOF(1), is used to check for the end of file #1. This function has a value of true if the file pointer has reached the end of the file; otherwise, it has a value of false. It is used as a test in a DO UNTIL statement to control the DO loop. After all information on the file has been read, the file is closed and the program ends.

Here are the results if a user specifies file TEST.DOC after it has been written by Example Program 5-2 and modified by Example Program 5-3.

```
Name of file? TEST.DOC

This is the first line of text.
This is the second line of text.
This is an appended line of text.
```

After writing a program to read a file, you can test it by reading any text file, including a QuickBASIC program file that has been saved as a text file.

Another example program reads a text file containing numbers. We assume that each number was written on a separate line of the file.

```
' Example Program 5-7
' Read a text file containing numbers and
' display these numbers on the screen.

INPUT "Name of file? ", FileName$
PRINT
OPEN FileName$ FOR INPUT AS #1
DO UNTIL EOF(1)
    INPUT #1, Number
    PRINT Number
LOOP
CLOSE #1
END
```

We show the results of reading the file NUMBERS.DAT from Example Program 5-5.

```
Name of file? NUMBERS.DAT

121.00
  3.75
 10.50
```

Our last example of reading text files is a variation of Example Programs 4-24 and 4-25. We read a sequence of numbers from file NUMBERS.DAT and calculate the average value, the maximum value, and the minimum value.

```
' Example Program 5-8
' Read a file of numbers and calculate
' average, maximum, and minimum values.

CONST MAXNUM = 3.4E+38
OPEN "NUMBERS.DAT" FOR INPUT AS #1
Count% = 0
Sum = 0
Largest = -MAXNUM
Smallest = MAXNUM
DO UNTIL EOF(1)
    INPUT #1, Number
    Count% = Count% + 1
    Sum = Sum + Number
    IF Number > Largest THEN Largest = Number
    IF Number < Smallest THEN Smallest = Number
LOOP
PRINT
PRINT "The average value is"; Sum / Count%
PRINT "The largest value is"; Largest
PRINT "The smallest value is"; Smallest
END
```

The following results are displayed.

```
The average value is 45.08333
The largest value is 121
The smallest value is 3.75
```

5.6 OTHER TYPES OF FILES

QuickBASIC supports two other types of files in addition to sequential text files. *Random-access files* store information in fixed-length records that can be accessed directly. Direct access means that you can move directly to any record in the file and write information on or read information from that record.

Binary files store information as a sequence of bytes with no concern about which data types these bytes represent. Binary files provide the most efficient method for storing information on a disk, but they are difficult to read and write and are not often used in simple application programs.

We discuss random-access files in Chapter 9 and refer you to the language reference manual for further information about binary files.

5.7 INTRODUCTION OF STANDARD FUNCTIONS

Functions are often used in expressions. They allow a broad variety of calculations to be made. Every version of BASIC has built-in or *standard functions*, but QuickBASIC has an especially large and comprehensive set, over 80 in number. We discuss many of the more common functions in this chapter and Chapter 6, and refer you to Appendix F for a complete list.

What is a standard function? It is a named identifier to which is passed one or more values in the form of constants, variables, or expressions. The function performs some calculation or manipulation and returns a new string or numeric value that has been assigned to the function name.

The EOF Function

We have already used the EOF(N) function to detect the end of text file number N. The file number value is passed to the function. It is called an *argument* of the function and must be the file number of an opened file. The EOF function is called a *logical* function because it returns a value of true or false, depending on whether the end of the file has been reached.

The SQR Function

Most functions return numeric or string values. An example of a numeric function is the square root function SQR(X). This function returns the square root of the argument X. **Remember that the square root of a negative number is not defined,** so if the argument is negative, you get an error message. Examples of this function are as follows.

```
SQR(9) is 3
SQR(2) is 1.414214
```

Here is a simple program using the SQR function.

```
' Example Program 5-9
' Calculate the square root of a number.
```

```
INPUT "Enter a number: "; Number
PRINT "The square root of"; Number; "is"; SQR(Number)
END
```

It might display the following output.

```
Enter a number: 25
The square root of 25 is 5
```

The LEN Function

As another example of a numeric function, we examine the LEN(A$) function that calculates the number of characters stored in the string variable A$. This value is called the length of the string. The string value stored in A$ is passed to the function LEN, which performs a calculation and returns the length of the string, as in the statement

```
Length = LEN(A$).
```

The numeric variable Length is assigned the length of the string stored in the variable A$. For example, if variable A$ has the value "TEST FLIGHT", Length is assigned a value of 11 (remember that a space is a valid character and must be counted).

Functions may be used, like variables, in many different BASIC statements. Here is an example program that uses the LEN function to display a string value centered in the screen width of eighty columns.

```
' Example Program 5-10
' Ask the user to enter a heading string and display it
' centered in the screen width. Assume the screen is
' eighty columns wide.

CONST SIZE = 80  ' width of screen in columns
LINE INPUT "Enter heading: "; Heading$
PRINT
IndentSpaces% = (SIZE - LEN(Heading$)) / 2
FOR I% = 1 TO IndentSpaces%
   PRINT " ";  ' a single space
NEXT I%
PRINT Heading$
END
```

The total amount of space available for both left and right margins is calculated by the expression (SIZE - LEN(Heading$)). The number of spaces to indent before printing the heading is half of this value. Here is an example of program output, although the position is not accurate because page width is not the same as screen width.

```
Enter heading: CHAPTER TWELVE
```

```
               CHAPTER TWELVE
```

This type of display is most often used with the CLS statement that clears the display screen (see Section 6.7).

The previously discussed functions have only a single argument. In general, functions have one or more arguments and these arguments may be constants, variables, or expressions, either string or numeric.

The UCASE$ and LCASE$ Functions

Function UCASE$(A$), an example of a string function, converts any lowercase letters in the argument A$ to uppercase letters. No other characters in A$ are affected. Function LCASE$(A$) does just the opposite, changing uppercase letters to lowercase. Here are two examples.

```
UCASE$("Bill Jones, Jr.") is BILL JONES, JR.
LCASE$("Bill Jones, Jr.") is bill jones, jr.
```

Note that if a function returns a string value, the last character in its name must be a dollar sign.

The LCASE$ or UCASE$ function is often used when you wish to compare two strings for equality, without regard for whether the characters are lowercase or uppercase. Here is a program that asks a user to enter a name and compares that name with names in a list.

The entered name is stored in the variable Name$ and changed to uppercase. As each name is read from the list, it is converted to uppercase and compared to Name$. All alphabetic characters in both strings are converted to uppercase before a comparison is made.

```
' Example Program 5-11
' Compare an entered name with names in a text file.
' In making comparisons, disregard any case differences.

CONST FALSE = 0, TRUE = NOT FALSE
OPEN "NAMES.DAT" FOR INPUT AS #1
INPUT "Enter your first name: ", Name$
Name$ = UCASE$(Name$)
Found% = FALSE
DO WHILE NOT EOF(1) AND Found% = FALSE
    LINE INPUT #1, ListName$
    IF Name$ = UCASE$(ListName$) THEN Found% = TRUE
LOOP
```

```
IF Found% = TRUE THEN
    PRINT "Your name is on the list."
ELSE
    PRINT "Your name is not on the list."
END IF
END
```

We use the variable Found% as a flag variable to indicate whether a comparison was successful. The value of Found% is initially set equal to the constant FALSE and is changed to TRUE only if a comparison is true. We check at the beginning of the loop and exit the loop if the end of the file has been reached or if the value of Found% is TRUE, meaning that the previous comparison was true. The last part of the program is a branch structure that displays an appropriate message, depending on the value of Found%. Here are the results from three runs of the program.

```
Enter your first name: bill
Your name is on the list

Enter your first name: BILL
Your name is on the list

Enter your first name: sally
Your name is not on the list
```

5.8 THE DEF FN STATEMENT

QuickBASIC provides the DEF FN statement, which allows a programmer to define a function within a program. In most cases, a function procedure (as discussed in Chapter 7) is preferable, but there are times when the DEF FN statement is useful.

Consider a financial program that often needs to calculate the future value of a principal sum where the interest is compounded annually and added to the principal. A statement like

```
DEF FNFutureValue (P, I, N) = P * ((1 + I / 100) ^ N)
```

defines a single-line function that calculates the future value of P dollars invested for N years at an interest rate of I percent. Note that the function name must start with the letters FN. This defining statement must be placed near the beginning of the program, preceding the first call to function FNFutureValue.

Here is an example program that prompts the user to enter information on principal, interest, and length of time. It displays the future value of the investment.

```
' Example Program 5-12
' Ask the user to enter the principal sum,
```

```
' interest rate, and length of investment.
' Display the future value of this sum at
' the end of the investment period.

DEF FNFutureValue (P, I, N) = P * ((1 + I / 100) ^ N)
INPUT "Principal sum in dollars"; P
INPUT "Rate of interest in percent"; I
INPUT "Investment time in years"; N
PRINT "The future value is ";
PRINT USING "$$####,.##"; FNFutureValue(P, I, N)
END
```

This program displays the following results.

```
Principal sum in dollars? 1000
Rate of interest in percent? 11.5
Investment time in years? 7
The future value is  $2,142.52
```

5.9 DEBUGGING QUICKBASIC PROGRAMS

The QuickBASIC environment provides several tools to help a programmer find program errors. We discuss two of the tools at this time.

Single-Step Execution of a Program

The ability to execute one statement at a time gives a programmer great insight into program behavior. Instead of pressing F5 (or Shift-F5) to run a program in the normal manner, press F8 to single-step through the program. Each time you press F8, the next statement is executed. As you proceed through the program, you will observe that the next statement to be executed is highlighted.

This debugging tool gives you a visual model of the flow of program logic. At any time, you can inspect the Output window by pressing F4. Pressing F4 again returns you to the View window. You can interrupt the single-step process at any time by pressing F5 and continue executing the program in the normal manner.

Watching Program Variables, QuickBASIC 4.5

Another useful debugging tool in QuickBASIC 4.5 gives you the ability to watch the values of selected variables as the program is executed, step by step. Select the Add Watch command from the Debug command menu. You are asked to enter the name of a variable to be watched. This variable name and its current value (if any) are then displayed in the Watch window, a new window opened just above the View window.

You can use the Add Watch command to add other variable names, one at a time. You can also use the Delete Watch command to delete watched variables, one at a time. The current value of each watched variable is displayed as the program executes, statement by statement.

Placing the cursor over any variable name and pressing Shift-F9 displays the current value of that variable. If you then press the Enter key, the selected variable is added to the list of watch variables and appears in the Watch window. This same action can be initiated by executing the Instant Watch command of the Debug command menu.

We recommend that you use these tools to examine Example Program 5-11. Designate the variables ListName$ and Found% and the function EOF(1) as watch variables. Single-step through the program and note how the loop is repeated until Found% becomes true (has a value of -1) or the end of the file is reached and EOF(1) becomes true. Note how the value of Found% determines which message is displayed.

Displaying Variable Values, QuickBASIC Interpreter

Watch variables are not available in the interpreter, so another method must be used to observe changes in variable values. Before starting to single-step through your program, press F6 to move from the View window to the Immediate window. Write a PRINT statement that includes those variables you are interested in observing. For example, referring again to Example Program 5-11, you might write the following statement for variables Found% and ListName$.

```
PRINT "Found% = "; Found%; " ListName$ = "; ListName$
```

Note that labels are used to distinguish the two displayed values. After writing the PRINT statement, press F6 again to move back to the View window and position the cursor at the beginning of the program.

The following procedure should be used to step through the program and observe changes in these two variable values.

1. Press F8 to execute a program statement and single-step to the next statement.
2. If you want to observe the selected variable values, press F6 to move to the Immediate window.
3. Make sure the cursor is at the end of the PRINT statement. If it is not there but at the beginning of the next line, you can move it to the proper location by pressing the Backspace key.
4. Press the Enter key to execute the PRINT statement. The values of all variables in the PRINT statement are displayed in the Output window.
5. Press any key to close the Output window and control will return to the Immediate window.
6. Press F8 again to move to the View window and execute the next program statement.

This process is slow and not as efficient as the Watch variables available in Quick-BASIC 4.5. It does provide one way, however, to observe changes in variable values when using the QuickBASIC Interpreter.

The various special keys used in debugging are listed in Fig. 5.2. In addition, the Add Watch and Delete Watch commands are available in the Debug command menu of QuickBASIC 4.5.

KEY	ACTION
F4	Toggles between the View and Output windows
F5	Stops single-step program execution and continues regular execution
F6	Toggles between the View and Immediate windows
F8	Starts single-step program execution
Shift F9	Displays value of variable under cursor, and makes it a watch variable when the Enter key is pressed

Figure 5.2   Special keys used in debugging.

Summary of Important Points

- Spaces or blank characters are not allowed in file names.
- It is good practice to close a file after you are through using it, especially if you have written new information on it.
- We recommend that you use the PRINT statement with only a single variable, expression, or constant when writing on a file.
- You cannot start reading somewhere in the middle of a sequential text file, only at the beginning. You cannot go to the middle of an existing sequential file and write new information.
- If you are reading string values from a text file, we recommend that you use the LINE INPUT statement.
- An item on a text file representing a number can be read into a numeric variable with the INPUT statement.
- You cannot take the square root of a negative number

Common Errors

- Trying to write new information in the middle of an existing text file.
- Choosing a file name that contains a space character.
- Opening a text file for input and then trying to write information on it.
- Failing to close a file after writing on it.
- Opening a text file for output and then trying to read information from it.
- Writing more than one item per line on a text file and then failing to tell every user of the file what you have done.
- Forgetting to include the disk drive letter in the path name when opening a file that is not on the disk in the current drive.
- Using the LINE INPUT statement to read ASCII digits from a text file and assign them to a numeric variable.
- Failing to use the EOF function properly by trying to read the end-of-file marker, and thus causing the program to crash or abort.
- When searching for a string value, failing to change all string values being compared to the same case.
- Not using the QuickBASIC debugger when your program is not running properly and producing the correct results. A good debugger is the most effective tool for finding and correcting program errors.

Self-Test Questions

Unless specified otherwise, the word "file" in these questions means a sequential text file.

1. What marker or delimiter is used to separate lines of text in a file?

2. Can you start to read a file
   (a) at the beginning of the file;
   (b) in the middle of the file?

3. Can you start to write new information on an existing file
   (a) at the beginning of the file;
   (b) in the middle of the file;
   (c) at the end of the file?

4. When you have opened a new file for writing but have not yet written anything on it, where is the file pointer?

5. Which of these file names are allowed in DOS?
   (a) HW1.DAT
   (b) NEW TEXT.DOC
   (c) 3WAYS.TXT
   (d) FINALLY
   (e) RESERVATIONS.DAT

6. If the first file opened in a program is assigned a file number of 1, does the next file opened have to be assigned a file number of 2?

7. Can the first file opened in a program be assigned a file number of
   (a) 9;
   (b) -9;
   (c) 100;
   (d) 900?

8. Is it possible to write information on a file that has not been assigned a file number?

9. What is a disadvantage, if any, of having more than one variable in a PRINT statement used to write information on a file?

10. If a file has been opened as file #1, what statement must you execute before you can open another file as file #1?

11. Can you read a file that has been opened with the statement

```
OPEN File$ FOR APPEND AS #3?
```

12. What is an advantage of the LINE INPUT statement over the INPUT statement when reading lines of text from a file?

13. If each line in file #1 represents a number, what statement or statements can you use to read a line and assign it to a variable named Number?

14. What is the value of the logical function EOF(1) if file #1 contains several lines of text and the file pointer is
   (a) at the beginning of the file;
   (b) at the end of the file?

15. A file is opened for reading with the statement

```
OPEN FileName$ FOR INPUT AS #1.
```

Assume that the current directory is the root directory of the disk in drive A. What value must be assigned to FileName$ if the desired file is named HOMEWORK and is located in a directory named CH10 on the disk in drive B?

16. Given the function SQR(9), what is
   (a) the value of the argument;
   (b) the value of the function?

17. What happens when you ask the computer to calculate SQR(-9)?

18. What is the value of the function LEN("Good try")?

19. What is the value of the function LCASE$("Upper Limit 05")?

Practice Programs

1. Write a text file consisting of lines of characters. The user specifies the file name and then enters text from the keyboard. Signify the end of text by entering an exclamation point as the first and only character in a line. Do not write this character on the file. Test your program by writing the first three lines of this problem statement on a file named FIRST.TXT.

2. Ask a user to specify the name of a text file. Read the file and display the text on the screen. Notify the user when the last line has been displayed. Test your program using the file FIRST.TXT written in Practice Program 1, or any other text file.

3. A text file named GRADES.DAT contains student grades stored as ASCII characters, one grade per line. Read the file and calculate the average grade, the minimum grade, and the maximum grade. Display these three values on the screen with appropriate labels.

4. A text file named NAMES.DAT contains customer names, stored one name per line in the format of first name, optional middle initial, last name. Two example names are shown.

> John H. Williams
> Judith Spencer

Enter a last name from the keyboard. Search through the file and display the names of all customers who have that last name. Test your program using the names WILLIAMS and SMITH.

5. Rewrite Practice Program 2 to print only 20 lines on the screen and then display the prompt "More?". A reply of "Y" or "y" displays 20 more lines. Any other reply stops the program. Test your program using the file PREFACE.TXT.

6. Two files maintain information on automotive parts in a distributor's warehouse. A file named PARTS.DAT is a text file with four lines of inventory information on each part. These four lines are called a file record and contain information as follows.

> part number
> part name
> quantity in stock
> unit cost

A file named ORDER.DAT is a text file whose file records contain three lines of ordering information on each part, as follows.

> part number
> minimum quantity before reordering
> quantity to reorder

The two files contain information on the same number of different parts. The corresponding file records in each file are for the same part. For example, the first record in each file might be for spark plugs, the second for distributors, and so forth.

Read the information for each part item from file PARTS.DAT and check the quantity in stock against the minimum quantity required for reordering, as shown in file ORDER.DAT. If an order is indicated (quantity in stock less than or equal to the minimum quantity required for reordering), display the information specified by the following column headings, using one line for each part item.

```
QUANTITY      PART NAME                  TOTAL COST
TO ORDER                                 OF ITEM
```

At the bottom of the screen, display the grand total cost of the entire order with an appropriate label. The information in this screen display could be used to generate an order for replacing inventory.

7. Ask a user to enter a time period expressed in seconds and display the same time period in hours, minutes, and seconds. Remember that Time$ is a reserved word in QuickBASIC. Consider using the MOD operator. Test your program using times of 136, 9,192, and 18,456 seconds.

8. Example Program 4-23 asks the user to enter the name of a city, and then displays the zip code of that city. Modify this program so that it is insensitive to case; that is, the entries Clarksburg, clarksburg, and CLARKSBURG should all return the same zip code, 20734. Test your program for the city names Clarksburg, CLINTON, and churchville.

9. Calculate the average length of the customer names stored in the text file NAMES.DAT. Calculate also the length of the longest name in that file. Display your results with appropriate labels.

6

STRING AND
OTHER FUNCTIONS;
LISTS AND ARRAYS

6.1 INTRODUCTION

We have already introduced the concept of string variables but have not yet written many programs with advanced string capabilities. We start this chapter by discussing a group of standard functions that can be used to process strings. We then examine other standard functions, including arithmetic, trigonometric, and conversion functions. We look at keyboard functions and screen functions.

In the second part of the chapter we introduce the concept of a list or array variable, a new type of data structure. We explain how to declare the size of an array. We discuss the concept of an index number used to identify a specific item in an array.

6.2 STRING FUNCTIONS

A powerful set of string functions in QuickBASIC allows string values to be manipulated. Some of these functions return string values and some return numeric values. We discuss a selected group of string functions in this section and refer you to Appendix E for a complete list of all QuickBASIC functions.

The LEFT$, RIGHT$, and MID$ Functions

These three functions allow substrings to be extracted from string expressions. Function LEFT$ has the syntax

```
LEFT$(Strg$, N)
```

where Strg$ is any string expression and N is the number of characters to be extracted from the left end of that expression. For example, the function

```
LEFT$("ABCDE", 2)
```

returns the substring value "AB".
Function RIGHT$ has the syntax

```
RIGHT$(Strg$, N)
```

where again Strg$ is any string expression and N is the number of characters to be extracted from the right end of the string. The example function

```
RIGHT$("ABCDE", 2)
```

returns the substring "DE", while function

```
RIGHT$("ABCDE", 6)
```

returns the original string "ABCDE".
Note in the last example that if N is equal to or greater than the length of the string expression, the original string is returned. The LEFT$ function behaves in a similar manner. If N has a value of zero, a null string is returned by both the LEFT$ and RIGHT$ functions.
The MID$ function extracts and returns a substring from the middle of a string of characters. The syntax is

```
MID$(Strg$, Start, Length)
```

where Strg$ is a string expression, Start is the character position in the string where the substring starts, and Length is the number of characters in the substring. If Length is omitted or if there are fewer than Length characters to the right of Start, all characters to the right of Start are returned. If Start is greater than the number of characters in Strg$, a null string is returned. For example, function

```
MID$("ABCDE", 3, 2)
```

returns the substring "CD".

As another example, consider a string variable Name$ with the value "Susan Smith". We can extract the first name and the last name, using one or more of the previously discussed functions. The following example statements illustrate this technique.

```
LEFT$(Name$, 5) has a value of "Susan"
MID$(Name$, 1, 5) has a value of "Susan"
RIGHT$(Name$, 5) has a value of "Smith"
MID$(Name$, 7, 5) has a value of "Smith"
```

The INSTR Function

QuickBASIC has a function named INSTR that returns the location of a substring within a string. The substring can have one or more characters, and the value of the function returns the character position of the first character in the first occurrence of the substring. The syntax is

```
INSTR(Target$, Pattern$)
```

where Pattern$ is the substring being searched for in the string Target$. Function INSTR returns the character position of the first character of Pattern$ occurring in Target$. A value of zero is returned if the substring cannot be found.

An optional third argument N can be added to specify the character position in Target$ where the search will start. The expanded syntax is

```
INSTR(Target$, Pattern$, N)
```

where N is the starting position. Here are some example statements.

```
INSTR("ABCDE", "C") has a value of 3
INSTR("ABCAB", "B") has a value of 2
INSTR("abcde", "A") has a  value of 0
INSTR("ABCAB", "B", 3) has a value of 5
```

Note that the INSTR function is case sensitive, so the third example returns a value of zero. In the fourth example, note that the value returned is the position of the second "B" in the string, not the first "B", because the search starts at the third character (after the first "B").

Remember that a blank space is a valid character in a string. If we have a person's full name (first name and last name only) in a string variable Name$, we can use the following program to extract and display the first name.

```
' Example Program 6-1
' Look for the first space in string Name$ and
' display the first name using the LEFT$ function.
```

```
DEFINT A-Z
PRINT "Enter your name, first and last only: ";
LINE INPUT Name$
Position = INSTR(Name$, " ")
IF Position > 0 THEN
    LengthFirst = Position - 1
    PRINT "Hello, "; LEFT$(Name$, LengthFirst)
ELSE
    PRINT "You seem to have only one name, "; Name$
END IF
END
```

The variable Position is assigned the position of the first space in the string Name$. If this value is zero, there is no space in Name$ and we assume that the user has only a single name. Otherwise, the first name starts at the first character in Name$ and goes to the character at position (Position - 1), the character just before the space. Thus the length of the first name is (Position - 1) characters. Here is the output from two program runs.

```
Enter your name, first and last only: Jennifer
You seem to have only one name, Jennifer


Enter your name, first and last only: Jennifer Scotch
Hello, Jennifer
```

A variation of the previous program extracts both the first name and the last name.

```
' Example Program 6-2
' Look for the first space in string Name$
' and display both the first and last names
' using the LEFT$ and RIGHT$ functions.

DEFINT A-Z
PRINT "Enter your name, first and last only: ";
LINE INPUT Name$
Position = INSTR(Name$, " ")
IF Position > 0 THEN
    LengthFirst = Position - 1
    PRINT "First name: "; LEFT$(Name$, LengthFirst)
    LengthLast = LEN(Name$) - Position
    PRINT "Last name: "; RIGHT$(Name$, LengthLast)
ELSE
    PRINT "You seem to have only one name, "; Name$
END IF
END
```

We calculate the value of variable LengthLast, which is the length of the last name. If the name is entered properly, we display both the first and last names. Once again, we show the program output.

```
Enter your name, first and last only: Jennifer Scotch
First name: Jennifer
Last name: Scotch
```

In place of the LEFT$ and RIGHT$ functions, we can accomplish the same results using only the MID$ function, as shown in the next example program.

```
' Example Program 6-3
' Look for the first space in string Name$
' and display both the first and last names.

DEFINT A-Z
PRINT "Enter your name, first and last only: ";
LINE INPUT Name$
Position = INSTR(Name$, " ")
IF Position > 0 then
    PRINT "First name: "; MID$(Name$, 1, Position - 1)
    LengthLast = LEN(Name$) - (Position - 1)
    PRINT "Last name: ";
    PRINT MID$(Name$, Position + 1, LengthLast)
ELSE
    PRINT "You seem to have only one name, "; Name$
END IF
END
```

This time we show the result if the user enters only a single name.

```
Enter your name, first and last only: James
You seem to have only one name, James
```

Note the use of two PRINT statements to display the last name; a single PRINT statement would have been too long to fit between the left and right margins of the page. You may find this technique useful when you have long PRINT statements in a program.

The STRING$ Function

The STRING$ function provides an easy way to create a string of identical characters. The syntax is

```
STRING$(N, Char)
```

where Char is the character appearing in the string and N is the number of characters. The argument Char may be a string constant, variable, or expression, or a number representing the ASCII value of a character. If Char is a string of more than one character, only the first character is used. Two examples are shown.

```
STRING$(10, "*") has a value of "**********"
STRING$(5, 66) has a value of "BBBBB"
```

In the last example, note that 66 is the ASCII value of the uppercase letter B. One common use of the STRING$ function is to create a long string of asterisks or dashes that can be used to separate sections of text, like the statement

```
PRINT STRING$(70, "-")
```

which displays a line of 70 dashes.

6.3 ARITHMETIC FUNCTIONS

Arithmetic functions are numeric functions that perform certain fundamental arithmetic calculations.

The ABS Function

The absolute value function is ABS(X) and returns a numeric value. It converts a negative numeric argument to a positive number. Here are two examples.

```
ABS(-5) has a value of 5
ABS(12) has a value of 12
```

The INT and FIX Functions

These two functions modify numeric variables or constants, changing them to integers. The integer function is INT(X) and has a numeric value. **It returns the greatest integer less than or equal to X.** Several examples are shown.

```
INT(100) has a value of 100
INT(125.9) has a value of 125
INT(125.1) has a value of 125
INT(-17.5) has a value of -18
```

Note in the last example that the value -18 is the greatest integer less than (more negative than) the value -17.5. You must be especially careful when using the INT function with a negative argument. The next three functions we discuss (FIX, CINT, and CLNG) are probably more useful and less likely to cause an error.

In contrast to the integer value of a number, the truncated value of a number is just that number with all digits after the decimal point truncated or chopped off. The function FIX(X) truncates its numeric argument X and returns a numeric value. Note that the results with a negative argument are different from those produced by the INT function.

```
FIX(100) has a value of 100
FIX(125.9) has a value of 125
FIX(125.1) has a value of 125
FIX(-17.5) has a value of -17
```

The CINT and CLNG Functions

These two functions are used to round numbers to the nearest integer. Both functions round the fractional part of the argument X and return a numeric value. CINT(X) returns an integer value while CLNG(X) returns a long integer value. These are true rounding functions, not truncating functions. Note particularly how negative numbers are rounded in the following examples.

```
CINT(3.49) has a value of 3
CINT(3.95) has a value of 4
CINT(-3.4) has a value of -3
CINT(-3.5) has a value of -4
CINT(-3.6) has a value of -4
```

If you use CINT to round a number that produces an integer greater than 32,767, you will receive an overflow error message. One solution is to use the CLNG function that returns a long integer, as shown in these examples.

```
CINT(99999.9) produces an overflow message
CLNG(99999.9) has a value of 100000
```

Here is an example program that rounds a number to two digits after the decimal point. Trailing zeros are not displayed.

```
' Example Program 6-4
' Use the CLNG function to display a decimal number
' rounded to two digits after the decimal point.
' Trailing zeros are not displayed.

INPUT "Enter a number: ", Number
Number = CLNG(100 * Number) / 100
PRINT "The rounded number has a value of"; Number
END
```

Multiplying the single-precision variable Number by 100 moves the decimal point two places to the right. Applying the CLNG function converts Number to a long integer. Dividing by 100 converts Number back to a single-precision variable and moves the decimal point two places to the left. Here is a typical result.

```
Enter a number: 53262.7544
The rounded number has a value of 53262.75
```

Note the difference between the results of this example program and the PRINT USING statement. This program actually changes the value of Number so that all decimal digits except the first two following the decimal point (7 and 5) are made zero. On the other hand, the PRINT USING statement does not change the value of Number, but rather controls its appearance as it is displayed on the screen.

6.4 TRIGONOMETRIC FUNCTIONS

If your knowledge of trigonometry is weak, you may need to review your high school mathematics textbook before reading this section. We use trigonometric functions in only a few of our example and practice programs.

The SIN Function

The function SIN(X) calculates the sine of X and returns a numeric value. **The argument X must be expressed in units of radians.** Remember that 2π radians equals 360 degrees. Two examples use a constant PI that has been declared equal to 3.141593.

```
SIN(PI/4) has a value of .7071068
SIN(PI/2) has a value of 1
```

The COS, TAN, and ATN Functions

Other trigonometric functions available in QuickBASIC are COS(X) for cosine of X and TAN(X) for tangent of X. The inverse trigonometric function ATN(Y), called the arctangent of Y, is also defined and returns the value in radians of an angle whose tangent is Y. Some examples follow.

```
COS(PI/4) has a value of .7071067
TAN(PI/4) has a value of 1
ATN(1.0) has a value of .7853982
```

Note the slight difference in the value of COS(PI/4) and the previous value of SIN(PI/4), probably due to the approximate value used for PI.

A familiar formula in trigonometry is the law of cosines, used to calculate the third side of a triangle when the other two sides and the included angle are known. The next example program uses this law.

```
' Example Program 6-5
' Given two sides of a triangle and the angle between
' them, calculate the length of the third side,

CONST PI = 3.141593
INPUT "Length of first side of triangle"; A
INPUT "Length of second side of triangle"; B
PRINT "Angle between 1st and 2nd sides in degrees";
INPUT Gamma
Gamma = Gamma * PI/180
C = SQR(A*A + B*B - 2*A*B*COS(Gamma))
PRINT "The length of the third side is"; C
END
```

Note that the angle is entered by the user in degrees but must be converted to radians before being used as an argument for the COS function. Here is an example of user interaction.

```
Length of first side of triangle? 12
Length of second side of triangle? 12
Angle between 1st and 2nd sides in degrees? 60
Length of third side is 12
```

6.5 OTHER NUMERIC FUNCTIONS

In this section we discuss several of the more specialized numeric functions. You may need to go back and review what you learned about logarithms and exponentials in high school mathematics.

The LOG and EXP Functions

The logarithmic function LOG(X) calculates the natural logarithm of X, as shown in the following example.

```
LOG(10) has a value of 2.302585
```

The exponential function EXP(X) calculates the natural number e (equal to 2.7128) raised to the X power. Recall that this number is the base of natural logarithms, so the EXP function is just the inverse of the LOG function. Here are two examples.

```
EXP(2.302585) has a value of 9.999998
EXP(LOG(10)) has a value of 10
```

Note the slight inaccuracy in the first result, probably due to the internal conversion of numeric values between decimal and binary forms. We discuss this matter further in Chapter 8.

The RND Function

The random number function is RND(N) and returns a random number less than 1 and greater than or equal to zero. The value of N controls the next random number, as shown in Fig. 6.1. Normally, the function is written as RND without a parameter.

When RND is used in a program without the modifying statement RANDOMIZE, it always produces the same sequence of random numbers each time the program is run. **If RANDOMIZE (with a different parameter or seed value) is executed prior to the use of the RND function, a different random number is returned every time the program is run.**

Value of N	Number Generated or Returned
N < 0	Same number for a given value of N
N > 0 or omitted	Next random number in the sequence
N = 0	The last number generated

Figure 6.1　Numbers generated by the RND function.

The RANDOMIZE statement requires a numeric modifier that serves as the seed for a random number sequence. A common choice of the seed is the function TIMER, which returns the number of seconds elapsed since midnight.

When developing a program that uses the RND function to produce a sequence of random numbers, we recommend that you do not include the RANDOMIZE statement. You will find it easier to locate and correct errors when the same sequence of random numbers is produced each time you run the program. After the program is producing correct results, add a RANDOMIZE statement with a variable seed so that each run produces a different sequence of random numbers.

Here is a sample program that simulates the roll of a pair of dice. It uses both the RND function and the RANDOMIZE statement.

```
' Example Program 6-6
' Simulate the roll of a pair of dice.
```

```
PRINT "Simulating the roll of a pair of dice."
PRINT "Press the Enter key for another roll"
PRINT "or press Q and then Enter to stop."
PRINT
RANDOMIZE TIMER
Count% = 1
DO
    Value1 = INT(6 * RND + 1)
    Value2 = INT(6 * RND + 1)
    PRINT "Roll";
    PRINT USING "###"; Count%;
    PRINT ":    ";
    PRINT USING "#   #"; Value1; Value2
    Count% = Count% + 1
    PRINT
    LINE INPUT Entry$
LOOP UNTIL UCASE$(LEFT$(Entry$, 1)) = "Q"
END
```

The expression (6 * RND + 1) produces a number between 1.0 and 6.9999..., where the latter notation means a number just less than 7. Note that the function INT(6.9999...) has a value of 6. The statement RANDOMIZE TIMER causes the program to print a different pair of numbers each time it is run. You might try running this program a few times without the RANDOMIZE statement to see what happens.

We have used a combination of different PRINT statements in this example program to format the screen display just the way we want it. Note the use of trailing semicolons and PRINT USING statements. Here is an example of program output.

```
Simulating the roll of a pair of dice.
Press the Enter key for another roll
or press Q and then Enter to stop.

Roll  1:    6    6

Roll  2:    6    4

Roll  3:    2    5


Q
```

6.6 CONVERSION FUNCTIONS

These functions return values that have the effect of converting a character to its ASCII value, and vice versa, and also of converting a numeric value to the corresponding string value, and vice versa.

The ASC and CHR$ Functions

The ASC(A$) function returns a numeric value equal to the ASCII code of the first character in the string A$. In practice, A$ is usually a single-character string. The complementary CHR$(X) function returns a single-character string whose ASCII code is X. Variable X must have a value between 0 and 255. Some examples are as follows.

```
ASC("A") has a value of 65
CHR$(66) has a value of "B"
CHR$(90) has a value of "Z"
```

Here is an example program that uses the ASC function to determine whether an entered character is an uppercase letter.

```
' Example Program 6-7
' Ask the user to enter an uppercase letter
' and display its ASCII value.

' Check for a single entered character.
DO
    PRINT
    INPUT "Enter an uppercase letter: ", Char$
    IF LEN(Char$) > 1 THEN
        PRINT "Enter only one character, please."
    END IF
LOOP UNTIL LEN(Char$) = 1

' Display the ASCII value of a valid character.
Code% = ASC(Char$)
IF Code% < 65 OR Code% > 90 THEN
    PRINT "Not an uppercase letter"
ELSE
    PRINT "Its ASCII value is"; Code%
END IF
END
```

The program asks a user to enter an uppercase letter and refuses to accept more than a single character. It then checks to see whether the ASCII value of the character is within the range of uppercase letters and prints an appropriate message.

Note that the ASCII value of Char$ is calculated only once and assigned to variable Code%. Otherwise, the function would have to be evaluated three times and the program would not run as quickly. Here are the results of two program runs.

```
Enter an uppercase letter: B
Its ASCII value is 66
Enter an uppercase letter: b
Not an uppercase letter
```

The VAL and STR$ Functions

The VAL(A$) function returns a numeric value equal to the number represented by the characters in A$. The string variable A$ may contain any characters that are valid in a number: Digits, a decimal point, plus and minus signs, and the letters E, e, D, or d. If A$ is not in valid numeric format, an error will occur when the function is executed.

The STR$(X) function returns a string whose characters are the same as those in the number X. Here are several examples.

```
VAL("123") returns the number 123
STR$(123) returns the string "123"
VAL("-1.2E+5") returns the number -120000
```

Remember that numbers and strings are stored in computer memory using different coding methods. The number 123 and the string "123" are not the same quantity and are not stored in the same manner.

It is sometimes convenient to enter a number as a string and then convert it to numeric form with the VAL function. If a user is asked to enter a number but enters some nonnumeric characters, the function cannot perform the conversion and the program aborts. **A well-designed program should tell the user what error has occurred and ask for input again.**

Our example is a simple version of a general numeric input program. A number is entered into a string variable named Entry$ and the program checks each character, accepting any character that is allowed in a number. If an invalid character is encountered, the program displays an error message and prompts the user to enter the number again. When a valid entry has been made, it is converted to a number using the VAL function.

```
' Example Program 6-8
' Check for the entry of a valid number
' Allow any characters to be entered and check for
' numeric characters. As written, this program does
' not handle numbers in exponential notation.

' Initialize constants and set variable type.

CONST FALSE = 0, TRUE = NOT FALSE
DEFINT A-Z
```

```
' Main loop for number input.
DO
   LINE INPUT "Enter number: ", Entry$
   ValidNumber = TRUE   ' flag for valid number
   NumPeriods = 0

   ' Check each character in the input.
   FOR I = 1 TO LEN(Entry$)
      Char$ = MID$(Entry$, I, 1)
      SELECT CASE Char$
      CASE "0" TO "9"
         ' do nothing, accept a digit character
      CASE "-", "+"   ' must be first character
         IF I > 1 THEN
            PRINT "Only the first character can ";
            PRINT "be a plus or minus sign."
            ValidNumber = FALSE
         END IF
      CASE "."   ' only one decimal point allowed
         NumPeriods = NumPeriods + 1
         IF NumPeriods > 1 THEN
            PRINT "Only one decimal point is allowed "
            ValidNumber = FALSE
         END IF
      CASE ELSE   ' other characters are invalid
         PRINT "Character '"; Char$; "' is not allowed."
         ValidNumber = FALSE
      END SELECT
   NEXT I
LOOP UNTIL ValidNumber = TRUE

' Convert input to a numeric value and display.
Number! = VAL(Entry$)
PRINT "Entry is a valid number equal to "; Number!
END
```

We use one of several CASE branches to check and accept valid characters. In some cases, if the same character appears more than a specified number of times, the entry is invalid and the ValidNumber flag is set to false. For example, there can be only one decimal point.

If a character is invalid, the CASE ELSE branch is used to display an error message and set the ValidNumber flag to false so that another number is requested. Here is an example of program output.

```
Enter number: +-55.7
```

```
Only the first character can be a plus or minus sign.
Enter number: -5.5.7
Only one decimal point is allowed.
Enter number: -55.7
Entry is a valid number equal to -55.7
```

Note that the program as written does not handle numeric strings in the exponential format. You might try to write a better program that will accept all valid numbers.

6.7 PRINT AND KEYBOARD FUNCTIONS

In this section we introduce functions used to modify PRINT statements, a function used to detect keyboard input, and several new statements used with input or output operations.

The TAB and SPC Functions

The TAB(X) and SPC(X) print functions allow some additional format control in the PRINT statement. They are not normal functions because they do not return a value, but rather change the location where the next expression in a PRINT statement is displayed. They can only be used in a PRINT statement.

TAB(X) moves the cursor to column X before the next expression is displayed. The left-hand column on the screen is column 1, and the right-hand column is usually column 80. Semicolons are used to separate this function from its neighboring expressions. For example, the statement

```
PRINT "A"; TAB(4); "B"; TAB(20); "XYZ"
```

produces the following display.

```
A   B               XYZ
```

Function SPC(X), when included in a PRINT statement, displays the number of spaces denoted by X. The statement

```
PRINT "A"; SPC(4); "B"; SPC(20); "XYZ"
```

produces the following display.

```
A    B                   XYZ
```

These functions are particularly useful when you use PRINT statements to display a table of values, as shown in the next example program. The text file PARTS.DAT contains part descriptions and quantities on hand.

```
' Example Program 6-9
' Display a table with column headings from
' information read from text file PARTS.DAT.

OPEN "PARTS.DAT" FOR INPUT AS #1
PRINT "Part Description"; TAB(30); "Quantity on Hand"
PRINT
DO UNTIL EOF(1)
    INPUT #1, Part$
    INPUT #1, Quantity%
    PRINT SPC(4); Part$; TAB(36); Quantity%
LOOP
CLOSE #1
END
```

This program produces the following table.

```
Part Description                    Quantity on Hand

        STARTER                             10
        ALTERNATOR                          25
        PANEL                               11
        REGULATOR                           87
```

The SPC function places four spaces at the beginning of each data row. Note that the TAB function does not directly control the space between displayed items. Instead, it controls the location of the item immediately following the TAB function, determining in which column that item is displayed. As always, an additional space is left in front of a numeric value for a possible minus sign.

The SPC function is used to create a space of specified length. The TAB function is used to move the next item to a specified position in a line.

The CLS and LOCATE Statements

CLS and LOCATE are actually statements, not functions, but it seems appropriate to introduce them here in order to explain our next example program. We wish to display a message at the center of the screen, allow the user to read it, and then allow the user to erase the message by pressing any key.

The CLS statement, in its simplest form, clears the display screen and places the cursor in the upper left-hand corner. This statement can also have a numeric modifier whose meaning is discussed in the QuickBASIC language manual and in the on-line help system. Remember that to get help on CLS while in the QuickBASIC system, place the cursor under any character in the CLS statement and press F1.

The LOCATE statement, among its other functions, moves the cursor to a specified place on the screen and turns the cursor off and on. The syntax is as follows.

```
LOCATE Row, Column, Cursor
```

This statement moves the cursor to the specified row and column. The third modifier (Cursor) is optional. A value of zero for Cursor turns the cursor off, while a value of 1 turns it on. If you want to use the statement only for turning the cursor on or off, you must still keep the two leading commas. For example, the statement

```
LOCATE ,, 0
```

turns the cursor off but does not move it. The LOCATE statement may have other optional modifiers and we again refer you to the manual and the help system.

The following program displays a message at the center of the screen. The cursor is also turned off but immediately turned back on by the LINE INPUT statement. Press the Enter key to continue when the program pauses.

```
' Example Program 6-10
' Clear the screen and display a message in its center.
' Press the Enter key to continue.

CLS
LOCATE 12, 20, 0
PRINT "Annual Financial Report for 1992-93"
LINE INPUT Dummy$
END
```

We do not show the output from this program, but urge you to run it yourself and see how it performs. In the next section we show a better way to pause while the screen is being observed.

The INKEY$ and INPUT$ Functions

The INKEY$ function returns a one-byte or two-byte string denoting a character entered from the keyboard. INKEY$ does not echo that character to the screen. The returned string contains the scan code of the key that was pressed. If no key is pressed, the function returns a null string value. Scan codes for the keys on IBM PC-compatible keyboards are listed in the computer manual.

The function is commonly used to make a program pause and suspend execution until a key is pressed. This action is accomplished by keeping the program in a small DO loop, as shown in the next example program.

```
' Example Program 6-11
' Use the INKEY$ function to create a wait loop
' in the preceding Example Program 6-10.
' Press any key to continue.

CLS
LOCATE 12, 20, 0
PRINT "Annual Financial Report for 1992-93"
DO
LOOP WHILE INKEY$ = ""
END
```

Note that this program terminates when any key, not just the Enter key, is pressed. In addition, the cursor is no longer visible while the message is being displayed. Once again, we ask you to run the program yourself and observe how it behaves.

Function INPUT$ is a similar function. It has the following syntax.

```
INPUT$(Count, #N)
```

This function accepts Count characters from the file designated by number N and returns that string of characters in INPUT$. If the file number is omitted, input is accepted from the standard input device, which is normally the keyboard. **Characters are not echoed on the screen.**

Here is a variation of Example Program 4-15 that uses the INPUT$ function. It also uses the LOCATE statement to turn on the cursor, which is normally turned off by the INPUT$ function.

```
' Example Program 6-12
' A variation of Example Program 4-15 that uses
' the INPUT$ function to accept user input and
' then determines if the answer is Y or N.

DEFINT A-Z
CONST FALSE = 0, TRUE = NOT FALSE
DO
    PRINT "Your answer?";    ' prompt user
    LOCATE , , 1             ' make cursor visible
    Ans$ = INPUT$(1)         ' accept one character
    PRINT                    ' move to next line
    SELECT CASE Ans$         ' select proper response
    CASE "Y", "y"
        PRINT "The answer is YES"
        ValidAnswer = TRUE
    CASE "N", "n"
        PRINT "The answer is NO"
```

```
        ValidAnswer = TRUE
     CASE ELSE
        PRINT "Please enter Y or N"
        ValidAnswer = FALSE
     END SELECT
  LOOP UNTIL ValidAnswer = TRUE
  END
```

This program produces the same output as Example Program 4-15, but characters entered by the user are not echoed on the screen.

6.8 ARRAYS WITH ONE DIMENSION

We have discussed how a variable can be thought of as a mailbox in which a value may be stored. As you now know, this mailbox is actually a memory location. There are times when it is convenient to be able to refer to a group of mailboxes rather than to a single mailbox, for example, when a group of mailboxes represents a collection of similar quantities. The group can be designated by a single name and each mailbox within the group can be identified by a number or *index*. This group of mailboxes or memory locations is called an *array variable*. Each individual mailbox is called an *array element*.

We look first at some examples of array variables. The index is a number and is enclosed in parentheses. Array variable Day$ represents the days of the week and each mailbox or element in the array is assigned the name of a day.

Day$(1) is day 1 (element 1) and contains a value of "Sunday".

Day$(6) is day 6 (element 6) and contains a value of "Friday".

Array variable Occupancy represents the occupied rooms in a motel and each element is assigned a value representing the number of occupants in that room.

Occupancy(10) contains the number of occupants in room 10.

Occupancy(35) contains the number of occupants in room 35.

The number of elements in an array is called the *size* of the array. Each element is identified by a numeric index that by default starts at zero for the first element (see the following discussion). In this section we discuss arrays with only one index and denote these arrays as *one-dimensional* arrays.

The rules for naming an array variable are the same as those for naming a simple variable (the kind of variable we have used in earlier chapters). An individual element is identified by the array name followed by an index number enclosed in parentheses. Arrays whose elements contain string values are called string arrays, and the last character in the array name must be a dollar sign. Numeric arrays have elements containing numeric values.

Array Bounds

The smallest or most negative value of the index is called the *lower bound* of an array. **The default value of the lower bound is zero.** However, if the statement

```
OPTION BASE 1
```

is placed at the beginning of a program before any arrays are declared, the default value of the lower bound of all arrays is set to 1. We usually set the lower bound of an array to 1 because human beings are accustomed to counting from 1 rather than from zero.

The largest or most positive value of the index is called the *upper bound* and has a default value of 10. If the lower bound starts at one, the upper bound is equal to the size of the array.

Dimensioning an Array

Before using an array in a BASIC program, you must identify the variable as an array variable and tell the computer its size. This is done with the DIM statement. **An array can be declared only once in a DIM statement. The same DIM statement cannot be executed more than once.** This means, for example, that a DIM statement cannot be placed in a loop where it would be executed on each pass through the loop.

The DIM statement not only sets the size of an array, it also initializes the array elements. All elements of a numeric array are initialized to zero, while those in a string array are initialized to null strings.

DIM statements are usually placed together near the beginning of a program. The program fragment

```
OPTION BASE 1
DIM Day$(7)
```

declares the array Day$ as an array with seven elements that can each hold a string value. Day$(1) is the first element and Day$(7) is the last element. When this array is used in a program, element Day$(1) might be assigned a value of "Sunday" and Day$(7) assigned a value of "Saturday".

QuickBASIC also allows both the lower bound and the upper bound to be specified in a DIM statement. The Day$ array can be declared by the following program statement.

```
DIM Day$(1 TO 7)
```

This is the preferred syntax for declaring an array and we recommend its use. Both the lower bound and the upper bound are clearly displayed. The size of the array is the same as before, but an OPTION BASE 1 statement is no longer needed. When using this form of the DIM statement, the bounds can be negative or positive numbers, as illustrated by the following example statement.

```
DIM Offset(-100 TO 100)
```

Static and Dynamic Arrays

The bounds of an array may be specified by constants, variables, or expressions. If a constant value or defined constant is used for both bounds, the array is called a *static array*. If either bound is specified by a variable or variable expression, the array is called a *dynamic array*. As you can see, our previously defined array Day$ is a static array.

Most arrays in BASIC are static arrays. This designation means that once the array size has been declared in a DIM statement, the array size cannot be changed later in the program. The memory space used by a static array is allocated when the program is compiled.

QuickBASIC also allows the creation of dynamic arrays. Dynamic arrays can be changed in size (made larger or smaller) by the REDIM statement. **All elements are reinitialized when the size is changed and thus all values already assigned to the array are erased and lost.** The memory space used by a dynamic array is allocated when the program is executed.

An example dynamic array is created by the following program fragment.

```
NumberOfRooms = 70
DIM Occupancy(1 TO NumberOfRooms)
```

This array has an initial size of 70, but its size can be changed in the program. The array is dynamic because a variable NumberOfRooms is used in the DIM statement to declare the upper bound.

The Occupancy array can also be dimensioned by the following program fragment.

```
FirstRoomNumber = 1
LastRoomNumber = 70
DIM Occupancy(FirstRoomNumber TO LastRoomNumber)
```

The array is still a dynamic array and its initial size has not changed.

Many arrays in QuickBASIC programs are declared as static arrays. These arrays can be accessed a little more quickly because of the way that memory space is allocated. On the other hand, if you anticipate ever having to change the size of an array, it should be declared as a dynamic array,

Here are two more DIM statements that specify both lower and upper bounds and show that the lower bound does not have to be zero or 1.

```
DIM Population(1950 TO 1999)
DIM Yield(LoVal TO HiVal)
```

The maximum number of elements in any dimension is 32,768. The system functions LBOUND(A) and UBOUND(A) return the values of the lower and upper bounds of

the array named A. In the preceding DIM statements, LBOUND(Population) has a value
of 1950 and UBOUND(Yield) has a value equal to the value of HiVal.

Array Indexing

The elements of an array variable can be used in most of the same ways that simple variables are used. An array element can be assigned a value, used in an expression, and have
its value displayed on the screen. An array element cannot be used as the index variable
in a FOR statement; that is, the statement

```
FOR A(2) = 1 TO 5  ' not allowed
```

is not a valid statement.

Here is a simple example program that does not do much, but does illustrate how
array elements can be manipulated. We use the OPTION BASE statement in this program
to show you how it works, but we will not use it in most subsequent programs.

```
' Example Program 6-13
' Manipulating an element in an array.

OPTION BASE 1
DIM Strength(20)              ' a static array
Strength(5) = 134.72
WorkingStrength = Strength(5) / 2
PRINT "Working strength is"; WorkingStrength
END
```

The array named Strength is declared large enough to hold 20 numeric values. A
value of 134.72 is assigned to the fifth element of the array, element Strength(5). Note
that the number in parentheses in the DIM statement is the upper bound of the array,
while the number in parentheses in the assignment statement is an index referring to a
particular element in the array. The element Strength(5) can be manipulated in an expression just like a simple variable. This program displays the following output.

```
Working strength is 67.36.
```

An array index can be a numeric constant, as in the preceding example, or it can be
a numeric variable. Because individual array elements can be designated by index and the
size of the array is known, arrays are often manipulated with FOR loops.

In the next example, we read values from a file and assign them to elements of an
array. We declare Structure as a dynamic array so we can change its size after we determine how many values are stored in the file.

```
' Example Program 6-14
' Use a variable index to load an array from a file
' and then display the array element values.

DEFINT A-Z
Size = 1   ' value will be changed by REDIM
DIM Structure!(1 TO Size)   ' dynamic array

' Open data file and count the number of values.
OPEN "STRUC.DAT" FOR INPUT AS #1
Count = 0
DO UNTIL EOF(1)
   LINE INPUT #1, Dummy$
   Count = Count + 1
LOOP
CLOSE #1

' Redimension the array.
Size = Count
REDIM Structure!(Size)

' Read the file again and fill the array.
OPEN "STRUC.DAT" FOR INPUT AS #1
FOR Index = 1 TO UBOUND(Structure!)
   INPUT #1, Structure!(Index)
NEXT Index
CLOSE #1

' Display the contents of the array.
PRINT "Old values:";
FOR Index = 1 TO UBOUND(Structure!)
   PRINT Structure!(Index);
NEXT Index
PRINT   ' move to next line
PRINT   ' put in a blank line

' Change the value of one element and display again.
Index = 2
Structure!(Index) = 133.55
PRINT "New values:";
FOR Index = 1 TO UBOUND(Structure!)
   PRINT Structure!(Index);
NEXT Index
PRINT
END
```

The array Structure! is declared a dynamic array with only a single element because we know it is going to be redimensioned. File STRUC.DAT is opened, the number of values in the file are counted, and the file is closed. The array Structure!, an array of single-precision numbers, is then redimensioned to a size equal to the number of values in the file, changing only the value of the upper bound.

The file is opened again and we start reading values from the beginning of the file and assign them to the array. This process of closing and then reopening the file sets the file pointer back to the beginning so the file can be read correctly.

A FOR loop is used to display the sequence of array values that were read from the file. A new value is then assigned to the element whose index is 2 and the sequence of array elements is displayed again. Note that the value of only one element has been changed. Here is the program output.

```
Old values: 128.21   167.33   135.01   142.84   134.72

New values: 128.21   133.55   135.01   142.84   134.72
```

The result of redimensioning an array containing data is shown in the next program, a shortened version of our preceding program.

```
' Example Program 6-15
' Show the results of redimensioning
' an array containing data.

DEFINT A-Z
Size = 5
DIM Structure!(1 TO Size)

' Fill the array from a file and display it.
OPEN "STRUC.DAT" FOR INPUT AS #1
FOR Index = 1 TO UBOUND(Structure!)
   INPUT #1, Structure!(Index)
NEXT Index
CLOSE #1
PRINT "Old values:";
FOR Index = 1 TO UBOUND(Structure!)
   PRINT Structure!(Index);
NEXT Index
PRINT
PRINT

' Redimension the array and display it again.
Size = 7
REDIM Structure!(1 TO Size)
PRINT "New values:";
```

```
FOR Index = 1 TO UBOUND(Structure!)
   PRINT Structure!(Index);
NEXT Index
PRINT
END
```

The original array contains five values. After redimensioning, it contains seven elements. Note that redimensioning erases all original element values and reinitializes the array so that each element has a value of zero. Program output now has the following appearance.

```
Old values: 128.21   167.33   135.01   142.84   134.72

New values: 0  0  0  0  0  0  0
```

Another example program assigns values to the array Day$ and then displays the day of the week corresponding to a number entered by the user.

```
' Example Program 6-16
' Create and use an array representing days of the week.

DEFINT A-Z
DIM Day$(1 TO 7)   ' static array

' Load names of days of week into an array.
FOR I = 1 TO 7
   READ Day$(I)
NEXT I
DATA Sunday, Monday, Tuesday, Wednesday
DATA Thursday, Friday, Saturday

' Ask user to enter a day number and
' display the corresponding day name.
PRINT "Enter a number between 1 and 7 and the"
PRINT "corresponding day of the week will be"
PRINT "displayed. Enter any other number to stop."
PRINT
INPUT "Day number? ", DayNumber
DO UNTIL DayNumber < 1 OR DayNumber > 7
   PRINT "Day number"; DayNumber; "is "; Day$(DayNumber)
   INPUT "Day number? ", DayNumber
LOOP
END
```

Here is the output produced by this program.

```
Enter a number between 1 and 7 and the
corresponding day of the week will be
displayed. Enter any other number to stop.

Day number? 2
Day number 2 is Monday
Day number? 7
Day number 7 is Saturday
Day number? 0
```

Note that a value of zero, which is not a valid day number, is entered to stop the program.

An Array as a List

We often think of a one-dimensional array as a list or more specifically, an indexed list. A list can have either string elements or numeric elements. The length of the list is declared in a DIM statement. We can refer directly to any element of the list by using its index number or position in the list.

There are times when we want to use an array for storing information but do not know how many items we will need to store. If the maximum number of items to be stored can be determined, however, we can set the size of the array to that value. The array can then be used for storing any number of items, up to the maximum number, while a counter keeps track of the actual number of items stored.

Here is an example of creating a list of names in a partially filled array. After all names have been entered, the number of names is displayed and the names are listed on the screen for verification.

```
' Example Program 6-17
' Store up to 100 names, entered from the keyboard,
' in an array. Enter a single period to stop.

DEFINT A-Z
DIM Names$(1 TO 100)     ' a static array
PRINT "Enter up to 100 names, one name per line."
PRINT "Enter a single period to stop the process."

' Keep accepting entered names until 100 names have
' been entered, or until a single period is entered.
Count = 0  ' initialize the counter
LINE INPUT "Name? ", Reply$
DO UNTIL Count >= 100 OR Reply$ = "."
   Count = Count + 1
   Names$(Count) = Reply$
   LINE INPUT "Name? ", Reply$
LOOP
```

```
' Display the results.
PRINT
PRINT "There are"; Count; "names in the list."
FOR I = 1 to Count
   PRINT "Name"; I; ": "; Names$(I)
NEXT I
END
```

The array Names$ is dimensioned to hold up to one hundred names. Each name is entered into a variable named Reply$. If the number of entered names exceeds 100 or the name is a single period, the entry process stops. If not, the counter Count is incremented and the name placed in the array Names$. After all names have been entered, a simple FOR loop uses the final value of Count to display the stored names. Here is an example of program output.

```
Enter up to 100 names, one name per line.
Enter a single period to stop the process.
Name? Bill
Name? Sally
Name? Jim
Name? .

There are 3 names in the list.
Name 1 : Bill
Name 2 : Sally
Name 3 : Jim
```

Note that both conditions for exiting the loop are tested in the DO statement. A name with an index value of 101 is requested but never actually assigned to the array. Another LINE INPUT statement is needed outside the loop to assign the initial name to the variable Reply$.

Summary of Important Points

- The INSTR function is case sensitive.
- A blank space is a valid character in a string.
- Function INT(X) returns the greatest integer less than or equal to X, not the integer part of X.
- The radian is the default unit of angular measure in trigonometric functions.
- The RANDOMIZE statement can be used to produce a different sequence of random numbers each time a program is run.
- A well-designed program should not stop when invalid input is entered but rather, should tell the user what error has occurred and ask for input again.

- Characters accepted by the INPUT$ function are not echoed on the screen.
- An array can be declared only once in a DIM statement. The same DIM statement cannot be executed more than once.
- The size of dynamic arrays can be changed but not the size of static arrays.
- When a dynamic array is redimensioned, the values of all elements are reinitialized.
- The default value of the lower bound of an array is zero.

Common Errors

- Using incorrect syntax for the INSTR function by reversing the order of the Target$ and Pattern$ arguments.
- Confusing the values produced by INT(X) and FIX(X) when X is a negative number.
- Forgetting to include a RANDOMIZE statement with a variable seed in the final version of a program that uses the RND statement.
- Using the VAL function with a string argument containing characters that are not allowed in a number.
- Failing to trap an invalid character in a VAL function argument and thus causing the program to crash.
- Confusing the behavior of the SPC function and the TAB function.
- Misunderstanding the different behavior of the INKEY$ and INPUT$ functions.
- Redimensioning a static array.
- Dimensioning an array with a DIM statement containing a single argument and not realizing that this creates an array whose first element has an index value of zero.
- Trying to read the value of an array element that has an index value greater than the upper bound or less than the lower bound.
- Losing information unexpectedly when an array is redimensioned and all its elements are reinitialized.
- Failing to record the number of items stored in a partially filled array, and subsequently reading information from an element that contains old data or "garbage."

Self-Test Questions

1.   What is the value of ABS(-12)?
2.   What is the value of each of the following functions?
     (a) INT(-12.85)
     (b) CINT(-12.85)
     (c) FIX(-12.85)
3.   Which is the default unit for measuring angles?

(a) the degree

(b) the radian

4. What statement can be included in a program to prevent the RND function from always producing the same sequence of random numbers?

5. Assume that you have a string variable named Line$ with a value such as "10,5,Duke". The first item is number of games won, the second is number of games lost, and the third is the name of the team. How do you calculate the value of a variable X representing the position of the first comma?

6. Using a string with the same format as the string in Question 5, how do you calculate the value of a variable Y representing the position of the second comma? You can assume that the value of X has already been calculated.

7. Assuming you have calculated the value of Y in Question 6, show how to create a string that contains only the team name.

8. What logical expression can you use to compare the values of Name1$ and Name2$, where the names are considered equal if they contain the same sequence of letters, either lowercase or uppercase?

9. If the value of ORD("A") is 65, what is the value of CHR$(65)?

10. A number is entered into a string variable Num$. How do you convert the value of Num$ to a numeric value and assign it to a variable Num?

11. Why might a program be designed so that numbers entered from the keyboard are assigned initially to a string variable rather than to a numeric variable?

12. Can the TAB function be used in any statements other than the PRINT statement? If so, in which statements?

13. What is
(a) an array;
(b) an array element;
(c) the dimension of an array;
(d) the size of an array dimension?

14. If an array is declared with the statement DIM Name$(50), can a value be assigned to
(a) the element Name$(0);
(b) the element Name$(50);
(c) the element Name$(51)?

15. If a variable N% has a value of 7, is the statement DIM Bound(N%) a valid statement? If not, why not?

16. If an array is dimensioned with DIM Structure(1 TO 5) and all its elements are assigned positive numeric values, is the statement

```
FOR I% = -1 TO Structure(3)
```

a legal statement? If not, why not?

17. Which of the following dimension statements are allowed?
(a) DIM Array(15)
(b) DIM Array(0-15)
(c) DIM Array(0 TO 15)
(d) DIM Array(0 THROUGH 15)

18.   What, if anything, is wrong with the following program?

```
FOR I = 1 TO 5
   DIM Value(1 TO 5)
   Value(I) = 0
NEXT I
END
```

19.   If an array is declared with DIM List$(100) and the program contains the statement OPTION
BASE 1, what is
(**a**) the value of UBOUND(List$);
(**b**) the value of LBOUND(List$)?

Practice Programs

1.   Ask a user for a positive or negative number and display it rounded to the nearest integer. If
11.5 is entered, 12 should be displayed. If -6.7 is entered, -7 should be displayed. Test your
program using the numbers 11.5, -6.7, 3.95, 9.11, and -3.95.

2.   Ask a user to enter a date in the mm/dd/yy format. The month and the day may be specified
by single digits; that is, by 1/5/85 rather than by 01/05/85. Separate the numbers representing
the month, day, and year and display each number on the screen with an appropriate label.
Remember that Date$ is a reserved word in QuickBASIC. Test your program using the dates
11/15/85, 12/08/86, 11/7/83, 2/27/81, and 3/1/99.

3.   Ask a user to enter a date in the mm/dd/yy format (see note in Practice Program 2). Display
the date in a format with the month named; that is, May 25, 1981. Assume that the date is in
the twentieth century. The month names should be read from DATA statements. Test your
program using the same dates as in Practice Program 2.

4.   Display an appropriately formatted table of the integers from 0 through 9, their square roots,
and their natural logarithms.

5.   Ask a user to enter a number between 1 and 5 inclusive. Your program should allow the user
to enter one or more characters. Check the input, and if it is longer than one character, is not
numeric, or is not in the proper range, display an error message that describes the specific
error. If the input is not correct, ask the user to try again. Test your program using the numbers 1, 0, 8, and 4, also the character strings Z, #3, and A1A.

6.   A palindrome is a sequence of characters that reads the same backward and forward. Punctuation marks and spaces are ignored. No distinction is made between lowercase and uppercase
letters. An example is the sequence "Name no one man." Ask a user to enter a string and
determine if this string is a palindrome. Test your program using the following string values.

> "Hannah"
> "winchester"
> "Madam, I'm Adam"
> "The time has come the Walrus said"

7.   Ask a user to enter a string and examine the value of each key as it is pressed. Display each
uppercase letter as it is entered and ignore any other character. Pressing the Enter key termi-

nates the input process. Assign the entered string of uppercase letters to a string variable named Entry$. Test your program using the following input string values.

"SUBROUTINE"
"123ABC"
"New York"
"HDK-468"

8. Read 10 names from a file specified by the user, using an array to store the names as they are read. After all names have been read, display the list of names in reverse order. Test your program using the file NAMES.DAT.

9. Enter a sentence from the keyboard. Place the alphabetic characters in the sentence into an array, one character per element, converting any uppercase characters to lowercase. Pass over any nonalphabetic characters, including spaces and punctuation marks. Display the array in reverse order. Test your program using the following sentence.

He said 'Hello! How are you?' and I smiled.

The last three programs are somewhat longer and more difficult than the previous programs.

10. Modify Example Program 6-8 so that it can also handle numbers in the exponential format. Test your program using the following values.

+1.25E7
3.22D-09
1e5
-5.5E+2
+5.5D-2
75E+-3

11. The TAB function can be used for displaying and printing simple graphs, provided that you plot the graph on its side with the X axis vertical and the Y axis horizontal. Any character may be used for plotting points, but we recommend the asterisk (*). Use a dash (—) to mark the Y axis and a vertical bar (|) to mark the X axis. Display a graph of the function $Y = 2^X$ for values of X ranging from -4 to 4 in steps of 0.5. The values of Y will be between 0 and 16.

12. A user enters an address on one line in the format CITY, STATE ZIP where STATE is a two-letter abbreviation and ZIP is a five-digit number. CITY may contain one or more words (examples are Chicago and New York). Your program should check whether the entered value for ZIP is a five-digit number and the value for STATE is a two-letter string. If an error is made in input, the program should loop and let the user try again. Extract the zip code and assign it to a numeric variable named Zip. Display this zip code value with an appropriate label. Test your program using the following string values.

"San Francisco, CA 94101"
"Boston, MA 021095"
"Worcester, 99 01601"
"West Menlo Park, CAL 95691"
"Adams, OR 9781A"

13. Two explorers sight a mountain in the distance and measure the angle of elevation of its peak. Call this angle A. They walk a distance toward the mountain and measure the angle of elevation again. Call this angle B. They look up a formula for the height of the mountain, as follows.

$$H = \frac{D}{\cot(A) - \cot(B)}$$

Variable D is the distance between measurements and A and B are the two angles of elevation in degrees. Write a program that calculates the height in feet of a mountain when a user enters the two angles of elevation (measured in degrees) and the distance between the two points of measurement. Test your program using angles of 25 and 37 degrees and a distance of 1 mile.

7

MODULAR PROGRAM STRUCTURE

7.1 INTRODUCTION

Modern computer languages allow a program to be designed with separate and independent procedure units. We discuss two such units that are available in QuickBASIC, the function procedure and the subroutine procedure.

Procedure parameters allow information to be passed to functions and subroutines and to be returned back to the original program. Local variables provide isolation between the main program and procedures and between individual procedures.

In the QuickBASIC 4.5 compiler, separate library modules or files of procedures can be created and saved on disk. Multimodule programs can then be written, making use of these library modules.

7.2 PROGRAM UNITS

Each program module or file consists of one or more program units. Up to this point, all our example programs contain only a single unit called the *main program*. We now introduce two other kinds of units, function procedures and subroutine procedures, that can also be used in QuickBASIC programs.

There are several advantages to writing programs with multiple units. Programs designed as a collection of units are easier to write and debug, easier to read and understand, and easier to maintain and modify. This type of design is called *modular program design*: dividing a large program into smaller program units. Note that this name has no direct connection with QuickBASIC modules, discussed in Section 7.5.

Top-Down Development and Modular Program Design

For example, suppose that we want to write a program to develop a classroom schedule. This is not a trivial problem to solve and we have not yet discussed all the techniques required to write this type of program. We can, however, analyze the problem and see how it can be divided into different tasks, as shown in Fig. 7.1. *Top-down development* means that we first identify the primary step or main task and then identify secondary steps or subtasks within that main task.

Main Task	Develop a classroom schedule.
Subtask A	Enter list of classes with time and size of each class. Enter list of classrooms with size of each room.
Subtask B	Sort classes by hour of the day. For each hour, sort classes by descending size. Sort classrooms by descending size.
Subtask C	For each hour, assign class to room, starting with the largest-size class. Note any class that cannot be assigned.
Subtask D	Print list of classes not assigned to rooms. Print list of rooms showing hours not assigned.

Figure 7.1   Outline of a scheduling program.

Whereas the main task is fairly complex and stated in general terms, each subtask is more specific and easier to understand. Any one of the listed subtasks may be divided further; for example, a sorting procedure might be a separate subordinate task within Subtask B. Just writing down an outline helps make the problem more understandable. After more experience, you will be able to write a program based on such a design outline.

Isolation

Isolation implies that each program unit is distinct and independent from all other units. Complete isolation means that a variable in one program unit is completely distinct from a variable with the same name in another program unit. Changes in the value of a variable are confined to a single program unit.

The importance of isolation is that a change in a variable value in one program unit can never cause an unexpected change in another program unit. These changes are called *side effects*. **Lack of program unit isolation can be a major source of hard-to-find errors in large programs.**

In practice, complete isolation may not be possible when we need to return or pass back information from a called program unit to the calling program unit. The goal of complete isolation is still desirable, however, and to the extent that this goal can be achieved, the chances of errors are reduced.

In view of these benefits, we will use top-down and modular program design in most of the example programs in this and subsequent chapters. The following units are the possible program units in a program file.

> The main program
>
> Function procedures
>
> Subroutine procedures

We define the *main program* as the type of QuickBASIC program that we have developed in previous chapters, always ending with an END statement. Additional statements called *module-level statements*, located outside the main program and all procedures, may be added. We discuss such statements in the next chapter.

A complete QuickBASIC program may have zero or more function procedures and zero or more subroutine procedures. Declaration statements must be included in the main program to name and identify all function procedures that follow the main program. Declaration statements may also be needed for some subroutine procedures.

7.3 FUNCTION AND SUBROUTINE PROCEDURES

Procedures allow a program to be divided into multiple units. We define function and subroutine procedures and show examples of their use in programs. In a program listing, all procedures follow the main program END statement.

Definition of a Function Procedure

We have already defined a standard function in Chapter 5. A similar definition describes a *function procedure* as a separate program unit (block of program statements) that is identified by name. It can have values passed to it from the calling program unit. The function performs some calculation or manipulation and returns a string or numeric value assigned to the function name. An example might be a function named Volume that calculates the volume of a box and returns the value in the function name Volume.

The function is invoked or *called* when its name is used in an expression. Within the function procedure itself, **a value must be assigned to the function name before**

control returns to the calling program unit. When we refer to a function in this section, we mean a function procedure.

We look in detail at a function named Volume that calculates the volume of a box. When we call this function, we have to pass it information on the length, width, and height of a particular box. To display the volume of a box that is 10 inches long, 5 inches wide, and 3 inches high, we might use the statement

```
PRINT Volume(10, 5, 3)
```

where the values 10, 5, and 3 are called *arguments* of the function.

The function procedure itself consists of the statements

```
FUNCTION Volume (L, W, H)
   Volume = L * W * H
END FUNCTION
```

where the function named Volume is assigned a value equal to the volume of the box. The variables L, W, and H are called *parameters* of the function Volume. When the function is called, value 10 is passed to variable L, value 5 to variable W, and value 3 to variable H. A prior declaration statement like

```
DECLARE FUNCTION Volume (L, W, H)
```

must appear in the main program to identify the name Volume as the name of a function.

A complete example program can be written using this function.

```
' Example Program 7-1
' Use a function procedure to calculate
' the volume of a box.

DECLARE FUNCTION Volume! (L!, W!, H!)
PRINT "Volume of box is"; Volume(10, 5, 3)
END

FUNCTION Volume (L, W, H)
   Volume = L * W * H
END FUNCTION
```

It displays the following output.

```
Volume of box is 150
```

Note that character type suffixes (in this case, exclamation points denoting single-precision numeric identifiers) have been added to the identifiers in the DECLARE statement. These suffixes are added automatically by the QuickBASIC system.

As mentioned previously, there must be a specific assignment statement in a function procedure that assigns a value to the function name. This value may be either numeric or string, depending on the function type. The value must be assigned before the END FUNCTION statement is executed. In our example program, the single statement in the function body assigns a value to Volume.

Definition of a Subroutine Procedure

In contrast to a function, we define the general purpose of a *subroutine procedure* as performing some task or carrying out some action, such as printing a standard business form. Like a function, a subroutine is a program unit identified by name.

Unlike a function, however, **no value is associated with a subroutine name.** A subroutine name cannot represent a string value and thus cannot have a dollar sign suffix. The name is used only to identify the subroutine.

A subroutine named Center might be written to display the value of a string parameter named Value$ on the screen, centered between the left and right margins.

```
SUB Center (Value$, Col)
   PRINT TAB((Col - LEN(Value$))/2); Value$
END SUB
```

Note that the second parameter Col represents the width of the screen in columns.

The subroutine can be called by the following CALL statement.

```
CALL Center ("Table III", 80)
```

It displays the title "Table III" (without quotation marks) in the center of a line that is 80 columns wide.

An alternative syntax can also be used for calling a subroutine, provided that the subroutine name has been previously declared. Here is the format.

```
Center "Table III", 80
```

Note that the arguments "Table III" and 80 are not enclosed in parentheses. When this syntax is used, a declaration statement is needed to define the identifier Center as the name of a subroutine. We seldom use this alternative syntax in our example programs.

The Procedure Heading

We now examine the syntax of procedures in more detail. The first statement in a procedure unit is the heading statement, written as follows.

```
FUNCTION/SUB Name (Parameters)
```

The notation FUNCTION/SUB means that the statement can be used with either a function or a subroutine procedure. The identifier Name is the procedure name and the word Parameters denotes a list of variable names, separated by commas. The procedure name must follow the same rules that apply to variable names (see Chapter 3). If the procedure is a function, its value can be either numeric or string. In the latter case, the function name must end with a dollar sign.

As discussed previously, an example heading statement is

```
FUNCTION Volume (L, W, H)
```

where the parameters are the variables L, W, and H.

Local Variables

We define *local variables* as variables that are declared in a program unit and are known only within that program unit. Each program unit in QuickBASIC (the main program, a function procedure, or a subroutine procedure) may have its own local variables. The concept of local variables is important because these variables provide isolation between different units. Local variables include any variables introduced and used in the function or subroutine procedure. We use only local variables in this chapter and introduce variables that are known in more than one unit in the next chapter.

Consider the case of a main program unit with a variable named Reply$ and a function procedure with a variable named Reply$. These two variables have the same name but they refer to different mailboxes or memory locations. Thus a value assigned to Reply$ in the function is placed in one mailbox, while the value of Reply$ in the main program is placed in another mailbox. The two variables may have the same name but are really completely different variables.

Procedure Parameters

Parameters are variables declared in a procedure heading. They are separated from one another by commas and are of type string or numeric. These parameter variables are also local variables because they are first used (the variables are declared) within the procedure itself. Information is passed to parameter variables when the procedure is called; that is, when a function procedure is used in an expression or a subroutine procedure is referenced in a CALL statement.

If a parameter variable is an array, the parameter name in the procedure heading statement must be followed by a set of empty parentheses. For example, the following statement indicates that the parameter Keywords$ is an array.

```
FUNCTION Parse (Keywords$())
```

The same format must be used for an array argument in a procedure call statement; the argument name must be followed by a set of empty parentheses.

Other Procedure Statements

The last statement in a procedure must be

```
END FUNCTION/SUB
```

where once again the notation means either the statement END FUNCTION or the statement END SUB. Only one such statement is allowed in a procedure.

A module or program file containing functions should have a declaration statement, containing the function name and list of parameters, for each function. The syntax of this statement is as follows.

```
DECLARE FUNCTION/SUB Name (Parameters)
```

A declaration is always required for functions. It is required for subroutines only if the alternative syntax (without the CALL statement) is used. A DECLARE statement must precede the first use of the procedure it declares.

If you are writing programs within the QuickBASIC environment (as we assume you are), declaration statements are usually generated automatically by the QuickBASIC system when the program is saved. Further information on the circumstances when QuickBASIC does or does not create a declaration statement is available in the language manual and the on-line help system.

If a procedure has no parameters, an empty set of parentheses should be included in the declaration statement. For example, the statement

```
DECLARE FUNCTION Second ()
```

declares a function named Second that has no parameters. An empty set of parentheses can also be included in the procedure heading statement but is not required.

A procedure normally reinitializes all local variables each time it is called. If you wish local variables (except parameters, of course) to preserve their values from one call to another, use the keyword STATIC in the procedure heading, as shown here.

```
FUNCTION/SUB Name (Parameters) STATIC
```

In the next section, we present Example Program 7-8 as a program that requires and uses a static function.

It is possible to exit a procedure at points other than the END FUNCTION/SUB statement by using the statement

```
EXIT FUNCTION/SUB
```

We discourage use of this statement, however, because we believe it is better programming practice (and reduces the likelihood of error) always to exit a procedure at its end.

When exiting a function by any means, an error occurs if the function has not been assigned a value before exiting.

Editing Programs Containing Procedures

We have not yet discussed the way the QuickBASIC editor displays and edits programs with procedures. Each program unit—main, function, or subroutine—is displayed in a separate window. When you use the Open Program command to view Example Program 7-1, you see only the main program unit. Pressing F2 or invoking the SUBs command from the View command menu displays a list of all units in the program. You can use the arrow keys to select any unit and press the Enter key to display the selected unit on the screen. Pressing F2 again allows another unit to be chosen.

If you are writing a new program, you normally start by writing the main program unit. As soon as you enter a procedure calling statement while writing your program, the QuickBASIC system immediately displays a new window containing the procedure heading and the procedure END statement. You can then proceed to enter the other procedure statements until the procedure has been completely written.

This same process can be repeated as many times as needed to write all procedures required by your program. When you have finished writing the program, you can run it by pressing F5 (or Shift-F5). As long as all program units are in a single module, the program will execute without DECLARE statements.

When the complete program is saved, the QuickBASIC system generates the necessary declaration statements and places them at the beginning of the main program unit. As mentioned earlier, a specific type character suffix is added to each procedure and parameter name in a DECLARE statement.

In our example programs, we have moved the declaration statements to a position after the initial comment statements. We think this format makes a program a little easier to read, but it certainly is not necessary. It is important, however, that the declaration statement for a procedure be executed before the procedure itself is called. Here is another example program with an additional subroutine Center that displays program output in the middle of a screen line.

```
' Example Program 7-2
' Use a function procedure to calculate the volume of a
' box and a subroutine procedure to display the result.

DECLARE FUNCTION Volume! (L!, W!, H!)
Result$ = "Volume of box is" + STR$(Volume(10, 5, 3))
CALL Center (Result$, 80)
END   ' Main Program

FUNCTION Volume (L, W, H)
   Volume = L * W * H
END FUNCTION   ' Volume
```

```
SUB Center (Value$, Col)
   PRINT TAB((Col - LEN(Value$)) / 2); Value$
END SUB  ' Center
```

This program produces the following output.

```
                Volume of box is 150
```

The output phrase displayed by subroutine Center is centered horizontally on the screen. Note that a comment is used to mark and identify the end of each program unit.

Be sure that you understand why example program listings do not appear on your screen as they appear in the book. On the screen you see either the main program or one of the procedures. You use F2 (as explained previously) to select whichever program unit you want to display. In the book you see the entire program as it might look if you printed the program file on a printer.

More about Parameters

When a procedure is called, the information passed to its parameters can be the values of constants (as in Example Program 7-1), the values of expressions, or the addresses of variables. **When a value is passed to a parameter, information flows in only one direction from the calling statement to the procedure.** The value of the local parameter variable in the procedure may be changed, but this change is not known in the calling program. We call this method of passing information *pass-by-value*. There is complete isolation between the calling program and the procedure.

When the address of a variable is passed to a parameter, however, any change in the value of the local parameter variable is known in the calling program. The parameter variable and the argument variable have the same address and thus share the same memory location and knowledge of its current value. If a change is made in the value of one of the local parameter variables in a procedure, the value of the corresponding argument variable in the calling program is also changed.

Passing information in this manner does not provide the complete isolation often desired between a procedure and its calling program unit. The argument variable name and the parameter variable name both refer to the same mailbox or memory location, and each variable has the value contained in that mailbox.

On the other hand, information can be passed back to the calling unit through the mailbox shared by the argument variable and the parameter variable. We call this method of passing information *pass-by-reference*. The different methods of passing information through parameters are used in Example Program 7-3 and diagrammed in Fig. 7.2.

```
' Example Program 7-3
' Use a function procedure to calculate volume of box.
' Use variable, expression, and constant arguments.
```

```
DECLARE FUNCTION Volume! (Length!, Breadth!, Height!)
L = 10
PRINT "Volume of box is"; Volume(L, L / 2, 3)
END  ' Main Program

FUNCTION Volume (Length, Breadth, Height)
   Volume = Length * Breadth * Height
END FUNCTION  ' Volume
```

The function call in the PRINT statement has variable L as its first argument and the address of this variable is passed to the function. Variables L and Length share the same address or memory location and always have the same value. The second argument, expression L/2, and the third argument, constant 3, have values that are passed to the parameters Breadth and Height. This program displays the same output as the two previous programs.

```
Volume of box is 150
```

Fig. 7.2 shows how information is passed to and from a function through its arguments and parameters. The same method of passing information applies also to subroutines. Single-headed arrows denote a value passing from an argument to a parameter. Double-headed arrows denote an address passing from an argument to a parameter.

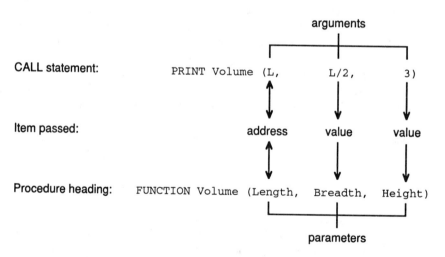

Figure 7.2   Passing information to and from procedures.

Here is a simple program that uses a subroutine procedure to halve a numeric parameter. A variable argument is used. The program contains many PRINT statements that show a user just what is going on at various points in the program. We suggest that you run this program and study its output if you are still uncertain about how parameter variables behave.

```
' Example Program 7-4
' Display values of argument and parameter variables
' when information is passed by reference.

INPUT "Type in a number...", Entry
PRINT "Before calling subroutine, Entry ="; Entry
CALL Halved (Entry)   ' argument is a variable
PRINT "After returning from subroutine, Entry =";
PRINT Entry
END   ' Main Program

SUB Halved (Value)
   ' Divide the parameter value by two.
   PRINT "Start of subroutine named Halved"
   PRINT "Entering the subroutine, Value ="; Value
   Value = Value / 2
   PRINT "After division, Value ="; Value
END SUB   ' Halved
```

The preceding example is a good illustration of how you can use PRINT statements to see what is happening inside a program. The address of variable Entry is passed to the local parameter variable Value. Thus both Entry and Value use the same mailbox or have the same memory location. When the value of Value is halved, the value of Entry is also halved. Here is the program output.

```
Type in a number...22
Before calling subroutine, Entry = 22
Start of subroutine named Halved
Entering the subroutine, Value = 22
After division, Value = 11
After returning from subroutine, Entry = 11
```

If information is passed by value, we get different results. **We change the argument in Example Program 7-4 into an expression by enclosing the variable Entry in another set of parentheses,** and name the new program Example Program 7-5.

```
' Example Program 7-5
' Display values of argument and parameter variables
' when information is passed by value.

INPUT "Type in a number...", Entry
PRINT "Before calling subroutine, Entry ="; Entry
CALL Halved ((Entry))   ' expression argument
PRINT "After returning from subroutine, Entry =";
PRINT Entry
END   ' Main Program
```

```
SUB Halved (Value)
   ' Divide the parameter value by two.
   PRINT "Start of subroutine named Halved"
   PRINT "Entering the subroutine, Value ="; Value
   Value = Value / 2
   PRINT "After division, Value ="; Value
END SUB   ' Halved
```

Note that the variable Entry is now enclosed in a second set of parentheses. Double parentheses are needed: the outer pair for the CALL statement syntax and the inner pair to change the variable into an expression. Example Program 7-5 produces the following results.

```
Type in a number...22
Before calling subroutine, Entry = 22
Start of subroutine named Halved
Entering the subroutine, Value = 22
After division, Value = 11
After returning from subroutine, Entry = 22
```

The only difference from Example Program 7-4 is in the last line of output. The revised value of parameter variable Value is not passed back to the main program, so Entry remains at its original value of 22.

This technique of using parentheses to change a variable into an expression only works with simple variables. It does not work with array variables which must be passed by reference (the address of the array variable must be passed).

7.4 ADDITIONAL EXAMPLE PROGRAMS

We write and discuss several example programs in this section. All these programs make use of procedures.

A Factorial Program

Our first example in this section uses a function procedure to calculate the factorial value of a positive number entered from the keyboard. For example, the factorial value of 5, denoted 5! by mathematicians, is equal to 1 x 2 x 3 x 4 x 5 or 120. By definition, 0! equals 1. This program prompts the user to enter a number from the keyboard, checks to see if the number is negative, and if it is, displays an error message and stops. Otherwise, it calculates and displays the factorial value of the number.

```
' Example Program 7-6
' Ask user to enter number and display its factorial
' value. Use a function for the factorial calculation.
```

```
DECLARE FUNCTION Factorial! (X!)
INPUT "Enter number: ", Number
IF Number < 0 THEN
    PRINT "Number must be positive."
ELSE
    PRINT "Factorial of"; Number; "is";
    PRINT Factorial((Number))
END IF
END  ' Main Program

FUNCTION Factorial (X)
    ' Calculate the factorial value of the parameter.
    Result = 1  ' initialize temporary variable Result
    FOR I = 1 to X
        Result = Result * I
    NEXT I
    Factorial = Result
END FUNCTION  ' Factorial
```

If the number is positive or zero, the function Factorial is called by the PRINT statement. The factorial value is calculated in the function and is returned to the main program. If X has a value of zero, the FOR loop is never executed and a value of 1 is assigned to Factorial.

Since there is no need to pass the value of X back to the main program, we provide better isolation between the main program and the function procedure by using an expression for an argument. Note that we enclose the variable Number in a double set of parentheses to make it an expression. The value of Number rather than its address is then passed to the function.

Here are two examples of user interaction with the program.

```
Enter number: 5
Factorial of 5 is 120

Enter number: -5
Number must be positive
```

A Palindrome Program

Another example uses string functions to determine if an entered string is a palindrome. A palindrome is defined as a sentence or sequence of letters that reads the same backward and forward. To test a palindrome, all letters must be converted to the same case (say, uppercase) and all nonalphabetic characters (including spaces or blanks) must be removed from the sentence.

The main program asks the user to enter a string from the keyboard. The standard function UCASE$ is called to convert all letters to uppercase. The user-defined function Remove$ is called to remove all nonalphabetic characters. Finally, the user-defined function Reverse$ is called to create a new string that is the reverse of the modified original string.

```
' Example Program 7-7
' Ask a user to enter a string and test
' if it is a palindrome.

DECLARE FUNCTION Remove$ (Phrase$)
DECLARE FUNCTION Reverse$ (Phrase$)
LINE INPUT "Enter string: ", Strg$
Strg$ = UCASE$(Strg$)
Strg$ = Remove$((Strg$))
RevStrg$ = Reverse$((Strg$))
IF Strg$ = RevStrg$ THEN
   PRINT "This string is a palindrome."
ELSE
   PRINT "This string is not a palindrome."
END IF
END  ' Main Program

FUNCTION Remove$ (Phrase$)
   ' Remove nonalphabetic characters from Phrase$.
   Result$ = ""   ' a null string
   FOR I = 1 TO LEN(Phrase$)
      Char$ = MID$(Phrase$, I, 1)
      IF Char$ >= "A" AND Char$ <= "Z" THEN
         Result$ = Result$ + Char$
      END IF
   NEXT I
   Remove$ = Result$
END FUNCTION   ' Remove$

FUNCTION Reverse$ (Phrase$)
   ' Reverse the order of characters in Phrase$.
   Result$ = ""
   FOR I = LEN(Phrase$) TO 1 STEP -1
      Char$ = MID$(Phrase$, I, 1)
      Result$ = Result$ + Char$
   NEXT I
   Reverse$ = Result$
END FUNCTION   ' Reverse$
```

Note that the string Result$ is initially assigned a null value in each function.

Selected characters from Phrase$ are then added to Result$, one by one. The two strings, Strg$ and RevStrg$, are compared and if they are the same, the original string is a palindrome. Here are two examples of user interaction.

```
Enter string: Madam, I'm Adam
This string is a palindrome.

Enter string: hello
This string is not a palindrome.
```

Note once again that in the two user-defined functions, information is passed by value because the modified string created by each function is returned to the main program through the function name. Double parentheses are not allowed in the standard function UCASE$; proper syntax requires that only a single set of parentheses be used.

A Summing Program

Each time a procedure is called, all nonparameter local variables are reinitialized by default, numeric variables to zero and string variables to the null string. You can prevent this reinitialization by declaring the procedure to be a static procedure.

The next example program shows how a local variable can be made to hold its value between function calls. A sum is accumulated in the variable Sum because it is not reset to zero each time the function is called. If the function is not declared to be static, the program does not work as expected.

```
' Example Program 7-8
' Display the sum of numbers entered from the keyboard,
' accumulating the sum in a local procedure variable.

DECLARE FUNCTION Add! (N!)
PRINT "Enter zero to stop data entry."
INPUT "Number"; Number
DO UNTIL Number = 0
   Result = Add((Number))
   INPUT "Number"; Number
LOOP
PRINT "The sum is"; Result
END   ' Main Program

FUNCTION Add (N) STATIC
   ' Add the parameter N to an existing sum.
   Sum = Sum + N
   Add = Sum
END FUNCTION   ' Add
```

Here is an example of program output.

```
Enter zero to stop data entry.
Number? 3
Number? 7
Number? 4
Number? 0
The sum is 14
```

Note that the variable Sum does retain its value between function calls, and its final value is the correct sum. Try running this program without the STATIC modifier and observe the error in the sum.

A Title-Display Program

It is possible to have one procedure call another procedure. **Remember that each procedure can have its own local variables.** Even if the same variable name is used in two different procedures, that name represents two different variables (two different mailboxes). Here is an example of a program that asks the user to enter a report title from the keyboard. It clears the screen and then calls a subroutine named Box that displays the centered title inside a box of asterisks or stars. The subroutine Center is used by Box to center each line of the boxed title on the screen.

The variable RetCode is a return variable that is set to a value greater than zero if the title in its box of asterisks will not fit between the margins. A screen width of 79 columns is assumed even though the column width of most screens is 80 columns. Some display units add an automatic line feed when displaying a line of 80 characters and we want to avoid that possibility.

```
' Example Program 7-9
' Ask user to enter a title and display it
' on the screen in a box of stars.

DEFINT A-Z
CONST SCREENWIDTH = 79
LINE INPUT "Enter title: ", Title$
RetCode = 0  ' initialize the return variable
CALL Box ((Title$), RetCode)
IF RetCode > 0 THEN PRINT "Title is too long."
END  ' Main Program

SUB Box (Name$, Code)
    ' Display the string Name$ in a box.
    Length = SCREENWIDTH - 4
    IF LEN(Name$) > Length THEN
```

```
            Code = LEN(Name$) - Length   ' title is too long
    ELSE
        CLS  ' clear the screen
        Stars$ = STRING$(LEN(Name$) + 4, "*")
        TitleLine$ = "* " + Name$ + " *"
        CALL Center ((Stars$), SCREENWIDTH)
        CALL Center ((TitleLine$), SCREENWIDTH)
        CALL Center ((Stars$), SCREENWIDTH)
    END IF
END SUB   ' Box

SUB Center (Value$, Col)
    ' Print a centered string in width of Col columns.
    PRINT TAB((Col - LEN(Value$)) / 2); Value$
END SUB   ' Center
```

The width of the screen, reduced by four columns to account for the asterisk and space at each end of the title, is stored in the local variable Length in procedure Box. The value of Length is compared with the length of the title string. If the title string is too long, the return variable is set to the number of characters by which the name exceeds the available space and the subroutine is exited. If the length is acceptable, subroutine Center is called to print a row of asterisks, the specified name with an asterisk and space at each end, and another row of asterisks. The CLS statement is used to clear the screen and the STRING$ function to create a row of asterisks.

The output of Example Program 7-9 looks as follows when the title "Analysis of 1993 Earnings" is entered.

```
            * * * * * * * * * * * * * * * * * * * * * * * * * * * *
            * Analysis of 1993 Earnings *
            * * * * * * * * * * * * * * * * * * * * * * * * * * * *
```

Note that function Box must pass the value of RetCode by reference because this value must be returned to the main program. On the other hand, function Center can pass information by value (a variable expression and a constant).

A Maximum Value Program

In our discussion of procedure syntax, we explained how an array can be passed as a parameter to a procedure. This example program reads a series of river depth values, measured at equidistant stations along the river, from a text file named DEPTH.DAT. The measured values are assigned to the elements of an array. A function is called that returns the station index corresponding to the maximum depth value. Note that the variable Count can be passed by value, but the array variable Depth must be passed by reference.

The first DO loop counts the number of depth readings in the file and uses this value to dimension the array Depth. The SEEK statement moves the file pointer back to the beginning of the file so that it can be read again. The function Station determines which array element contains the maximum depth reading and returns the index value of that element. Here is the program.

```
' Example Program 7-10
' Read river depths from text file DEPTH.DAT
' and assign value to an array. A function
' returns the index of the greatest depth.

DECLARE FUNCTION Station (Depth(), N)
OPEN "DEPTH.DAT" FOR INPUT AS #1
Count = 0
DO UNTIL EOF(1)
   LINE INPUT #1, Dummy$
   Count = Count + 1
LOOP
DIM Depth(1 TO Count)
SEEK #1, 1  ' set file pointer to beginning of file
FOR I = 1 TO Count
   INPUT #1, Depth(I)
NEXT I
Index = Station(Depth(), (Count))
PRINT "A maximum depth of"; Depth(Index)
PRINT "feet was measured at station"; Index
END   ' Main Program

FUNCTION Station (Depth(), N)
   ' Find the station index with the
   ' greatest depth value.
   Greatest = 0
   DeepPlace = 1
   FOR I = 1 TO N
      IF Depth(I) > Greatest THEN
         Greatest = Depth(I)
         DeepPlace = I
      END IF
   NEXT I
   Station = DeepPlace
END FUNCTION
```

It produces the following output.

```
A maximum depth of 55.7 feet was measured at station 2
```

We discuss the SEEK statement in more detail when we introduce random-access files. In the case of a sequential file, however, the SEEK statement is primarily useful for moving to the beginning of the file. The statement

```
SEEK #1, 1
```

moves the file pointer in file #1 to the beginning of the first byte. This location is the same as the beginning of the file. Using the SEEK statement is an alternative to closing and then reopening the file, as we did in Example Program 6-14.

7.5 PROGRAM MODULES, QUICKBASIC 4.5

> **QBI Note:** The QuickBASIC Interpreter does not support program modules, either as regular library files or as Quick libraries. Modular development of small programs is still possible (as shown in the preceding examples), but all program units must reside in a single file. Sections 7.5 and 7.6 thus apply only to the QuickBASIC compiler, not to the interpreter.

A *program module* is defined in QuickBASIC as a file that contains an executable part of a computer program. A complete program can be contained in one module or can be divided among two or more modules.

One module is called the *main module.* Program execution always starts with the first executable statement in the main module. Every program must have a main module. Other modules may contain other parts of the main program, or more commonly, only function and subroutine procedures. The QuickBASIC system helps you keep track of the various modules that make up a particular program, as discussed in Section 7.6.

Modules containing only procedures, sometimes called *library modules,* can often be used with more than one program. Remember that each module is a separate file. These procedures in the library modules should be written in general terms so they can be used in as many applications as possible. Programmers should be encouraged to make use of existing procedures instead of writing new ones.

Programs with multiple modules are usually medium-sized to large programs, which is one of the reasons that we have not introduced the concept until now. Several benefits result from dividing a large program into multiple modules.

Separate Modules of Procedures

A module containing only procedures can be used over and over again in different programs. Some care should be taken to group similar procedures in the same module. For example, one module might contain text-processing procedures, while another might contain matrix procedures. These procedures can often be tested more thoroughly and effectively outside the program environment.

Although we say that the module contains only procedures, this is not strictly correct. A library module often contains module-level or initialization code, consisting of such items as constant and type definitions and error-handling statements.

Team Development of Programs

Two or more programmers, working as members of a programming team, may be developing different parts of a large program at the same time. If each programmer is writing a separate module, there is little chance that they will interfere with each other. It is important, however, that each team programmer follow a previously-agreed-upon program outline.

Reuse of Procedures

Modules of well-designed and error-free procedures can be created and used in many different programs. A procedure that does a particular job and does it well does not have to be written over and over again. It can be placed in a module, and that module can be made a part of any new program you write. In a sense, these procedures become Quick-BASIC language extensions.

7.6 LIBRARY MODULES, QUICKBASIC 4.5

Function and subroutine procedures can be stored in separate modules or files. They can also be stored in special library files called Quick libraries. One disadvantage of Quick libraries is that they tend to be quite large and so are most useful with very large and complex programs. For programs of moderate size, modules of procedures (which we call library modules) are probably more convenient.

As we have explained previously, a module is the same as a file. A QuickBASIC program can consist of a single module or multiple modules. All the example programs we have written so far have been single-module programs.

In order to develop multimodule programs, the Full Menu option must be used. Select the Options command menu and press the letter F key to shift from Easy Menus to Full Menus. You will notice many additional commands that are explained in the language manual and the on-line help system.

Writing the Library Module and Include File

Write a program module that contains only procedures and no main program. You would normally use the New Program command and after writing the module, save it as a text file (recommended) or a QuickBASIC file. Here is an example of a library module named STRGLIB.BAS that contains several useful procedures for handling strings. Constant definitions are included as module-level code and placed at the beginning of the module.

```
' Example library module STRGLIB.BAS.
' A collection of procedures for handling strings.

CONST FALSE = 0, TRUE = NOT FALSE
CONST SCREENWIDTH = 80

SUB Center (Strg$)
   ' Display a string centered in the screen width.
   Space% = (SCREENWIDTH - LEN(Strg$)) \ 2
   PRINT TAB(Space%); Strg$
END SUB  ' Center

SUB Outline (Strg$)
   ' Display a string in a box.
   ' The following constants are the extended ASCII
   ' values of characters used to draw a box.
   ' UL = upper left corner, LL = lower left corner
   ' UR = upper right corner, LR = lower right corner
   ' VT = vertical line, HZ = horizontal line
   CONST UL = 218, LL = 192, UR = 191
   CONST LR = 217, VT = 179, HZ = 196
   Length% = LEN(Strg$)
   Space% = (SCREENWIDTH - Length%) \ 2
   PRINT TAB(Space% - 2); CHR$(UL);
   PRINT STRING$(Length% + 2, CHR$(HZ));
   PRINT CHR$(UR)
   ' Add leading and trailing spaces to Strg$
   Strg$ = " " + Strg$ + " "
   PRINT TAB(Space% - 2); CHR$(VT); Strg$; CHR$(VT)
   PRINT TAB(Space% - 2); CHR$(LL);
   PRINT STRING$(Length% + 2, CHR$(HZ));
   PRINT CHR$(LR)
END SUB  ' Outline

FUNCTION Remove$ (Phrase$)
   ' Remove nonalphabetic characters from Phrase$.
   Result$ = ""  ' a null string
   FOR I% = 1 TO LEN(Phrase$)
      Char$ = MID$(Phrase$, I%, 1)
      IF Char$ >= "A" AND Char$ <= "Z" THEN
         Result$ = Result$ + Char$
      END IF
   NEXT I%
   Remove$ = Result$
END FUNCTION  ' Remove$
```

```
FUNCTION Reverse$ (Phrase$)
   ' Reverse the order of characters in Phrase$.
   Result$ = ""
   FOR I% = LEN(Phrase$) TO 1 STEP -1
      Char$ = MID$(Phrase$, I%, 1)
      Result$ = Result$ + Char$
   NEXT I%
   Reverse$ = Result$
END FUNCTION   ' Reverse$

SUB Vertical (Strg$, Column%)
   ' Print a vertical string of characters
   ' in the specified column.
   FOR I% = 1 TO LEN(Strg$)
      PRINT TAB(Column%); MID$(Strg$, I%, 1)
   NEXT I%
END SUB   ' Vertical
```

In addition to the library module, an include file containing declaration statements must be created. This include file is known as the *declaration include file.*

After saving the library module, use the NewProgram command to erase memory and write an include file. This file must contain a DECLARE statement for each of the procedures in STRGLIB.BAS. When we save the file, we name it STRGLIB.BI, where the extension BI means a QuickBASIC include file. We recommend saving the include file in the Text format. Here is the include file for our library module.

```
' Example include file STRGLIB.BI.
' Declarations for procedures in STRGLIB.BAS.

DECLARE FUNCTION Remove$ (Phrase$)
DECLARE FUNCTION Reverse$ (Phrase$)
DECLARE SUB Center (Strg$)
DECLARE SUB Outline (Strg$)
DECLARE SUB Vertical (Strg$, Column%)
```

The library module may be given any legal DOS file name. We recommend that you use a name containing the letters LIB to identify a library module and to distinguish it from a QuickBASIC program. The include file of declarations should have the same file name as its library module but with the extension BI.

Writing a Multimodule Program

Once again, we use the New Program command to write a main program. This program may use any of the procedures contained in STRGLIB.BAS. It also must have a special type of REM statement, using the following syntax, that specifies the name of the declaration include file.

```
REM $INCLUDE: 'include file name'
```

This REM statement is called a metacommand or *compiler directive.* It is an instruction to the compiler, not a regular program statement, and should be written on a line by itself. The REM reserved word can be replaced by a single quotation mark ('). Note that the name of the include file is enclosed in single quotation marks, not the usual double quotation marks. Here is our example program, a modified version of Example Program 7-7.

```
' Example Program 7-11
' A modified palindrome program.
' Library module STRGLIB.BAS and the declaration
' include file STRGLIB.BI are part of this program.

REM $INCLUDE: 'STRGLIB.BI'

LINE INPUT "Enter string: ", Strg$
Strg$ = UCASE$(Strg$)
Strg$ = Remove$((Strg$))
RevStrg$ = Reverse$((Strg$))
IF Strg$ = RevStrg$ THEN
    PRINT "This string is a palindrome."
ELSE
    PRINT "This string is not a palindrome."
END IF
END
```

Before this program will run successfully, the library module must be loaded into memory. With the Full Menus option active, we use the Load File command from the File command menu. This command loads a file without erasing any existing file in memory. In our case we must load the library module file STRGLIB.BAS in addition to the already loaded main program module file EX07-11.BAS.

Note that if you use the Load File command to load all program modules, you must load the main program module first. After that module is loaded, you can load any other modules. QuickBASIC considers the first module loaded to be the main module and starts execution with the first executable statement in that module.

The program can now be run as before. Functions Remove$ and Reverse$ are available in the library module, while function UCASE$ is a standard function. The output results are the same as those produced by Example Program 7-7.

When this program is saved, another file named EX07-11.MAK is also created and saved. This file, called a *make file,* tells the QuickBASIC system that any time program file EX07-11.BAS is loaded, the library module STRGLIB.BAS must also be loaded. The

QuickBASIC system automatically loads all files listed in the make file after the first file has been loaded. The make file is a simple text file and in the case of our example program, contains the two following lines.

```
EX07-11.BAS
STRGLIB.BAS
```

Once all the necessary files have been created, as discussed in the preceding paragraphs, you can load program EX07-11.BAS using the Open Program command and the library module will be loaded with it. You must, however, be using the Full Menus option. If not, the QuickBASIC system changes to that option after displaying a warning message .

You must be careful that two procedures in your program do not have the same name, whether they are located in a library module loaded with the program or written as part of the main program. You can, of course, load more than one library module with your main program. Each library module should have its own declaration include file, and a compiler directive for all these files must be included in the main program.

Summary of Important Points

- Lack of isolation between program units can be a major source of hard-to-find errors in large programs.
- A value must be assigned to the function name before control returns to the calling program unit.
- No value is associated with a subroutine name.
- The notation FUNCTION/SUB means that the statement can be used with either a function or a subroutine procedure.
- When a value is passed to a parameter, information flows in only one direction, from the calling statement to the procedure.
- When an address is passed to a parameter, any change in the value of the local parameter variable is known in the calling program.
- Enclosing a simple variable in parentheses makes it an expression rather than a variable. This technique does not work with array variables.
- Each procedure in a program can have its own local variables.
- DECLARE statements must be included in the main program for all procedures that are called from library modules.
- A make file is created when a multimodule program is saved. This file automatically loads all required modules when the main program is loaded.

Common Errors

- Writing a subroutine procedure whose name ends with a dollar sign.
- Leaving a function procedure before assigning a value to the function name.

- Using the alternative method (no CALL statement) of calling a subroutine without including a declaration statement in the program unit.
- Failing to declare a procedure as static when the value of a local procedure variable must be preserved between procedure calls.
- Writing a procedure without parameters and failing to include a set of empty parentheses in its declaration statement.
- Using an EXIT statement to exit a procedure that could just as easily have been exited through the END statement.
- Passing an address to a parameter rather than passing a value when maximum isolation is desired between the calling unit and the procedure unit.
- Passing a value to a parameter rather than passing an address when information must be passed back through the parameter from the procedure unit to the calling unit.
- Forgetting to place an additional set of parentheses around a simple variable that is being passed by value.
- Placing an additional set of parentheses around an array variable.
- Trying to calculate the factorial value of a negative number.
- Testing a string to determine if it is a palindrome without converting all letter characters to the same case.
- Trying to execute a program that uses a library module while running under the Quick-BASIC Interpreter.
- Keeping a program file and its make file in different directories.
- Selecting the Easy Menus option when executing a program that uses a library module.

Self-Test Questions

1. What is an advantage of writing a program as a sequence of small program units?
2. What is meant by the concept of isolation between program units?
3. Can the dollar sign character be included as part of
    (a) a subroutine name;
    (b) a function name?
4. Does a function procedure require an assignment statement to assign a value to the procedure name?
5. What is meant by a local variable in a procedure?
6. If a local variable (not a parameter) named Number in a procedure is assigned a value of 5, what will be the value of the same variable Number when the procedure is called again? Explain your answer.
7. (a) Is a value assigned to a subroutine name when the subroutine is called?
    (b) Is a value assigned when control returns to the calling program?
8. Are the following words palindromes?
    (a) William
    (b) Hannah
    (c) baby

9. What is the factorial value of 4 (in mathematical notation, what is the value of 4!)?

10. How can a variable argument be changed to an expression argument?

11. If a main program unit has a variable named Count and a function procedure declares a variable named Count as the control variable in a FOR loop, do these two variables refer to the same or different memory locations? Explain your answer.

12. What statement must be the last statement in
    (a) a function procedure;
    (b) a subroutine procedure?

13. What is meant by the term *pass-by-value*?

14. Under what circumstances is the reserved word CALL needed to call a subroutine procedure?

15. What is meant by the term *pass-by-reference*?

16. Are values passed to a procedure through
    (a) variable arguments;
    (b) constant arguments;
    (c) expression arguments?

17. Are addresses passed to a procedure through
    (a) variable arguments;
    (b) constant arguments;
    (c) expression arguments?

18. Can a library module be used with the QuickBASIC Interpreter?

Practice Programs

In these problems we ask you to write procedures. To show how each procedure works, you must also write a short program, called a *stub program*, that tests the procedure. For example, you might write a subroutine procedure called Exchange in Practice Program 1 and test this procedure using the following stub program.

```
' Test subroutine of Practice Program 1.
A = 5
B = 10
PRINT "Before exchange, A ="; A; "and B ="; B
CALL Exchange (A, B)
PRINT "After exchange, A ="; A; "and B ="; B
END
```

1. Write a subroutine to exchange or swap the values of two numeric variables that are passed as parameters. Test your subroutine using values of 0 and 1.

2. Write a subroutine to swap the values of two string variables that are passed as parameters. Test your subroutine using values of "TRUE" and "FALSE".

3. Write a function PRED$ that returns the predecessor (in the ASCII table) of a single-character string parameter. If the parameter string is longer than one character, the function returns the predecessor of the first character. Test your function using the string values "C", "A", "@", and "qed".

4. Write a function SUCC$ that returns the successor (in the ASCII table) of a single-character string parameter. If the parameter string is longer than one character, the function returns the successor of the first character. Test your function using the string values "C", "z", "*", and "ABC".

5. Write a function CUBE that returns the cube of its numeric parameter. Test your function using the numbers 2, 5, and 132.

6. Write a function DECIMAL that returns the decimal part of its numeric parameter. Test your function using the numbers 12.75, 35, 3.3333333, and -1.001.

7. Write a subroutine GRID that clears the entire screen and fills it with an 80-by-24 grid of dots. Such a subroutine might be used in a computer-aided drafting program.

8. Write a function SPHERE that returns the volume of a sphere whose radius is passed as a parameter. If you have forgotten the formula for the volume of a sphere, look it up in a dictionary or encyclopedia. Test your function using radii of 5, 10, and 2.32 units.

9. Write a function WORD$ that returns the English word corresponding to its single-digit numeric parameter; that is, TWO for parameter 2, SEVEN for 7, and so forth. Test your function using the digits 0, 9, and 5.

10. Write a function TODAY$ that returns the current date in an expanded format, for example, March 13, 1990. This problem assumes that your computer has a built-in clock or that you entered the correct date and time when you turned on the system. Review the date and time functions in Appendix E.

11. Write a function COMPARE% that compares two string parameters, returning the value of 1 if they are equal and zero if not equal. Test your function using the following pairs of string values.

        "abc" and "xyz"
        "aaa" and "aaa"
        "abc" and "abcdef"
        "abc" and "ABC"

12. Write a function WORDS that returns the number of words in a string. Assume that there is a word (no initial blank) at the beginning of the string and a word (no final blank) at the end of the string. Any other sequence of one or more characters surrounded by blanks is defined as a word. Assume only one blank between words. Test your function using the following phrases.

        This is a test string.
        Will you dance? Will you dance? Will you dance?

13. Write a function OCCURRENCES that returns the number of times that a character appears in a string. The function should be insensitive to uppercase and lowercase differences in characters. For example, the function should show that the character T appears four times in the string "This is the straight way." Both the string and the character are parameters. Test your function using the following values.

        "T" in "This is the straight way"
        "X" in "Use the Xerox machine"
        "*" in "***********"

14.   Write a function AVERAGE that returns the average word length in a string parameter. Use the function developed in Practice Program 12. Test your function using the following sentences.

> Dependents must furnish evidence of eligibility.
> Now is the time for all good men to fight or flee.

8

DESIGNING PROGRAMS AND CORRECTING ERRORS

8.1 INTRODUCTION

A large fraction of the time spent developing a computer program is devoted to finding and eliminating errors. We discuss several techniques for helping a programmer find errors, including more information on the built-in program debugger. We also discuss a program structure for trapping and handling errors.

In addition to learning how to find errors, it is important to learn how to write computer programs that contain few errors. We present a recommended procedure for writing programs that are likely to run correctly the first time they are executed. We discuss the important subject of program testing. We illustrate our recommendations with an example program.

8.2 FINDING AND CORRECTING ERRORS

We discussed the QuickBASIC debugging system in Chapter 5 and will discuss it further in this chapter. There are other methods, however, that can be used to find errors and we introduce them in this section. These methods are especially useful if you are using the QuickBASIC Interpreter.

Testing Individual Units

We have recommended that your program be divided into multiple units, consisting of the main program and separate procedures. Ideally, the main program should consist almost entirely of calls to procedures. Each of these procedures should be tested independently to make sure it is working properly. Whenever possible, reuse a procedure you have already tested and used before.

If the procedure is new, it is a good idea to test it with a short main program, often called a *stub program*. Look at the stub program listed at the beginning of the Practice Program section in Chapter 7 for an example. Once you are certain that each procedure is working correctly, you have eliminated many of the likely causes of error in your program. You will probably find that your program runs perfectly.

Playing Computer

Our goal is to write programs that contain no errors. It is usually an impossible goal to attain, but we need to learn how to reduce the number of errors to a minimum. At the same time, we must develop skill in finding errors and then removing them from our programs.

One of the easiest methods for finding errors is to read through a computer program pretending that you are the computer. You make all the calculations and decisions that would normally be made by the computer. Many simple errors will be revealed.

This method is easy to understand and to apply but it can be slow and tedious. You will find it most useful for examining small sections of a program. You will make better progress if you write down intermediate results on paper in a systematic format. If complicated arithmetic calculations are involved, you can speed up the process by using a hand calculator or the Immediate window of QuickBASIC.

In spite of the limitations, we recommend that you try this method first, especially with small programs. It is a natural way to find errors if a program is not working properly.

Temporary PRINT Statements

Student programmers often say "I know that the value of variable X at this point in the program is 15.2, but when I make a calculation using X and print the results, they are wrong." Our automatic response is "How do you know that the value of X is 15.2?"

One way to answer the question is to put a temporary PRINT statement into your program and see what the value of X actually is at the point of calculation. It is surprising how often it will be different from what you thought it should be.

It is not unusual to insert half a dozen temporary PRINT statements in a program before finding an error. Often it is helpful to include a label in a PRINT statement to help identify its location.

For example, the statement

```
PRINT "In Report section: X ="; X
```

identifies the variable being displayed and the program section where it has this value. A single PRINT statement can also be used to print out the values of several different variables, as shown in the following statement.

```
PRINT "After first search: I,Sum = ";I; Sum
```

You must, of course, remember to delete all temporary PRINT statements after you have found the error.

You probably have noticed that these temporary statements provide essentially the same information as do watch variables in the QuickBASIC debugger. Programmers using the QuickBASIC 4.5 compiler quickly adapt to using the debugger and watch variables, while users of the QuickBASIC Interpreter are limited to PRINT statements. As suggested earlier, it may be more convenient to place these PRINT statements in the Immediate window.

Once you have become thoroughly familiar with the debugger, you will probably use it frequently. It is helpful, however, to know about other error-finding techniques that can supplement the debugger. In many cases, these two techniques, playing computer and inserting temporary PRINT statements, are sufficient to identify programming errors.

8.3 MORE ON THE QUICKBASIC DEBUGGER

We return now to our discussion of the QuickBASIC debugger and examine some of its other capabilities.

Debugging Procedures

We have learned how to write programs with separate procedures, and in many cases these procedures have been thoroughly debugged before the whole program is put together. In such cases, we are interested in debugging the main program and skipping over the procedures.

Pressing F8 performs a single-step trace through an entire program, including all procedures. Pressing F10, on the other hand, performs the same trace but skips over all procedure statements.

When debugging short programs or on the first attempt to debug a longer program, the F8 key is normally used. Once you are convinced, however, that all the procedures are executing properly, you can save time by using the F10 key for single-step tracing.

Breakpoints

If a program is long and most of its statements contain no errors, it is a waste of time to single step through many valid statements in order to reach a section of the program where an error is thought to exist. The QuickBASIC debugger solves this problem by allowing one or more breakpoints to be set in the source program.

A breakpoint is a designated line where the program stops execution and waits for some action by the user. Most often, a breakpoint is set just before a section of code where an error is suspected, and when the program halts, the F8 or F10 key is used to single step through that section.

The Toggle Breakpoint command in the Debug command menu sets the line marked by the cursor as a breakpoint. Placing the cursor under any character in the desired line and pressing F9 has the same effect. The program is then executed using the normal Run (Shift-F5) command and execution stops when the breakpoint is reached. At this point, pressing F8 or F10 starts a single-step trace of the program. Single stepping can be interrupted at any time by pressing F5 or executing the Continue command in the Run command menu.

You can clear or release a breakpoint by placing the cursor on the line containing the breakpoint and pressing F9 again. You can also clear all breakpoints with the Clear All Breakpoints command in the Debug command menu.

Fig. 8.1 is an expanded version of the list of debugging keys shown in Chapter 5. In addition, there are other commands in the full Debug command menu that do not have special keys.

KEY	ACTION
F4	Toggles between Edit and Output windows
F5	Continues regular program execution from the current line
F8	Starts single step-program execution
F9	Toggles a breakpoint on and off at this line
F10	Same as F8, but skips over procedures
Shift-F5	Starts regular program execution from the beginning of the program
Shift-F9	Displays value of variable under cursor and makes it a watch variable by pressing the Enter key

Figure 8.1   Expanded list of debugging keys.

Tracing a Program in Slow Motion

We have discussed the process of manually single stepping through a program. That process can be automated by activating the Trace On command of the Debug command menu. When this command is active, a bullet (•) appears next to the Trace On command in the command window. Pressing Shift-F5 or F5 starts the program executing in slow motion. Each line is highlighted as it is executed. The system displays the Output window when necessary to show output or accept input. If you are using the QuickBASIC 4.5 compiler, you can have the Watch window open while executing the program in this mode and watch how the values of selected variables change.

At any time, execution can be stopped by pressing the interrupt key (Ctrl-Break). Execution can be started again by pressing F5. If you wish to go back to regular program execution, just invoke the Trace On command again and it acts as a toggle, turning off slow motion execution.

Unfortunately, the speed of statement execution in the Trace On mode cannot be adjusted and you may find it too fast to be useful. We believe the combination of break-points and the single-step mode is a more satisfactory debugging technique.

The art of program debugging can be learned only by experience. It can be time consuming and frustrating, but if you persist, you should be able to find and eliminate most program errors.

8.4 CALCULATION ERRORS

Most calculation errors are due to incorrect programs, but some are due to limitations of the computer or the language. These latter errors are hard to find and require some understanding of how your computer works. We discuss a typical example that can cause unexpected problems in a QuickBASIC program.

Computers use binary arithmetic for manipulating and storing numbers. Programs are usually written to use decimal arithmetic for numeric calculations. This difference means that computers running a program must often convert between binary and decimal representations of numbers.

In binary arithmetic as in decimal arithmetic, certain fractions can only be represented by nonterminating sequences of digits. A familiar example in decimal arithmetic is the value of 0.333... (a nonterminating sequence of the digit 3) for the fraction 1/3. If the sequence is terminated, it is not exactly equal to the fraction. For example, the sequence 0.33333 is not exactly equal to 1/3.

The fraction 1/10 or 0.1 is represented in binary arithmetic as a nonterminating sequence of binary digits. If the binary sequence is terminated, as it must be if the number is stored in a computer, it is no longer exactly equal to the fraction 1/10.

This type of error causes problems when an equality is used to make a program decision. Here is an example.

```
' Example Program 8-1
' Failure of an equality test in a loop
' with display of partial results.

X = 0
PRINT X;
```

```
DO UNTIL X = 1
   X = X + .1
   PRINT X;
LOOP
END
```

The problem with this program is that the value of X is never exactly equal to 1 even though the PRINT statement displays a value of 1. Thus the loop will continue indefinitely or until stopped by pressing the interrupt key (Ctrl-Break). Here are some partial results.

```
0  .1  .2  .3  .4  .5  .6  .7  .8000001  .9000001  1
1.1  1.2  1.3 ... 2.899999  2.999999  3.099999 ...
```

Note that some of the conversion errors are visible in the displayed values. Other values appear correct as displayed but errors may exist in the internal representations of the numbers. In particular the value of the expression X = 1 is never true.

A better program can be written by testing whether the value of X differs by only a small amount (small compared to the increment of 0.1) from 1. Here is a program that works, stopping when the value of X equals 1.

```
' Example Program 8-2
' A successful equality test in a loop
' with display of several variables.

CONST EPSILON = .000001
PRINT " X"; TAB(21); "ABS(X - 1)"; TAB(41); "EPSILON"
PRINT
X = 0
PRINT X; TAB(20); ABS(X - 1); TAB(40); EPSILON
DO UNTIL ABS(X - 1) < EPSILON
   X = X + .1
   PRINT X; TAB(20); ABS(X - 1); TAB(40); EPSILON
LOOP
END
```

This program produces tabular results as follows.

X	ABS(X - 1)	EPSILON
0	1	.000001
.1	.9	.000001
.2	.8	.000001
.3	.7	.000001

.4	.6	.000001
.5	.5	.000001
.6	.4	.000001
.7	.3	.000001
.8000001	.1999999	.000001
.9000001	.0999999	.000001
1	1.192093E-07	.000001

Note how the error in X increases as its value approaches one. The last value of X appears to be accurate because only seven digits are printed (with trailing zeros deleted), while the error is in the eighth digit. Note also that if the value of EPSILON is made too small (say, 1E-7), Example Program 8-2 fails to work properly because expression ABS(X - 1) is larger than EPSILON. The conclusion to draw from these two examples is to **avoid using an equality between two numeric values as a condition in a logical expression. Use an inequality instead.**

This and similar types of errors can occur in computer programs written in almost any language. Try the sample programs yourself on your computer. Simple test programs such as the ones we have listed can be written quickly and easily to determine how QuickBASIC will behave on your particular computer. With a little care, you can write computer programs that avoid calculation errors.

8.5 ERROR TRAPPING AND HANDLING

Program errors can be divided into several general classes. Syntax errors (also called compile errors) are errors in statement syntax detected while each program line containing one or more statements is being compiled or accepted (see the following QBI Note) These errors are identified quickly after each line is entered. You can either use the editor to correct the line or just backspace and enter the line again. If the syntax is correct, each statement is accepted and all its reserved words are changed to uppercase.

> **QBI Note:** The interpreter checks the syntax of each statement and accepts it if it is correct. It does not, however, compile each statement as the line is entered into the computer.

Logic errors are the result of mistakes in logic when the program was designed or written. The program may run perfectly but produces meaningless results. These errors are hard to find and can be corrected only by thoroughly testing the program.

Run-time errors occur while the program is executing. These errors may be caused by logic errors or by other mistakes when writing the program. They are usually fatal and cause the program to stop, displaying an error code or message. Computer programmers say the program has crashed. A list of run-time error codes appears in Appendix F. QuickBASIC provides a facility for trapping and handling run-time errors that allows the user to correct these errors in many cases and continue executing the program.

The ON ERROR Statement

The statement for trapping errors is the ON ERROR statement with the following syntax.

```
ON ERROR GOTO label
```

The label is any numeric or alphanumeric line identifier or label. This statement must be located in the program before any statement that might produce an error we want to trap. We recommend the use of an alphanumeric label which consists of any sequence of up to 40 letters or digits, starting with a letter and ending with a colon. Some valid labels are shown in the following list.

```
ErrorHandler:
Messages:
Table3A:
```

When used with the ON ERROR statement, the label identifies the beginning of a block of program code that is invoked when a run-time error occurs. **This block should be located so that it is never executed during normal running of the program.** The error-handling block is usually placed after the END statement in the main program or in the initialization section of a library module.

Shared Variables

An ON ERROR statement may be placed within a procedure unit rather than in the main program unit The associated error-handling block cannot be placed in the procedure itself or in the main program, but rather is placed in the file or module as a block of module-level statements (see Section 7.2). Normally the error-handling code is placed after the main program END statement and before the first procedure heading statement.

Variables in the main program are known in or shared with any module-level code, including the error-handling block, but local variables in a procedure are not known in that block. Moreover, variable values cannot be passed as parameters from a procedure to the error-handling block because the block is not part of either the main program or the procedure.

One way to solve this problem is to introduce the concept of a *shared variable*. Shared variables can be declared in any procedure using the SHARED statement. The syntax is

```
SHARED Variable1, Variable2,...
```

These variables are known in or shared with the single procedure in which they are declared and with any module-level code, including the main program, but not with any other procedure in the program. Note that this type of SHARED statement must always appear in a procedure (see Section 11.5 for a discussion of shared global variables).

It is usually preferable to pass variable values as parameters but that is impossible in this case. The use of shared variables should be kept to a minimum because it removes some of the isolation normally present between program units. Shared variables are used in the file-opening procedures of Example Program 8-4.

The RESUME Statement

The last statement in the error-handling block is normally a RESUME or RESUME NEXT statement. RESUME returns control to the statement that caused the error. RESUME NEXT returns control to the statement after the one that caused the error. It is also possible to return control to a specific line, using the syntax

```
RESUME line identifier
```

Here is a sample program that uses error trapping and error handling. The system function ERR returns the error code number, which is 11 for division by zero (see Appendix F).

```
' Example Program 8-3
' Calculate the inverse of a number, trapping
' and handling the error of division by zero.

CONST FALSE = 0, TRUE = NOT FALSE
ON ERROR GOTO ErrorHandler
DO
    NoError = TRUE
    INPUT "Enter number: ", Number
    Result = 1 / Number
    IF NoError = TRUE THEN
        PRINT "Inverse of"; Number; "is"; Result
    END IF
LOOP UNTIL NoError = TRUE
END


ErrorHandler:
IF ERR = 11 THEN
    PRINT "The inverse of zero cannot be calculated."
ELSE
    PRINT "Unexpected error"; ERR
END IF
NoError = FALSE
PRINT "Please enter number again."
PRINT
RESUME NEXT
```

The user is asked to enter a number and the inverse of that number is calculated and displayed. We use the flag variable NoError to signal whether an error has occurred. If the error is division by zero, we describe the type of error. If not, we display the error number. After displaying error information, we ask the user to enter the number again.

Note that we terminate the error-handler block with a RESUME NEXT statement. This statement transfers control past the IF statement (NoError is false) to the LOOP statement, resulting in the loop being executed again and the user being given another opportunity to enter a number.

It is important that the error-handler code be able to handle any type of error. An unexpected error is trapped and the error code number is displayed. The program remains in a loop until a valid, nonzero number is entered. Program output might look as follows.

```
Enter a number: 0
The inverse of zero cannot be calculated.
Please enter number again.

Enter a number: 10
Inverse of 10 is .1
```

Error trapping is an example of good defensive programming. You should anticipate the possibility of run-time errors in your program and develop plans to handle these errors when they occur. Nothing is more discouraging to the user of an application program than to have the program suddenly stop and display an error message that is not understood. A well-written program always gives the user an opportunity to recover from an error, especially an error such as misspelling a name that is entered during input.

8.6 HINTS FOR WRITING CORRECT PROGRAMS

Most of our discussion in this chapter has been about methods for finding and correcting program errors. An equally important topic is how to write programs that have no errors in the first place, a topic that we discussed briefly in Chapter 2.

When we say that a program is error-free, we mean that extensive testing has revealed no errors. There is no way of knowing absolutely that every single error has been found and corrected. Unfortunately, some errors may never be found until the program has been used by many people in many different applications.

Throughout the book we stress logical program design, development of a program in small modules, and use of clear, simple structures for looping and branching. Keep these points in mind as we discuss some hints for writing better programs.

Understand the Problem

You cannot write a program to solve a problem until you completely understand the problem. We made this statement in an earlier chapter, but it bears repeating. A lot of people start to write a program before they understand clearly what the program must do. Keep asking questions or investigate further until you do understand the problem.

Plan First, Program Later

You must plan how you will write your program before you write the first statement. If you fail to plan carefully, you may find halfway through writing the program that you have to start all over again. There are two steps you should take.

First, you must choose an algorithm to solve the problem. It is helpful if the algorithm is simple and in many cases, the algorithm must also be efficient. Second, **you must write an outline of your program.** We discussed these two steps in Chapter 2 and mention them again because of their importance. Too often we have seen students struggling with large programs that have been put together without any serious planning or thought and then modified at random when they would not run. When asked for help, the best advice we can give is to start over again and we feel as badly as the students about the time that has been wasted and lost. Only when you have taken these two steps are you ready to start writing the program itself.

Write Simple Programs

Use all the techniques that we have discussed to write a program that is easy to read and understand. Use variable names that are descriptive. Use indentation to show which statements make up the body of a branch or loop. Use comments to explain the logical action of the program, not just what an individual statement does.

Avoid program structures that are tricky or hard to understand. There is usually no justification for writing programs that are complicated in order to make them more efficient. Remember that computer memory is becoming less expensive and computers are becoming faster. In most cases, programs should be written to minimize the time required for maintenance rather than to minimize execution time or the amount of memory used.

Most important, **if your program is longer than a page of code, write it as a series of short procedures,** as independent from one another as possible. No procedure should be longer than a single page. Include general procedures that you have written previously, and if you are using QuickBASIC 4.5, make use of library modules as often as you can.

Thoroughly test each procedure before adding it to your program. Small procedures tend to be easier than large programs to write and debug. If each procedure is free of errors, the resulting program should also be error-free.

Test and Debug Carefully

If you are careful in writing your program, it should contain few errors. **Test your program for as many conditions as possible that might cause an error.** Look carefully at extreme conditions, such as the largest and smallest values of key variables. Ask someone else to run your program and see if they can make it fail.

Beginning programmers tend to overlook the importance of adequate program testing and do not budget enough time for this critical phase of program development. In a school or college environment, a programming assignment is often finished just before the due date and tested on only one or two simple cases. You should assume that a user (or your instructor) will test the program with a wide variety of input data.

If you are developing a program for a commercial or governmental application, it is worthless unless it has been thoroughly tested. You may have heard the story (possibly false) about the space probe that missed Mars because a programmer failed to find and correct a simple bug in a computer program. There is concern that many commercial programs will fail on January 1, 2000 because no testing was ever done using dates in the twenty-first century. Testing is important and we discuss it further in the next section.

A common type of error is called the off-by-one bug. This is the error that occurs, for example, when you are counting and the sum turns out to be 1 less or 1 greater than it should be. It often occurs because computers start counting at zero, while people start counting at 1. Look carefully at your logic and you should be able to find the mistake.

In summary, your ability to write error-free programs should improve quickly if you follow these suggestions. There will be times, however, when in spite of your best efforts you cannot get a program to work. You should then go back and examine your program outline. If you are not satisfied with it, you may save time by starting over again. It is difficult to write a good program from a bad outline.

8.7 DEVELOPMENT OF A COMPUTER PROGRAM

We recommend the following steps when developing a computer program: (1) Start with a general outline of the program, (2) refine the outline until you are thoroughly satisfied with it, and (3) only at that point start to write program statements.

This is the same method used by experienced writers when developing a book or article. If you start from a general program outline, you are more likely to avoid logical errors and produce a program whose component parts all work together properly.

We recommend that you write the outline of your program on paper as a sequence of steps. These outline steps are often called *pseudocode* statements. If any of the steps in your outline are long or complicated, write out a secondary outline of each complicated step. After carefully reviewing the outline, start writing the program statements that will carry out the steps you have written down.

We stress the importance of writing the program outline, not just creating it in your mind. If your program is of any size (say, over 20 statements in length), there is too much chance of forgetting some point in the outline if it is not written down.

Pseudocode versus Flowcharts

Many older textbooks on computer programming advise students to draw flowcharts rather than write program outlines. A flowchart is a diagram that shows how a computer program works, using boxes and arrows as symbols for such actions as looping, branching, and I/O (input and output) operations. The symbols are joined by lines with arrowheads showing the direction of flow of program control. Fig. 8.2 is an example of a section of a flowchart.

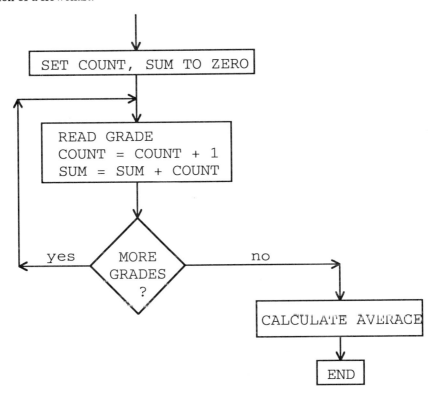

Figure 8.2   Part of a computer program flowchart.

Our experience indicates that flowcharts are not needed to explain small programs and they become too complicated and difficult to draw for large programs. In either case it is questionable whether the benefit is worth the extra work. It is a fact that in many commercial programming operations, flowcharts are used primarily to document large programs and are drawn after the programs have been completed.

On the other hand, we find that program outlines written in pseudocode are easy to produce (once you understand the problem) and provide invaluable guidance during program development. We strongly recommend their use.

The Program Outline

We now look at an example of program development. We have a relatively simple problem, namely, to compute the average grade of each student in a class and the average class grade. Student names and individual student grades are stored in a file whose name is entered by the user. Here is part of a typical grade file. For each student it contains the student's name and several grades, all on separate lines.

```
Susan Litchfield
75
82
89
78
92
Jim Bishop
91
87
93
85
95
```

The user must enter the number of grades per student. Before computing average grades, the user can exercise an option of dropping each student's lowest grade. Each student's name and average grade is displayed on the screen and written on an output file specified by the user. The class average for all students is also calculated and displayed on the screen. Here is an outline of the program.

Ask user for name of grade file and open as input file.

Ask user for name of output file and open it.

Ask user for number of grades per student.

Ask if lowest grade is to be dropped and set flag.

Initialize the variables for sums and counts.

Display column headings on the screen.

Top of loop: Call a procedure to do the following and exit at end of file.

   Read a student's name.

   Read a student's individual grades.

   Calculate the average grade, dropping lowest grade if requested.

   Display name and average grade on the screen.

   Write name and average grade on output file.

   Increment the count of students.

   Add new average grade to sum of average grades.

Bottom of loop.

Calculate and display the class average.

End of program.

Modular Development of the Program

As we have discussed previously, it is desirable to write a program as a main program unit and a group of procedures. Looking at our outline, we can identify at least three separate procedures.

Procedure 1:	Opens the student grade file for input.
Procedure 2:	Opens the class average file for output.
Procedure 3:	Calculates and displays the average grade for an individual student.

Procedures for Opening Files

Many computer programs need to open files. At this point in our discussion of Quick-BASIC, we have learned about and used sequential text files. An OPEN statement must be executed before reading information from an existing file, writing information on a new file, overwriting information on an existing file, or appending information to the end of an existing file.

We first develop a group of procedures for opening files. An error-handling section should be included in any program that uses these procedures, allowing a user to try again if an incorrect file name is entered or if a file name is misspelled. These procedures will be part of this and future example programs, so we make them as general as possible.

Here are the error-handling statements that should be placed right after the main program END statement. The statement

```
CONST FALSE = 0, TRUE = NOT FALSE
```

must be included in the main program.

```
ErrorHandler1:
   ' Set NameOK to false if file does not exist.
   IF ERR = 53 THEN
      PRINT "File does not exist - try again"
      NameOK = FALSE
      RESUME NEXT
   ELSE   ' unexpected error, halt the program
      ON ERROR GOTO 0
   END IF


ErrorHandler2:
   ' Set OverWrite to true if file does not exist.
```

```
IF ERR = 53 THEN   ' no existing file
   OverWrite = TRUE
   RESUME NEXT
ELSE   ' unexpected error, halt the program
   ON ERROR GOTO 0
END IF
```

ErrorHandler1 is used when opening a file for reading or appending. In both cases, an existing file is expected. Error code number 53 is returned if a file does not exist and cannot be found. The most probable reason for not finding a file is that its name was entered incorrectly or misspelled, so flag NameOK is set to false. This flag value is returned to the procedure and causes the program to ask for the file name again. If an error is found other than error 53, the error handler uses the special statement

```
ON ERROR GOTO 0
```

to halt the program and then displays the QuickBASIC error message.

ErrorHandler2 is used when opening a file for writing and the question is whether or not to overwrite an existing file. If there is no existing file, flag OverWrite is set to true and the flag value returned to the procedure. If the returned flag value is false, the user is asked if the existing file should be overwritten.

Here are the procedures themselves, including one procedure to check for a "Y" or "N" answer and three procedures to open files.

```
SUB CheckAnswer (Prompt$, Flag)
   ' Display prompt, get answer, and set flag
   ' to TRUE or FALSE if answer is YES or NO.
   ' Otherwise, prompt for answer again.
   ' Main program defines constants TRUE and FALSE.
   DO
      PRINT Prompt$;
      INPUT Ans$
      Ans$ = UCASE$(LEFT$(Ans$, 1))
      SELECT CASE Ans$
      CASE "Y"
         Flag = TRUE
      CASE "N"
         Flag = FALSE
      CASE ELSE
         PRINT "Please answer Y or N"
      END SELECT
   LOOP UNTIL Ans$ = "Y" OR Ans$ = "N"
END SUB   ' CheckAnswer
```

```
SUB OpenAppFile (Prompt$, N)
   ' Open an existing file for appending.
   ' If file does not exist, ask user
   ' to enter name again.
   SHARED NameOK
   ON ERROR GOTO ErrorHandler1
   DO
      NameOK = TRUE
      PRINT Prompt$;
      INPUT FileName$
      OPEN FileName$ FOR APPEND AS #N
   LOOP UNTIL NameOK = TRUE
END SUB   ' OpenAppFile

SUB OpenInFile (Prompt$, N)
   ' Open an existing file for reading.
   ' If file does not exist, ask user
   ' to enter name again.
   SHARED NameOK
   ON ERROR GOTO ErrorHandler1
   DO
      NameOK - TRUE
      PRINT Prompt$;
      INPUT FileName$
      OPEN FileName$ FOR INPUT AS #N
   LOOP UNTIL NameOK = TRUE
END SUB   ' OpenInFile

SUB OpenOutFile (Prompt$, N)
   ' Open a file for writing.
   ' If file already exists, ask user
   ' if it is OK to overwrite it.
   SHARED OverWrite
   ON ERROR GOTO ErrorHandler2
   DO
      NameOK = FALSE
      OverWrite = FALSE
      PRINT Prompt$;
      INPUT FileName$
      ' Open for input to see if file exists
      OPEN FileName$ FOR INPUT AS #N
      ' ErrorHandler2 is called if file does not exist
      ' and returns flag OverWrite as TRUE
      CLOSE #N
```

```
            IF OverWrite = TRUE THEN
               OPEN FileName$ FOR OUTPUT AS #N
               NameOK = TRUE
            ELSE
               CheckAnswer "Overwrite this file", OverWrite
               IF OverWrite = TRUE THEN
                  OPEN FileName$ FOR OUTPUT AS #N
                  NameOK = TRUE
               END IF
            END IF
         LOOP UNTIL NameOK = TRUE
      END SUB   ' OpenOutFile
```

Subroutine OpenInFile uses a module-level routine named ErrorHandler1. It contains a flag variable NameOK that is declared as a shared variable. Variable NameOK is originally set to true in the subroutine and is changed to false by the error-handling routine if the requested file does not exist. The loop that requests a file name repeats until the name of an existing file is entered. At that point, the file is opened for input.

Subroutine OpenOutFile checks first to see if the file already exists by attempting to open it for input. This procedure uses ErrorHandler2 and flag OverWrite, which is also a shared variable. If an error is created when the file is first opened for input (meaning that it does not exist), flag OverWrite is set to true. In this case, a new file is opened for output.

If the file does exist, it is closed and the user is asked if it should be overwritten. If the answer is yes, the file is opened for output and overwritten. If the answer is no, the user is asked for another file name.

Subroutine CheckAnswer is a simple procedure used by the other procedures and the main program to check answers for "Y" or "N". Subroutine OpenAppFile opens an existing file so that text can be appended, but it is not used in this program.

Other Procedures

Our next task is to write the procedure for calculating and displaying the average grade of a single student and writing this information on the output file. The procedure must have as parameters the input file and output file numbers, the number of grades per student, and the value of the flag to drop the lowest grade. The individual average grade must also be a parameter because this information is passed back to the main program and used to calculate the class average.

```
      SUB ReadGrades (N1, N2, NumGrades, Drop, AvgGrade)
         ' Student grades are read from file #N1. The average
         ' grade is calculated for a student, displayed on
         ' the screen, and written with the student's name on
         ' file #N2. Lowest grade is dropped if Drop is TRUE.
```

```
      Sum = 0
      MinGrade = 100
      LINE INPUT #N1, StudentName$
      FOR I = 1 TO NumGrades
          INPUT #N1, Grade
          IF Grade < MinGrade THEN MinGrade = Grade
          Sum = Sum + Grade
      NEXT I
      IF Drop = TRUE THEN
          Sum = Sum - MinGrade
          AvgGrade = Sum / (NumGrades - 1)
      ELSE
          AvgGrade = Sum / NumGrades
      END IF
      PRINT StudentName$; TAB(40);
      PRINT USING "###"; AvgGrade
      PRINT #N2, StudentName$
      PRINT #N2, AvgGrade
   END SUB   ' ReadGrades
```

The subroutine is straightforward in its design and implementation. It reads the specified number of grades from the grade file, calculates the average grade, and writes both the student name and the average grade on the screen and on the output file.

The Example Program

The main program requests information from the user, opens the required files, calls procedure ReadGrades for each student's average grade, and calculates and displays the class average. Here is the source code.

```
   ' Example Program 8-4
   ' Calculate and display average student grades
   ' and average class grade from a file of class grades.

   CONST FALSE = 0, TRUE = NOT FALSE

   ' Get information from the user.
   CALL OpenInFile ("Name of class grade file", 1)
   CALL OpenOutFile ("Name of class average file", 2)
   INPUT "Number of grades per student? ", NumGrades
   CALL CheckAnswer ("Drop the lowest grade", Drop)

   ' Call subroutine ReadGrades in a loop to read and
   ' display student names and grades.
```

```
Count = 0
TotalAverages = 0
PRINT
PRINT "STUDENT NAME"; TAB(40); "GRADE"
PRINT
DO UNTIL EOF(1)
   CALL ReadGrades (1, 2, (NumGrades), (Drop), AvgGrade)
   Count = Count + 1
   TotalAverages = TotalAverages + AvgGrade
LOOP
CLOSE #1, #2

' Calculate and display the class average,
PRINT
PRINT "Class average:"; TAB(40);
PRINT USING "##.#"; TotalAverages / Count
END   ' Main Program


ErrorHandler1:
   ' Set NameOK to false if file does not exist.
   IF ERR = 53 THEN
      PRINT "File does not exist - try again"
      NameOK = FALSE
      RESUME NEXT
   ELSE  ' unexpected error, halt the program
      ON ERROR GOTO 0
   END IF


ErrorHandler2:
   ' Set OverWrite to true if file does not exist.
   IF ERR = 53 THEN  ' no existing file
      OverWrite = TRUE
      RESUME NEXT
   ELSE  ' unexpected error, halt the program
      ON ERROR GOTO 0
   END IF


SUB CheckAnswer (Prompt$, Flag)
   ' Display prompt, get answer, and set flag
   ' to TRUE or FALSE if answer is YES or NO.
   ' Otherwise, prompt for answer again.
   ' Main program defines constants TRUE and FALSE.
```

```
      DO
         PRINT Prompt$;
         INPUT Ans$
         Ans$ = UCASE$(LEFT$(Ans$, 1))
         SELECT CASE Ans$
         CASE "Y"
            Flag = TRUE
         CASE "N"
            Flag = FALSE
         CASE ELSE
            PRINT "Please answer Y or N"
         END SELECT
      LOOP UNTIL Ans$ = "Y" OR Ans$ = "N"
   END SUB    ' CheckAnswer

   SUB OpenInFile (Prompt$, N)
      ' Open an existing file for reading.
      ' If file does not exist, ask user
      ' to enter name again.
      SHARED NameOK
      ON ERROR GOTO ErrorHandler1
      DO
         NameOK = TRUE
         PRINT Prompt$;
         INPUT FileName$
         OPEN FileName$ FOR INPUT AS #N
      LOOP UNTIL NameOK = TRUE
   END SUB    ' OpenInFile

   SUB OpenOutFile (Prompt$, N)
      ' Open a file for writing.
      ' If file already exists, ask user
      ' if it is OK to overwrite it.
      SHARED OverWrite
      ON ERROR GOTO ErrorHandler2
      DO
         NameOK = FALSE
         OverWrite = FALSE
         PRINT Prompt$;
         INPUT FileName$
         ' Open for input to see if file exists
         OPEN FileName$ FOR INPUT AS #N
         ' ErrorHandler2 is called if file does not exist
         ' and returns flag OverWrite as TRUE
         CLOSE #N
```

```
      IF OverWrite = TRUE THEN
         OPEN FileName$ FOR OUTPUT AS #N
         NameOK = TRUE
      ELSE
         CheckAnswer "Overwrite this file", OverWrite
         IF OverWrite = TRUE THEN
            OPEN FileName$ FOR OUTPUT AS #N
            NameOK = TRUE
         END IF
      END IF
   LOOP UNTIL NameOK = TRUE
END SUB   ' OpenOutFile


SUB ReadGrades (N1, N2, NumGrades, Drop, AvgGrade)
   ' Student grades are read from file #N1. The average
   ' grade is calculated for a student, displayed on
   ' the screen with the student's name, and written on
   ' file #N2. Lowest grade is dropped if Drop is TRUE.
   Sum = 0
   MinGrade = 100
   LINE INPUT #N1, StudentName$
   FOR I = 1 TO NumGrades
      INPUT #N1, Grade
      IF Grade < MinGrade THEN MinGrade = Grade
      Sum = Sum + Grade
   NEXT I
   IF Drop = TRUE THEN
      Sum = Sum - MinGrade
      AvgGrade = Sum / (NumGrades - 1)
   ELSE
      AvgGrade = Sum / NumGrades
   END IF
   PRINT StudentName$; TAB(42);
   PRINT USING "###"; AvgGrade
   PRINT #N2, StudentName$
   PRINT #N2, AvgGrade
END SUB   ' ReadGrades
```

Note that the call to subroutine ReadGrades uses value parameters for variables
NumGrades and Drop by enclosing them in parentheses and making them appear as (and
thus behave like) expressions. The use of a value parameter reduces the possibility of
inadvertent errors when there is no need to return information through that parameter.
The output file contains the name and average grade of each student in the class with each
item of information on a separate line. Here is a sample of program output.

```
Name of class grade file? GRADES.DAT
Name of class average file? AVERAGE.DAT
Number of grades per student 5
Drop the lowest grade? y

STUDENT NAME                                      GRADE

Susan Litchfield                                   85
Jim Bishop                                         92
Florence Green                                     78

Class average:                                    84.8
```

If you save your program and then load it at a later time, you will notice that the QuickBASIC system has placed a list of DECLARE statements at the beginning of the program. These statements are required for functions but not for subroutines that are called with CALL statements. Unfortunately, QuickBASIC writes a declaration statement for every procedure whether needed or not. Even if you delete the unnecessary statements, they are added once more if the program is saved again. There appears to be no way to turn off this action.

Program Testing

After a program has been designed and written, and any errors removed so that it compiles successfully, it must be tested. The first test is to see if it produces reasonable results, in the expected format. Further tests are run to determine (1) if the results are accurate, (2) if the program runs without error for a wide range of input data, and (3) if the output format agrees exactly with the design specifications. **Program testing is an important and necessary part of program development.**

In our example program, we first ask for several user inputs. Subroutines OpenIn-File and OpenOutFile already incorporate error-handling routines that avoid most illegal file names. Subroutine CheckAnswer forces a user to answer yes or no. The request for number of grades per student, however, is not checked in any way.

This last item, number of grades per student, is especially sensitive because a wrong number creates problems in reading the input file and the program aborts. There is no way to determine if an entered number is correct other than actually counting the number of grades in the file. If the number of grades has been counted, however, there is no need to ask a user to enter the number.

We decide at this point to improve the design of our program and eliminate the question by counting the grades of the first student in the file. We write a subroutine CheckGradeFile that reads as follows:

```
SUB CheckGradeFile (N1, NumGrades)
    ' Read the first record from file #N1 and count
    ' the number of grades. Reset the file to its
    ' beginning after reading.
    LINE INPUT #N1, Entry$    ' read the first name
    NumGrades = 0
    Finished = FALSE
    DO
        LINE INPUT #N1, Entry$  ' read next entry
        Value = ASC(LEFT$(Entry$, 1))
        IF Value >= 48 AND Value <= 57 THEN
            NumGrades = NumGrades + 1
        ELSE
            Finished = TRUE
        END IF
    LOOP UNTIL Finished = TRUE OR EOF(1)
    SEEK #N1, 1
END SUB   ' CheckGradeFile
```

The first line of the file is read and discarded because it is a student name. Each succeeding line of the file is then read in a loop. If the ASCII value of the first character indicates the line contains a number, the counter NumGrades is incremented and the loop continues as another line is read. If the first character is not a digit, the loop terminates. Note the use of an EOF function to terminate the loop if there is only one student in the file. A SEEK statement moves the imaginary file pointer back to the beginning of the first line in the file, allowing the file to be read again.

There is one additional test we should make. Subroutine OpenInFile checks to see if the specified file already exists and if it does not, asks the user to enter the file name again. No check is made, however, to see if the input file exists but is empty. Here is a new version of this procedure that checks for an empty file.

```
SUB OpenInFile (Prompt$, N)
    ' Open an existing file for reading.
    ' If file does not exist or is empty,
    ' ask user to enter name again.
    SHARED NameOK
    ON ERROR GOTO ErrorHandler1
    DO
    ' Check if the file exists.
        DO
            NameOK = TRUE
            PRINT Prompt$;
            INPUT FileName$
            OPEN FileName$ FOR INPUT AS #N
        LOOP UNTIL NameOK = TRUE
```

```
            ' Check if the file contains data.
            IF EOF(N) THEN
               PRINT "This file is empty,";
               PRINT " please try again."
               CLOSE #N
               NameOK = FALSE
            END IF
      LOOP UNTIL NameOK = TRUE
   END SUB  ' OpenInFile
```

We have added another file name check and placed both it and the original check within an outer DO loop. The new check uses the EOF function to determine if the file is empty. Here is our revised program containing both the new and the modified procedures.

```
' Example Program 8-5
' Calculate and display average student grades
' and average class grade from a file of class grades.

CONST FALSE = 0, TRUE = NOT FALSE
' Get information from the user.
CALL OpenInFile ("Name of class grade file", 1)
CALL OpenOutFile ("Name of class average file", 2)
CALL CheckAnswer ("Drop the lowest grade", Drop)
' Determine the number of grades per student.
CALL CheckGradeFile (1, NumGrades)

' Call subroutine ReadGrades in a loop to read and
' display student names and grades.
Count = 0
TotalAverages = 0
PRINT
PRINT "STUDENT NAME"; TAB(40); "GRADE"
PRINT
DO UNTIL EOF(1)
   CALL ReadGrades (1, 2, (NumGrades), (Drop), AvgGrade)
   Count = Count + 1
   TotalAverages = TotalAverages + AvgGrade
LOOP
CLOSE #1, #2

' Calculate and display the class average,
PRINT
PRINT "Class average:"; TAB(40);
PRINT USING "##.#"; TotalAverages / Count
END  ' Main Program
```

```
ErrorHandler1:
    ' Set NameOK to false if file does not exist.
    IF ERR = 53 THEN
        PRINT "File does not exist - try again"
        NameOK = FALSE
        RESUME NEXT
    ELSE    ' unexpected error, halt the program
        ON ERROR GOTO 0
    END IF

ErrorHandler2:
    ' Set OverWrite to true if file does not exist.
    IF ERR = 53 THEN   ' no existing file
        OverWrite = TRUE
        RESUME NEXT
    ELSE    ' unexpected error, halt the program
        ON ERROR GOTO 0
    END IF

SUB CheckAnswer (Prompt$, Flag)
    ' Display prompt, get answer, and set flag
    ' to TRUE or FALSE if answer is YES or NO.
    ' Otherwise, prompt for answer again.
    ' Module defines constants TRUE and FALSE.
    DO
        PRINT Prompt$;
        INPUT Ans$
        Ans$ = UCASE$(LEFT$(Ans$, 1))
        SELECT CASE Ans$
        CASE "Y"
            Flag = TRUE
        CASE "N"
            Flag = FALSE
        CASE ELSE
            PRINT "Please answer Y or N"
        END SELECT
    LOOP UNTIL Ans$ = "Y" OR Ans$ = "N"
END SUB   ' CheckAnswer

SUB OpenInFile (Prompt$, N)
    ' Open an existing file for reading.
    ' If file does not exist or is empty,
    ' ask user to enter name again.
    SHARED NameOK
    ON ERROR GOTO ErrorHandler1
```

```
    DO
    ' Check if the file exists.
        DO
            NameOK = TRUE
            PRINT Prompt$;
            INPUT FileName$
            OPEN FileName$ FOR INPUT AS #N
        LOOP UNTIL NameOK = TRUE
        ' Check if the file contains data.
        IF EOF(N) THEN
            PRINT "This file is empty,";
            PRINT " please try again."
            CLOSE #N
            NameOK = FALSE
        END IF
    LOOP UNTIL NameOK = TRUE
END SUB  ' OpenInFile

SUB OpenOutFile (Prompt$, N)
    ' Open a file for writing. If file already exists,
    ' ask user if it is OK to overwrite it.
    SHARED OverWrite
    ON ERROR GOTO ErrorHandler2
    DO
        NameOK = FALSE
        OverWrite = FALSE
        PRINT Prompt$;
        INPUT FileName$
        ' Open for input to see if file exists
        OPEN FileName$ FOR INPUT AS #N
        ' ErrorHandler2 is called if file does not exist
        ' and returns flag OverWrite as TRUE
        CLOSE #N
        IF OverWrite = TRUE THEN
            OPEN FileName$ FOR OUTPUT AS #N
            NameOK = TRUE
        ELSE
            CheckAnswer "Overwrite this file", OverWrite
            IF OverWrite = TRUE THEN
                OPEN FileName$ FOR OUTPUT AS #N
                NameOK = TRUE
            END IF
        END IF
    LOOP UNTIL NameOK = TRUE
END SUB  ' OpenOutFile
```

```
SUB CheckGradeFile (N1, NumGrades)
   ' Read the first record from file #N1 and count
   ' the number of grades. Reset the file to its
   ' beginning after reading.
   LINE INPUT #N1, Entry$  ' read the first name
   NumGrades = 0
   Finished = FALSE
   DO
      LINE INPUT #N1, Entry$  ' read next entry
      Value = ASC(LEFT$(Entry$, 1))
      IF Value >= 48 AND Value <= 57 THEN
         NumGrades = NumGrades + 1
      ELSE
         Finished = TRUE
      END IF
   LOOP UNTIL Finished = TRUE OR EOF(1)
   SEEK #N1, 1
END SUB  ' CheckGradeFile


SUB ReadGrades (N1, N2, NumGrades, Drop, AvgGrade)
   ' Student grades are read from file #N1. The average
   ' grade is calculated for a student, displayed on
   ' the screen, and written with the student's name on
   ' file #N2. Lowest grade is dropped if Drop is TRUE.
   Sum = 0
   MinGrade = 100
   LINE INPUT #N1, StudentName$
   FOR I = 1 TO NumGrades
      INPUT #N1, Grade
      IF Grade < MinGrade THEN MinGrade = Grade
      Sum = Sum + Grade
   NEXT I
   IF Drop = TRUE THEN
      Sum = Sum - MinGrade
      AvgGrade = Sum / (NumGrades - 1)
   ELSE
      AvgGrade = Sum / NumGrades
   END IF
   PRINT StudentName$; TAB(42);
   PRINT USING "###"; AvgGrade
   PRINT #N2, StudentName$
   PRINT #N2, AvgGrade
END SUB  ' ReadGrades
```

This program produces almost the same output as Example Program 8-4 but does not ask the user to enter the number of grades per student.

```
Name of class grade file? GRADES.DAT
Name of class average file? AVERAGE.DAT
Overwrite this file? y
Drop the lowest grade? n

STUDENT NAME                                   GRADE

Susan Litchfield                                 83
Jim Bishop                                       90
Florence Green                                   76

Class average:                                 83.0
```

As you can see, thoroughly testing a program is a long and complicated process. There are probably additional improvements that can be made. We believe, however, that Example Program 8-5 is a reasonably robust and well-tested program that will do the job it is designed to do.

8.8 LIBRARY MODULE FOR QUICKBASIC 4.5

Users of the QuickBASIC 4.5 compiler have the capability to write library modules. The error-handling routines and procedures for opening files can be placed in a separate library module and this module made part of any program. As discussed in the preceding chapter, a make file tells the system which files are included in the program. Here is a library module named FILELIB.BAS that opens files.

```
' Module FILELIB.BAS
' Library module of procedures for opening
' sequential text files. Common errors in the
' OPEN statement are trapped and the user is
' given a chance to enter the file name again.

CONST FALSE = 0, TRUE = NOT FALSE

ErrorHandler1:
   ' Set NameOK to false if file does not exist.
   IF ERR = 53 THEN
      PRINT "File does not exist - try again"
      NameOK = FALSE
      RESUME NEXT
```

```
    ELSE  ' unexpected error, halt the program
       ON ERROR GOTO 0
    END IF

ErrorHandler2:
    ' Set OverWrite to true if file does not exist.
    IF ERR = 53 THEN  ' no existing file
       OverWrite = TRUE
       RESUME NEXT
    ELSE  ' unexpected error, halt the program
       ON ERROR GOTO 0
    END IF

SUB CheckAnswer (Prompt$, Flag)
    ' Display prompt, get answer, and set flag
    ' to TRUE or FALSE if answer is YES or NO.
    ' Otherwise, prompt for answer again.
    ' Module defines constants TRUE and FALSE.
    DO
       PRINT Prompt$;
       INPUT Ans$
       Ans$ = UCASE$(LEFT$(Ans$, 1))
       SELECT CASE Ans$
       CASE "Y"
          Flag = TRUE
       CASE "N"
          Flag = FALSE
       CASE ELSE
          PRINT "Please answer Y or N"
       END SELECT
    LOOP UNTIL Ans$ = "Y" OR Ans$ = "N"
END SUB  ' CheckAnswer

SUB OpenAppFile (Prompt$, N)
    ' Open an existing file for appending.
    ' If file does not exist, ask user
    ' to enter name again.
    SHARED NameOK
    ON ERROR GOTO ErrorHandler1
    DO
       NameOK = TRUE
       PRINT Prompt$;
       INPUT FileName$
       OPEN FileName$ FOR APPEND AS #N
    LOOP UNTIL NameOK = TRUE
```

```
END SUB   ' OpenAppFile

SUB OpenInFile (Prompt$, N)
   ' Open an existing file for reading.
   ' If file does not exist or is empty,
   ' ask user to enter name again.
   SHARED NameOK
   ON ERROR GOTO ErrorHandler1
   DO
   ' Check if the file exists.
      DO
         NameOK = TRUE
         PRINT Prompt$;
         INPUT FileName$
         OPEN FileName$ FOR INPUT AS #N
      LOOP UNTIL NameOK = TRUE
      ' Check if the file contains data.
      IF EOF(N) THEN
         PRINT "This file is empty,";
         PRINT " please try again."
         CLOSE #N
         NameOK = FALSE
      END IF
   LOOP UNTIL NameOK = TRUE
END SUB   ' OpenInFile


SUB OpenOutFile (Prompt$, N)
   ' Open a file for writing.
   ' If file already exists, ask user
   ' if it is OK to overwrite it.
   SHARED OverWrite
   ON ERROR GOTO ErrorHandler2
   DO
      NameOK = FALSE
      OverWrite = FALSE
      PRINT Prompt$;
      INPUT FileName$
      ' Open for input to see if file exists
      OPEN FileName$ FOR INPUT AS #N
      ' ErrorHandler2 is called if file does not exist
      ' and returns flag OverWrite as TRUE
      CLOSE #N
      IF OverWrite = TRUE THEN
         OPEN FileName$ FOR OUTPUT AS #N
         NameOK = TRUE
```

```
        ELSE
            CheckAnswer "Overwrite this file", OverWrite
            IF OverWrite = TRUE THEN
                OPEN FileName$ FOR OUTPUT AS #N
                NameOK = TRUE
            END IF
        END IF
    LOOP UNTIL NameOK = TRUE
END SUB   ' OpenOutFile
```

Remember that the Load File command from the full menu must be used to load two or more modules into a single program. In this case, file EX08-06.BAS must be loaded first, followed by file FILELIB.BAS. This program produces the same output as Example Program 8-5.

```
' Example Program 8-6
' Calculate and display average student grades
' and average class grade from a file of class grades.

CONST FALSE = 0, TRUE = NOT FALSE
' Get information from the user.
CALL OpenInFile ("Name of class grade file", 1)
CALL OpenOutFile ("Name of class average file", 2)
CALL CheckAnswer ("Drop the lowest grade", Drop)
' Determine the number of grades per student.
CALL CheckGradeFile (1, NumGrades)
' Call subroutine ReadGrades in a loop to read and
' display student names and grades.
Count = 0
TotalAverages = 0
PRINT
PRINT "STUDENT NAME"; TAB(40); "GRADE"
PRINT
DO UNTIL EOF(1)
    CALL ReadGrades (1, 2, (NumGrades), (Drop), AvgGrade)
    Count = Count + 1
    TotalAverages = TotalAverages + AvgGrade
LOOP
CLOSE #1, #2

' Calculate and display the class average,
PRINT
PRINT "Class average:"; TAB(40);
PRINT USING "##.#"; TotalAverages / Count
END   ' Main Program
```

```
SUB CheckGradeFile (N1, NumGrades)
   ' Read the first record from file #N1 and count
   ' the number of grades. Reset the file to its
   ' beginning after reading.
   LINE INPUT #N1, Entry$  ' read the first name
   NumGrades = 0
   Finished = FALSE
   DO
      LINE INPUT #N1, Entry$  ' read next entry
      Value = ASC(LEFT$(Entry$, 1))
      IF Value >= 48 AND Value <= 57 THEN
         NumGrades = NumGrades + 1
      ELSE
         Finished = TRUE
      END IF
   LOOP UNTIL Finished = TRUE OR EOF(1)
   SEEK #N1, 1
END SUB  ' CheckGradeFile

SUB ReadGrades (N1, N2, NumGrades, Drop, AvgGrade)
   ' Student grades are read from file #N1. The average
   ' grade is calculated for a student, displayed on
   ' the screen, and written with the student's name on
   ' file #N2. Lowest grade is dropped it Drop is TRUE.
   Sum = 0
   MinGrade = 100
   LINE INPUT #N1, StudentName$
   FOR I = 1 TO NumGrades
      INPUT #N1, Grade
      IF Grade < MinGrade THEN MinGrade = Grade
      Sum = Sum + Grade
   NEXT I
   IF Drop = TRUE THEN
      Sum = Sum - MinGrade
      AvgGrade = Sum / (NumGrades - 1)
   ELSE
      AvgGrade = Sum / NumGrades
   END IF
   PRINT StudentName$; TAB(42);
   PRINT USING "###"; AvgGrade
   PRINT #N2, StudentName$
   PRTNT #N2, AvgGrade
END SUB  ' ReadGrades
```

Library modules provide a convenient way to store procedures in QuickBASIC 4.5.

Summary of Important Points

- Use lots of temporary PRINT statements to help locate program errors.
- Avoid using an equality between two numeric values as a condition in a logical expression; use an inequality instead.
- An error-handling block must be located so that it is not executed during normal running of the program.
- You must understand the problem before writing a program to solve the problem.
- Always write down a program outline before starting to write program statements.
- If your program is longer than a page of code, write it as a series of short procedures.
- Do not use tricky or complicated logic in order to make a program shorter or more efficient.
- Program testing is an important and necessary part of program development. Test your program for as many conditions as possible that might cause an error.

Common Errors

- Starting to write program statements before writing a program outline.
- Assuming that you know the value of a variable when you can easily check the value with a PRINT statement.
- Failing to put labels on temporary PRINT statements and then not knowing which value belongs to which variable.
- Changing a statement or adding a new statement when the program is paused at a breakpoint.
- Using noninteger numeric values in an equality expression that controls a loop or decision branch.
- Placing error-handling routines inside a procedure or before the main program END statement.
- Attempting to use a library module with the QuickBASIC Interpreter.
- Using the RESUME statement when you should use the RESUME NEXT statement.
- Writing your program outline or flowchart after you have finished writing the program, when it can provide no help in writing the code.
- Forgetting to define the constants TRUE and FALSE in a program whose procedures use these values.
- Starting to design and write a program so late that there is not enough time to test it thoroughly before it is due.
- Writing a long main program without procedures.
- Assuming that the user of a program will always enter proper and accurate data and thus failing to check for data entry errors.
- Allowing a program to crash when incorrect data is entered by the user rather than trapping the error and giving the user another chance.

Self-Test Questions

1. What is meant by the term *debugging?*
2. What is the method of playing computer?
3. What statement can you insert into a program to display the value of a variable?
4. Which key is used in QuickBASIC to
   (a) step through an entire program line by line;
   (b) step through the main program but skip over all procedures?
5. If the cursor is on a line that you wish to use as a breakpoint, which key should you press to turn on the breakpoint?
6. Immediately after a program has been loaded, what is the difference between pressing F5 and Shift-F5?
7. (a) What problem may occur when you use an expression like $X = 5$ in a program to test whether a process (such as a loop) should be stopped?
   (b) How can you avoid the problem?
8. What is the difference between a syntax error and a logic error?
9. What statement is used in QuickBASIC for error trapping?
10. Can error-trapping code be located
    (a) in the main program before the END statement;
    (b) in the main program after the END statement;
    (c) in a procedure?
11. What is your estimate of the percentage of total program development time you use in actually writing the source code?
12. If you are designing a procedure that asks a user for a file name and then opens that file for reading data from the disk, what specific checks should your procedure make on the entered file name?
13. What tests, other than those on user input, might you make in the process of thoroughly testing a new program?
14. (a) What is an algorithm?
    (b) How important is it, in your opinion, that an algorithm be efficient?
15. Why is a written program outline preferable to a mental outline?
16. Why is it important to write programs that are clear and easy to understand?

Practice Programs

1. You are asked to calculate the roots of the standard quadratic equation, written as

$$Ax^2 + Bx + C = 0$$

Recall that the roots are given by the two following expressions.

$$x_1 = \frac{-B + \sqrt{B^2 - 4AC}}{2A}, \quad x_2 = \frac{-B - \sqrt{B^2 - 4AC}}{2A}$$

You write the following program to solve this problem.

```
' Program with a logical error.
INPUT "Value of A"; A
INPUT "Value of B"; B
INPUT "Value of C"; C
X1 = (-B + SQR(B*B - 4*A*C)) / (2*A)
X2 = (-B - SQR(B*B - 4*A*C)) / (2*A)
PRINT "The roots are"; X1; "and"; X2
END
```

A user enters a value of 3 for A, 2 for B, and 2 for C. The program responds with a run-time error. What is wrong? Write a corrected program that will handle this set of values.

2. Practice Programs 2 and 3 in Chapter 6 ask a user to enter a date in mm-dd-yy format. The month and the day may be specified by single digits; that is, by 1-5-85 rather than by 01-05-85. Write a program that requests such a date and then checks the validity of the entry. If a user enters an invalid date, the program should loop back and allow the date to be entered again. Assume 29 days in February. Test your program using the following values.

> 13-20-85
> 2-30-81
> 11-31-88
> 1-17-77

3. If you have not already done so, write Practice Program 1 as a procedure with error handling. Use the same numeric entries to test your program.

4. A user is asked to enter two numbers assigned to variables A and B and the quotient A/B is displayed. Use error trapping to trap the error if division by zero is attempted. If an error occurs, display the text of an appropriate error message. Test your program using the following number pairs.

> 13.5, 7.7
> 0, 33.2
> 125, 0
> 25, 5

5. Write a program similar to Example Program 6-6 that uses error trapping and the VAL function to warn a user if an entry is not a valid number. Test your program using the following values.

> 125.99
> 11,234.50
> 13.2E-3
> 13.2E+-3
> +e+e+e
> -55

6. Modify subroutine OpenInFile in the FILES.BAS module so that it can handle illegal file names without causing the program to abort. A short explanatory message should be displayed and the user given a chance to enter another file name. Test your subroutine in a stub program with the file names ABC, 1+2, and $$$.

9

ARRAYS, RECORDS, AND FILES

9.1 INTRODUCTION

We introduce multidimensional arrays with two or more dimensions. We use these arrays in programs to create tables and to read information from tables.

We then discuss a new file structure consisting of records containing individual fields. We use this structure first in sequential text files and show how information can be stored in these files. We next introduce random-access files and the user-defined record type. Example programs show how to store information in files and later retrieve this information.

9.2 MULTIDIMENSIONAL ARRAYS

The arrays we discussed in previous chapters have a single index and are called one-dimensional arrays. An example is the familiar list. We can also have arrays with two or more indices, called *multidimensional arrays*. An example of a multidimensional array is a two-dimensional array or table that has several rows and several columns. The location of an element in the table is specified by two indices, one index specifying the row number and the other specifying the column number. We will restrict our discussion of multidimensional arrays to two-dimensional arrays, although QuickBASIC supports arrays with arrays with more than two dimensions. **Note that a one-dimensional array and a two-dimensional array in the same program cannot have the same name.**

Two-Dimensional Array Notation

An example two-dimensional array containing string values is named Salesman$. Fig. 9.1 shows how the array might look with labels and numbers added to identify rows and columns.

Column	1	2	3
Row			
1	John Adams	Chicago	312-202-5674
2	Bill Cullins	New York	212-405-1298
3	Gary Despio	Atlanta	404-813-8824
4	Bill Morris	Miami	305-222-5141
5	Jack Williams	Boston	617-267-0351

Figure 9.1 Table of salesmen.

If you visualize the array as a table, the horizontal lines of element values are called rows and the vertical lines are called columns. The normal convention is to use the first index to refer to the row number and the second index to refer to the column number. For example, the element in the third row and first column is designated as Salesman$(3,1) and has a value of "Gary Despio".

Tables are often organized in a manner similar to our example array, with each column referring to a different kind of information and each row referring to a different person or item. For example in row three, the element Salesman$(3,1) in column one refers to a salesman's name, Salesman$(3,2) in column two refers to a salesman's city, and Salesman$(3,3) in column three refers to a salesman's telephone number.

Dimensioning Two-Dimensional Arrays

Arrays with two dimensions are declared with the DIM statement, in a manner similar to one-dimensional arrays. As an example, the statement

```
DIM Salesman$(1 TO 100, 1 TO 3)
```

declares an array with 100 rows and 3 columns. This array can hold 300 string values. There is now a size associated with each dimension. The index of the first dimension ranges from 1 to 100 and has a size of 100, while the index of the second dimension ranges from 1 to 3 and has a size of 3.

Remember that a string array is initialized just like any other string variable, with a null string assigned to each element. As with one-dimensional arrays, if you wish to assign another value to one or more elements, you must individually assign a new value to each modified element. If the array of Fig. 9.1 was dimensioned with the foregoing statement, note that information is assigned only to the elements in the first five rows. As discussed previously, this example array is only partially filled.

Reading and Writing Two-Dimensional Arrays

Here is an example program to read numbers from DATA statements, assign these numbers to elements of a two-dimensional array, and then display the array. We use a small array with three rows and five columns so that it will fit easily on the screen. We put five values in each DATA statement and read values into the array by row. This program demonstrates the use of FOR loops for reading two-dimensional arrays and for printing these arrays in a formatted display.

```
' Example Program 9-1
' Fill an array and display it on the screen.

DEFINT A-Z
DIM Table(1 TO 3, 1 TO 5)

' Fill the array from DATA statements.
FOR Row = 1 to 3
   FOR Column = 1 to 5
      READ Table(Row, Column)
   NEXT Column
NEXT Row

' Display the array on the screen.
FOR Row = 1 to 3
   FOR Column = 1 to 5
      PRINT Table(Row, Column);
   NEXT Column
   PRINT   ' move to next row
NEXT Row

DATA 3, 5, 7, 3, 8
DATA 4, 1, 0, 3, 4
DATA 5, 2, 7, 5, 3
END
```

For each value of Row in the outer loop, the variable Column runs through its set of values from 1 to 5 in the inner loop. Each element in the row is assigned a value. This process is repeated for each row (or value of Row) from 1 to 3. We say that the program assigns values to the array elements by row.

Note also that the outer FOR loop must completely surround and contain the inner FOR loop. If the two NEXT statements are reversed, the loops overlap and the program will not work. **Nested FOR loops cannot overlap.** Indentation should always be used to show how the inner loop nests within the outer loop.

In the display module, the semicolon at the end of the first PRINT statement causes all values in a row to be displayed on the same line (this does not work if there are too many columns to fit on the screen). The second PRINT statement moves the cursor to the next line on the screen after a row of values has been displayed. This program produces the following display.

```
3   5   7   3   8
4   1   0   3   4
5   2   7   5   3
```

Two-Dimensional Arrays as Parameters

Two-dimensional arrays can be passed as parameters to subroutines and functions. As discussed previously, **an array used as a procedure heading parameter or a call statement argument must have a pair of dummy parentheses after the array name**.

The functions UBOUND and LBOUND can still be used, but they now require two parameters. The first parameter is the name of the array and the second parameter is the number of the dimension. For example, UBOUND(Table, 1) is the upper bound of the first dimension of the array Table, while UBOUND(Table, 2) is the upper bound of the second dimension.

Our next example passes the values of a two-dimensional array to a function that calculates the *trace* of an array. The trace is a mathematical value that can be calculated for any *square array* of numeric values where the number of rows equals the number of columns. It is equal to the sum of all elements whose row and column indices are the same. For example, in the array

$$
\begin{array}{ccc}
1 & 3 & 6 \\
2 & 7 & 8 \\
9 & 2 & 4
\end{array}
$$

the trace is $1 + 7 + 4$ and equals 12.

```
' Example Program 9-2
' Read an array and calculate its trace.

DEFINT A-Z
DIM A(1 TO 3, 1 TO 3)
DECLARE FUNCTION Trace (A())
```

```
PRINT "The array is"
FOR I = 1 TO UBOUND(A, 1)
   FOR J = 1 TO UBOUND(A, 2)
       READ A(I, J)
       PRINT A(I, J);
   NEXT J
   PRINT
NEXT I
PRINT "Its trace is"; Trace((A()))

DATA 1,3,6,2,7,8,9,2,4
END   ' Main Program

FUNCTION Trace (X())
   ' Calculate the trace of X.
   Sum = 0
   FOR I% = 1 TO UBOUND(X, 1)
      Sum = Sum + X(I%, I%)
   NEXT I%
   Trace = Sum
END FUNCTION   ' Trace
```

In the present case, the trace equals the sum of $X(1, 1)$, $X(2, 2)$ and $X(3, 3)$. As before, the array is dimensioned in the calling program. Note the upper limit of the FOR statement in the function Trace. **We can use either UBOUND(X, 1) or UBOUND(X, 2) because the two dimensions of X are the same size.** Here is the output produced by this program.

```
The array is
1   3   6
2   7   8
9   2   4
Its trace is 12
```

Example Program Using a Table

An example of a two-dimensional numeric array is the table, often found on road maps, showing distances between cities. We use the variable Distance to represent this table. If you want to find the distance between Boston and New York, you go down the left margin of the table until you find the row labeled Boston and then across that row until you find the column labeled New York. Where this row and column intersect, you find the distance in miles. If Boston is the label for row two and New York the label for column six, then the distance between these two cities is given by the value of the element Distance(2,6). Here is the outline of a program to create and use such a table.

Read a list of cities.

Read a mileage table of distances between cities.

Ask the user to enter the names of two cities.

Look up and display the distance between cities.

End the program.

We read the city names and the distances between cities from two text files. File CITIES.DAT contains a list of cities, one per line. File DISTANCE.DAT contains a sequence of numbers representing distances, again one per line. We write subroutines for reading the list of cities (a one-dimensional array) and the table of distances (a two-dimensional array). We use the same library procedures that we used in Chapter 8 to open these files. The list of cities we have chosen is shown in Fig. 9.2.

1	ATLANTA
2	BOSTON
3	CHICAGO
4	DETROIT
5	MIAMI
6	NEW YORK
7	WASHINGTON

Figure 9.2 List of cities.

Here is a straightforward subroutine to read the list of cities. The array Cities$ and the file number N are parameters.

```
SUB ReadList (Cities$(), N)
   ' Read the list of city names from file #N
   ' and assign them to the elements of Cities$.
   FOR I = 1 TO UBOUND(Cities$)
      INPUT #N, Cities$(I)
   NEXT I
END SUB
```

Another subroutine reads the DISTANCE.DAT file and assigns the values to a two-dimensional array named Distance. In our example, this information will be placed in an array with seven rows and seven columns. We need to look carefully at how information is assigned to this array or table of distances.

The table must have the same number of rows and columns because each row represents one of the cities in the list and each column represents one of the cities in the same list. We use the same order of city names for both rows and columns.

The table of distances is shown in Fig. 9.3.

	1	2	3	4	5	6	7
1	0	1065	675	715	665	850	605
2	1065	0	965	710	1515	215	445
3	675	965	0	270	1335	790	695
4	715	710	270	0	1370	620	520
5	665	1515	1335	1370	0	1300	1080
6	850	215	790	620	1300	0	230
7	605	445	695	520	1080	230	0

Figure 9.3   Table of distances between cities.

Note that the distance between two cities with the same name is zero; that is, Distance(1, 1) is zero, Distance(2, 2) is zero, and so forth. All these zero values lie along what we call the *principal diagonal,* the diagonal running from the upper left corner of the table to the lower right corner. In general, all elements with identical indices, of the form Distance(I, I), must equal zero.

Note further that the elements lying below the principal diagonal contain the same information as those lying above this diagonal. For example, element Distance(1, 2) represents the distance between cities 1 and 2 (in our case, ATLANTA and BOSTON). Distance(2, 1) represents the distance between cities 2 and 1. These distances must, of course, be the same and each is equal to 1065 miles. In general terms, any element Distance(I, J) must equal the corresponding element Distance (J, I).

We now discuss in some detail how the subroutine assigns values to the table of distances. We first set all elements along the principal diagonal equal to zero. We then read, from the file DISTANCE.DAT, the 21 elements lying above the principal diagonal and after we read each value, assign it also to the corresponding element lying below the principal diagonal. Here is the subroutine to read the table of distances.

```
SUB ReadTable (Distance(), N)
   ' Read the table of distances using
   ' data in file #N.
   FOR I = 1 TO UBOUND(Distance, 1)
      Distance(I, I) = 0
   NEXT I
```

```
    FOR I = 1 TO (UBOUND(Distance, 1) - 1)
        FOR J = (I + 1) TO UBOUND(Distance, 2)
            INPUT #N, Distance(I, J)
            Distance(J, I) = Distance(I, J)
        NEXT J
    NEXT I
END SUB
```

Note particularly the FOR loops used to read file information. We read values and assign them only to elements in rows one through six because these rows include all elements lying above the principal diagonal (row seven lies below the principal diagonal). Thus variable I ranges from 1 to 6, or in more general notation, from 1 to UBOUND(Distance, 1) - 1.

In row one we start reading at column two, in row two at column three, and so forth.; that is, we start reading values in row I at column (I + 1). Thus J (the column number) ranges from (I + 1) to 7 or in more general notation, from (I + 1) to UBOUND(Distance, 2). The result is that we read values only for elements lying above the principal diagonal.

One disadvantage of using an array to hold the distance values is that we waste over half the storage space in the array because we store so many duplicate distances. This might become a problem with very large tables, but we use comparatively little memory space in our example. A compensating advantage is that a two-dimensional array is probably the simplest data structure to use for the table of distances, and this method of storing information produces a simple and easy-to-understand program.

A function is used to calculate the numerical position of any city in the list of cities. We need this information to calculate the indices of the appropriate distance table element. The name of the city is passed to the function as parameter Name$, along with the array parameter Cities$ containing the list of cities. The position in the list of the specified city is assigned to the function Location.

```
FUNCTION Location (Name$, Cities$())
    ' Find the location of a city specified by Name$
    ' in the list of cities named Cities$.
    CityNum = 0
    Count = 1
    DO
        IF Name$ = Cities$(Count) THEN
            CityNum = Count
        END IF
        Count = Count + 1
    LOOP UNTIL CityNum > 0 OR Count > UBOUND(Cities$)
    Location = CityNum
END FUNCTION
```

Note that if a city name cannot be found, a value of zero is returned by the function.

Finally, the main program is written and all the procedures are added to it The name of the first city is First$ and its location in the city list is First. The second city is Second$ and its location is Second. The distance between these two cities is simply the array element Distance(First, Second).

```
' Example Program 9-3
' Calculate the distance between two cities.

DEFINT A-Z
CONST FALSE = 0, TRUE = NOT FALSE
DECLARE FUNCTION Location (Name$, Cities$())
DIM Cities$(1 TO 7), Distance(1 TO 7, 1 TO 7)

CALL OpenInFile ("Name of cities file", 1)
CALL OpenInFile ("Name of distance file", 2)
CALL ReadList (Cities$(), 1)
CALL ReadTable (Distance(), 2)

INPUT "Name of first city? ", First$
First$ = UCASE$(First$)
First = Location((First$), Cities$())
INPUT "Name of second city? ", Second$
Second$ = UCASE$(Second$)
Second = Location((Second$), Cities$())
PRINT

IF First = 0 OR Second = 0 THEN
   PRINT "One of the city names is not in the list."
ELSE
   PRINT "Distance between "; First$; " and ";
   PRINT Second$; " is"; Distance(First, Second);
   PRINT "miles."
END IF
END  ' Main Program

ErrorHandler1:
   ' Set NameOK to false if file does not exist.
   IF ERR = 53 THEN
      PRINT "File does not exist - try again"
      NameOK = FALSE
      RESUME NEXT
   ELSE  ' unexpected error, halt the program
      ON ERROR GOTO 0
   END IF
```

```
ErrorHandler2:
    ' Set OverWrite to true if file does not exist.
    IF ERR = 53 THEN  ' no existing file
       OverWrite = TRUE
       RESUME NEXT
    ELSE   ' unexpected error, halt the program
       ON ERROR GOTO 0
    END IF

SUB CheckAnswer (Prompt$, Flag)
    ' Display prompt, get answer, and set flag
    ' to TRUE or FALSE if answer is YES or NO.
    ' Otherwise, prompt for answer again.
    ' Module defines constants TRUE and FALSE.
    DO
       PRINT Prompt$;
       INPUT Ans$
       Ans$ = UCASE$(LEFT$(Ans$, 1))
       SELECT CASE Ans$
       CASE "Y"
          Flag = TRUE
       CASE "N"
          Flag = FALSE
       CASE ELSE
          PRINT "Please answer Y or N"
       END SELECT
    LOOP UNTIL Ans$ = "Y" OR Ans$ = "N"
END SUB   ' CheckAnswer

FUNCTION Location (Name$, Cities$())
    ' Find the location of a city specified by Name$
    ' in the list of cities named Cities$.
    CityNum = 0
    Count = 1
    DO
       IF Name$ = Cities$(Count) THEN
          CityNum = Count
       END IF
       Count = Count + 1
    LOOP UNTIL CityNum > 0 OR Count > UBOUND(Cities$)
    Location = CityNum
END FUNCTION   ' Location

SUB OpenInFile (Prompt$, N)
    ' Open an existing file for reading.
```

```
   ' If file does not exist or is empty,
   ' ask user to enter name again.

   SHARED NameOK
   ON ERROR GOTO ErrorHandler1
   DO
   ' Check if the file exists.
      DO
         NameOK = TRUE
         PRINT Prompt$;
         INPUT FileName$
         OPEN FileName$ FOR INPUT AS #N
      LOOP UNTIL NameOK = TRUE
      ' Check if the file contains data.
      IF EOF(N) THEN
         PRINT "This file is empty,";
         PRINT " please try again."
         CLOSE #N
         NameOK = FALSE
      END IF
   LOOP UNTIL NameOK = TRUE
END SUB   ' OpenInFile


SUB ReadList (Cities$(), N)
   ' Read the list of city names from file #N
   ' and assign them to the elements of Cities$.
   FOR I = 1 TO UBOUND(Cities$)
      INPUT #N, Cities$(I%)
   NEXT I
END SUB   ' ReadList


SUB ReadTable (Distance(), N)
   ' Read the table of distances using
   ' data in file #N.
   FOR I = 1 TO UBOUND(Distance, 1)
      Distance(I, I) = 0
   NEXT I

   FOR I = 1 TO (UBOUND(Distance, 1) - 1)
      FOR J = (I + 1) TO UBOUND(Distance, 2)
         INPUT #N, Distance(I, J)
         Distance(J, I) = Distance(I, J)
      NEXT J
   NEXT I
END SUB   ' ReadTable
```

A user is asked to enter the name of two cities. If both cities are in the city list, the distance between them is displayed. If not, an error message appears on the screen. Here is a sample of program output.

```
Name of cities file? cities.dat
Name of distance file? distance.dat
Name of first city? atlanta
Name of second city? boston

Distance between ATLANTA and BOSTON is 1065 miles.
```

Redimensioning Arrays

The DIM statement establishes the size of an array, often specifying only the upper bound of each dimension. If the array is too large, we discussed in Chapter 6 how only part of the array may be used (see Example Program 6-17). If the array is too small, we cannot write a new DIM statement with larger upper bounds. We can, however, redimension the array if it is a dynamic array.

The REDIM statement allows us to change the size of one or more dimensions of a dynamic array. Remember that either the lower or upper bound of the dimension being changed must be a variable or expression, not a constant. In fact, both the upper and lower bounds can be variables or expressions and the values of both bounds can be changed. The new lower and upper bound values may be larger or smaller than the original values. **Redimensioning cannot be used to change the number of dimensions.**

A major disadvantage of redimensioning is that all elements in the array are reinitialized: numbers to zero and strings to null strings. Thus any information stored in an array is lost when the array is redimensioned.

For example, assume that a dynamic array has been dimensioned with the following program fragment.

```
Upper1 = 5
Upper2 = 4
DIM Ratio(1 TO Upper1, 1 TO Upper2)
```

The additional statements

```
Upper1 = 10
Upper2 = 3
REDIM Ratio(1 TO Upper1, 1 TO Upper2)
```

change the size of Ratio and reinitalize its elements to zero. Note that the lower bound of each dimension remains at 1.

If you cannot determine what size you need for an array before it is dimensioned, it should be created as a dynamic array, as shown in the following program.

```
' Example Program 9-4
' Dimension and fill a square array.

DEFINT A-Z
INPUT "Size of the square array? ", N
PRINT
DIM Table(1 TO N, 1 TO N)
FOR I = 1 TO N
   FOR J = 1 TO N
      PRINT "Element("; LTRIM$(STR$(I));
      PRINT ","; STR$(J); ")";
      INPUT Table(I, J)
   NEXT J
NEXT I

PRINT
PRINT "Here is the array"
FOR I = 1 TO N
   FOR J = 1 TO N
      PRINT Table(I, J);
   NEXT J
   PRINT
NEXT I
END
```

The following results are produced.

```
Size of the square array? 3

Element(1, 1)? 1
Element(1, 2)? 2
Element(1, 3)? 3
Element(2, 1)? 4
Element(2, 2)? 5
Element(2, 3)? 6
Element(3, 1)? 7
Element(3, 2)? 8
Element(4, 3)? 9

Here is the array

 1   2   3
 4   5   6
 7   8   9
```

The program asks a user first to specify the size of a square array and then enter the element values. Note our use of the STR$ function to convert each index value to a string. We then use the LTRIM$ function to trim leading blanks from row values. The row and column indices are now properly formatted to be used in element labels for the INPUT statement.

Another example program allows a user to specify the maximum number of items that can be stored in an array and then redimensions the array. The array starts out with sufficient space for 100 items, but fewer than 100 items can be stored.

```
' Example Program 9-5
' Store names in an array.
' Enter a single period to stop.

DEFINT A-Z
N = 100
DIM Names$(1 TO N)
PRINT "The array has room for"; UBOUND(Names$); "names."
PRINT "If you want to change the size of the array,"
PRINT "specify the new number; otherwise, just press"
PRINT "the Enter key.  Size? ";
LINE INPUT Entry$
IF Entry$ <> "" THEN
   N = VAL(Entry$)
   REDIM Name$(1 TO N)
END IF

PRINT
PRINT "Enter up to"; N; "names, one name per line."
PRINT "Enter a single period to stop the process."
Count = 0
LINE INPUT "Name? ", Reply$
DO UNTIL Count >= N OR Reply$ = "."
   Count = Count + 1
   Names$(Count) = Reply$
   LINE INPUT "Name? ", Reply$
LOOP
PRINT
PRINT Count; "names have been entered."
PRINT "Here is the list:"
PRINT
FOR I = 1 to Count
   PRINT SPC(5); Names$(I)
NEXT I
END
```

In this program we use the technique of entering a numeric value (the array size) into a string variable named Entry$. This allows us to use the LINE INPUT statement and signal no change in array size by just pressing the Enter key. We convert Entry$ to a number before redimensioning the array.

Remember that redimensioning an array also reinitializes the array. For this reason we redimension the array before entering any information. Program output looks as follows.

```
The array has room for 100 names.
If you want to change the size of the array,
specify the new number; otherwise, just press
the Enter key.  Size? 5

Enter up to 5 names, one name per line.
Enter a single period to stop the process.
Name? Sally
Name? Mary
Name? Joan
Name? .

3 names have been entered.
Here is the list:

Sally
Mary
Joan
```

9.3 STORING INFORMATION IN SEQUENTIAL FILES

We introduced sequential text files in Chapter 5 and discussed the process of writing information on and reading information from such files. You may remember that we recommended writing only one item of information per line.

We now modify this recommendation and discuss a useful structure for organizing information stored in computer files. **In this structure, a file consists of a sequence of components or records, each record containing a sequence of fields.** The record may contain information on one person or on one item. Each field within the record contains information on selected attributes of the person or item, as shown in Fig. 9.4. A user must know the record structure or determine it by inspection before using a file.

The sequential file structure that we introduce has one record of information per line. This means that a single line may contain several field values. We shall separate field items from one another by commas and enclose string fields in quotation marks. This structure allows commas to be included in strings without being mistaken as field separators.

RECORD	FIELDS
Employee	Name Age Salary
Automobile	Stock number Type Color Date Price

Figure 9.4 Examples of records and fields.

The WRITE Statement

We use the statement

```
WRITE #N, Field1, Field2, Field3,...
```

to write a record of information on file #N. **The WRITE statement differs from the PRINT statement in that it separates all fields or items by commas and encloses all string values in quotation marks.**

For example, the statement

```
WRITE #1, Name$, Age, Salary
```

might write the following line of information on file #1.

```
"Joseph O'Grady, Jr.",37,28500
```

In contrast, the statement

```
PRINT #1, Name$, Age, Salary
```

writes a different line of information on file #1, as shown here.

```
Joseph O'Grady, Jr.        37              28500
```

The record produced by the WRITE statement can be read from the file by the familiar INPUT statement.

```
INPUT #1, Name$, Age, Salary
```

If we tried to use this INPUT statement to read the record produced by the PRINT statement, we would get an error. The comma in the name would be interpreted as a field separator, and the value read into variable Age would be of the wrong type.

Note that the individual fields in a sequential file record can be either numbers or strings, but they cannot be arrays. Each record is written or read field by field; it is not possible to write or read the entire record as a single variable.

A sequential file with this new structure behaves just like a normal text file. All items of information are stored as ASCII characters. A new file can be written or information can be appended to the end of an existing file. A file containing information can only be read sequentially from the beginning of the file. **The record structure of a sequential file can be determined by displaying a file record on the screen.**

An Example Program

We first show an example program that writes several records containing automobile information on a sequential file.

```
' Example Program 9-6
' Use a sequential file for storing data records.
' Type a zero for stock number to stop
' entering information.

' Write records on the data file AUTO1.DAT.
OPEN "AUTO1.DAT" FOR OUTPUT AS #1
Count = 0
DO
    PRINT "Record"; Count + 1
    INPUT "Stock number: ", Num
    IF Num = 0 THEN EXIT DO
    LINE INPUT "Type of car:  ", Type$
    LINE INPUT "Color of car: ", Color$
    INPUT "Year of car:  ", Year
    INPUT "Sales price:  ", Price
    WRITE #1, Num, Type$, Color$, Year, Price
    Count = Count + 1
    PRINT
LOOP
CLOSE #1
PRINT "File AUTO1.DAT closed after ";
PRINT "writing"; Count; "records.";
END
```

Here is an example of user interaction with the program.

```
Record 1
Stock number: 1011
Type of car:  Dodge truck, 4-wheel drive
Color of car: tan
Year of car:  1982
Sales price:  3400

Record 2
Stock number: 1012
Type of car:  Lincoln Continental
Color of car: dark gray
Year of car:  1985
Sales price:  17300

Record 3
Stock number: 1013
Type of car:  Mazda RX-7
Color of car: blue
Year of car:  1986
Sales price:  11200

Record 4
Stock number: 0
File AUTO1.DAT closed after writing 3 records.
```

The file written by Example Program 9-6 contains the following lines of information.

```
1011,"Dodge truck, 4-wheel drive","tan",1982,3400
1012,"Lincoln Continental","dark gray",1985,17300
1013,"Mazda RX-7","blue",1986,11200
```

The next example program reads the records from file AUTO1.DAT and displays their contents on the screen.

```
' Example Program 9-7
' Read records from file AUTO1.DAT and
' display their contents on the screen.

OPEN "AUTO1.DAT" FOR INPUT AS #2
CLS   ' clear the screen
Record = 1
DO WHILE NOT EOF(2)
    PRINT "Record"; Record
    INPUT #2, Num, Type$, Color$, Year, Price
    PRINT "Stock number: "; Num
```

```
          PRINT "Type of car:   "; Type$
          PRINT "Color of car:  "; Color$
          PRINT "Year of car:   "; Year
          PRINT "Sales price:   "; Price
          PRINT
          Record = Record + 1
     LOOP
     CLOSE #2
     END
```

Here is the program output.

```
     Record 1
     Stock number: 1011
     Type of car:  Dodge truck, 4-wheel drive
     Color of car: tan
     Year of car:  1982
     Sales price:  3400

     Record 2
     Stock number: 1012
     Type of car:  Lincoln Continental
     Color of car: dark gray
     Year of car:  1905
     Sales price:  17300

     Record 3
     Stock number: 1013
     Type of car:  Mazda RX-7
     Color of car: blue
     Year of car:  1986
     Sales price:  11200
```

In a practical application, the data file would be much longer and contain many more records. We have kept it short for demonstration purposes. The main disadvantage of this file structure is that anyone writing a program to read the file must know the record structure. On the other hand, this record structure does create a shorter and better organized file. It is always possible to examine the file with a text editor and determine the record structure.

9.4 STORING INFORMATION IN RANDOM-ACCESS FILES

Random-access files contain the same record and field structure that we discussed in the preceding section. They differ from sequential files in that any specific record can be read directly without reading all preceding records. This ability to read any particular record in a file is called *random access.*

A random-access file is not a pure text file. Information is written in this type of file in a coded format containing some ASCII characters and some binary data. In general, it is not possible to read a random-access file with a text editor, and under no circumstances should a random-access file be modified with a text editor.

A major feature of random-access files is that a program can directly access any record in the file. This means that a program must be able to calculate where a specified record starts; that is, the distance in bytes from the beginning of the file to the beginning of the specified record. In order to make this calculation, all records in the file must be the same length.

Opening Random-Access Files

The OPEN statement is used to open a random-access file for either reading or writing. An additional parameter should be specified, the length of the file record in characters or bytes. The syntax is

```
OPEN FileName$ FOR RANDOM AS #N LEN = L
```

where N is the file number and L is the record length in characters or bytes. If a record length is not specified, a default value of 128 bytes is used.

The GET and PUT Statements

Information is written on random-access files by the PUT statement and read by the GET statement. Here is the syntax for these statements.

```
PUT #N, R, Item
GET #N, R, Item
```

The file number is denoted by variable N and the record number by variable R. Record numbers in a random-access file start with the number 1. The variable Item may be a number, a fixed-length string, or a user-defined record (the latter two types are discussed in the following sections). It cannot be a regular string variable.

The LEN clause in the OPEN statement must specify the length of Item. For numeric records, the proper length is 2 bytes for an integer, 4 bytes for a long integer, 4 bytes for a single-precision real number, and 8 bytes for a double-precision real number.

Fixed-Length Strings

The records of a random-access file may be fixed-length strings. The string variables we have used so far are called dynamic strings because the actual length of their values can vary between zero and the defined length. Thus the amount of space occupied on a file by the value of a dynamic string will vary. On the other hand, the value of a fixed-length string variable always takes the same amount of file space.

Fixed-length string variables can be defined in one or more DIM statements as shown in the following program fragment

```
DIM Employee AS STRING * 30, Address AS STRING * 50
```

where the number following the asterisk is the length of the string in characters. Note that the string variable name cannot end with a dollar sign. The variable Employee must always contain exactly 30 characters.

If you assign fewer characters, as shown in the following statement, trailing blanks are added to bring the total number of characters to the defined length. For example, the statement

```
Employee = "Jennifer Jones"
```

when displayed by the PRINT statement

```
PRINT "***"; Employee; "***"
```

produces the following output.

```
***Jennifer Jones                ***
```

The assigned characters are left-justified in the defined width of thirty characters.

The reason that only fixed-length strings can be used in random-access files is that records must have a fixed length, as specified in the OPEN statement. Remember that a fixed record length is a necessary requirement for accessing a specific record in a file.

User-Defined Record Types

QuickBASIC allows a user to define a new record type containing multiple field variables. **These field variables can be numbers, fixed-length strings, or even other user-defined record variables. They cannot be variable-length strings.** Most random-access files have records that are user-defined types. The TYPE statement defines a new record type and specifies the names of the field variables that make up that record. A DIM statement can then be used to declare a variable of the new record type.

Here is a user-defined record type based on our previous examples.

```
TYPE AutoRecord
   Num AS INTEGER
   CarType AS STRING * 30
   CarColor AS STRING * 10
   Year AS STRING * 4
   Price AS SINGLE
END TYPE
```

Note that we use variable names CarType and CarColor instead of Type$ and Color$ (the variable names we used in Example Program 9-7). Dollar signs are not allowed in fixed-length string names, and the identifiers Type and Color are reserved words in Quick-BASIC. The other predefined types for field variables (not used in this example) are LONG for long integers and DOUBLE for double-precision real variables.

The difference between type names and variable names must be fully understood. A type name simply identifies a new type structure. The newly defined type AutoRecord can be used in most ways like any predefined type such as integer or string. A value cannot be assigned to AutoRecord just as a value cannot be assigned to the identifier integer or string. The field variables in AutoRecord, however, are true variables and can have values assigned to them.

Before a new type structure can be used in any practical way, a variable of that type must be declared with the DIM statement. Here is an example.

```
DIM AutoInfo AS AutoRecord
```

The variable AutoInfo has a value that consists of the values of its individual field variables. Variables like AutoInfo (of type AutoRecord) are often the components or records of a random-access file.

The individual fields in record variable AutoInfo are identified by a notation that combines the record variable name and the field variable name, separated by a period. For example, to assign a value to the first field in AutoInfo, we use the following assignment statement.

```
AutoInfo.Num = 1015
```

This notation is used in the INPUT statements of Example Program 9-8.

The LEN Function

The length of a record variable is just the sum of its field lengths. It can be calculated by the LEN function, using a statement like the following.

```
Length = LEN(AutoInfo)
```

In our case of the record type AutoRecord, Length has a value of 50 bytes.

An Example Program

We now develop a program similar to Example Program 9-6 that stores its information in a random-access file.

```
' Example Program 9-8
' Use random-access file AUTO2.DAT for storing
```

```
' data records. Type a zero for the stock number
' to stop entering information.

' Define the record type.
TYPE AutoRecord
    Num AS INTEGER
    CarType AS STRING * 30
    CarColor AS STRING * 10
    Year AS STRING * 4
    Price AS SINGLE
END TYPE
' Write records on the data file.
DIM AutoInfo AS AutoRecord
OPEN "AUTO2.DAT" FOR RANDOM AS #1 LEN = LEN(AutoInfo)
Count = 0
DO
    PRINT "Record"; Count + 1
    INPUT "Stock number: ", AutoInfo.Num
    IF AutoInfo.Num = 0 THEN EXIT DO
    LINE INPUT "Type of car:  ", AutoInfo.CarType
    LINE INPUT "Color of car: ", AutoInfo.CarColor
    INPUT "Year of car:  ", AutoInfo.Year
    INPUT "Sales price:  ", AutoInfo.Price
    Count = Count + 1
    PUT #1, Count, AutoInfo
    PRINT
LOOP
CLOSE #1
PRINT "File AUTO.DAT closed after ";
PRINT "writing"; Count; "records.";
END
```

User interaction is the same as Example Program 9-6 and so we do not show it again. We cannot show you the contents of file AUTO2.DAT because these contents cannot be displayed on the screen. We define the record type in our program and use the appropriate identifiers in the INPUT statements. Once values have been assigned to all fields in a record, we use the PUT statement to write that entire record on the file.

The next example program reads a specified record from the file AUTO2.DAT and displays that record on the screen. The GET statement reads the entire record and each field is displayed with a PRINT statement. Remember that user-defined records are read from and written on files as whole objects, but are typed in from the keyboard and displayed on the screen field by field.

A new function, the LOF function, returns the length in bytes of a random-access file. If the file length is divided by the record length using integer division, the number of records in the file can be calculated. We call the number of records N and stop the program if the entered record number is greater than N or less than 1. The user is reminded by the prompt that the record number must be between 1 and N.

```
' Example Program 9-9
' Read a specified record from file AUTO2.DAT
' and display its contents on the screen.
' Type record number of zero to stop.

TYPE AutoRecord
    Num AS INTEGER
    CarType AS STRING * 30
    CarColor AS STRING * 10
    Year AS STRING * 4
    Price AS SINGLE
END TYPE
DIM AutoInfo AS AutoRecord
OPEN "AUTO2.DAT" FOR RANDOM AS #2 LEN = LEN(AutoInfo)
CLS
N = LOF(2) \ LEN(AutoInfo)
PRINT "Record number ( 1 to"; N; ")";
INPUT Record
DO UNTIL Record < 1 OR Record > N
    GET #2, Record, AutoInfo
    PRINT "Stock number:"; AutoInfo.Num
    PRINT "Type of car:  "; AutoInfo.CarType
    PRINT "Color of car: "; AutoInfo.CarColor
    PRINT "Year of car: "; AutoInfo.Year
    PRINT "Sales price: "; AutoInfo.Price
    PRINT
    PRINT "Record number ( 1 to"; N; ")";
    INPUT Record
LOOP
CLOSE #2
END
```

Here is a sample of program output.

```
Record number ( 1 to 3 )? 3
Stock number: 1013
Type of car:  Mazda RX-7
Color of car: blue
Year of car: 1986
Sales price: 11200

Record number ( 1 to 3 )? 0
```

A comparison of the two file types, sequential and random access, is in order. The two files are probably comparable in the amount of storage space they use for a given amount of information. Sequential files have the advantage that they are text files and can be displayed on the screen. You can always determine the record structure of a sequential file by looking at one of the records. Sequential files must be read sequentially, starting at the beginning of the file.

On the other hand, random-access files have the advantage that any record can be accessed directly. The record structure, however, cannot be determined by inspecting the file, and thus must be documented and known before a program can be written that uses the file.

Summary of Important Points

- An array used as a procedure heading parameter or a call statement argument must have a pair of dummy parentheses after the array name.
- Use the UBOUND function to specify the upper bound of an array in a subprogram.
- A one-dimensional array and a two-dimensional array in the same program cannot have the same name.
- It is common convention for the first index of an array variable to refer to the row number and the second index to refer to the column number.
- Nested FOR loops cannot overlap.
- Redimensioning cannot be used to change the number of dimensions in an array.
- The record structure of a sequential file can be determined by displaying a file record on the screen.
- A major disadvantage of redimensioning is that all elements in the array are reinitialized to zero numbers or null strings.
- A useful file structure for storing information consists of a sequence of components or records, each record containing a sequence of fields.
- The WRITE statement differs from the PRINT statement in that it separates all fields or items by commas and encloses all string values in quotation marks.
- A major feature of random-access files is that a program can directly access any record in the file.
- The field variables of a user-defined record type can be numbers, fixed-length strings, or even other user-defined record variables, but not variable-length strings.

Common Errors

- Trying to display the contents of a random-access file on the screen.
- Writing only one argument in the UBOUND function for a two-dimensional array.
- Redimensioning an array after data has been assigned to it and thus losing all that data.
- Reversing the positions of the row and column indices in the DIM statement of a two-dimensional array.

- Redimensioning a static array.
- Including an array as one of the fields in a user-defined record type.
- Naming a fixed-length string variable with a name that ends in a dollar sign.
- Assigning a value to the record type name rather than to the record variable name.

Self-Test Questions

1. If an array is dimensioned with the statement

    ```
    DIM Value(-5 TO 5, 1 TO 10)
    ```

    how many elements are contained in the array?

2. Which of the following dimension statements are valid?
    (a) DIM Array(10,10)
    (b) DIM Array(1,10)
    (c) DIM Array(10;10)
    (d) DIM Array(1-10,10)
    (e) DIM Array(1 TO 10,10)
    (f) Do all the preceding valid statements produce the same array?

3. If a two-dimensional array named Structure is passed as the only parameter to a subroutine named Analyze, what is the proper form of
    (a) the subroutine call statement;
    (b) the subroutine heading statement?

4. If an array is dimensioned in the main program unit and passed as a parameter to a function, should it be dimensioned again in the function unit?

5. (a) What function returns the upper bound value of the second dimension of the two-dimensional array named Result?
    (b) What function returns the lower bound value of the same dimension?

6. What is meant by the principal diagonal of a square array?

7. What, if anything, is special about the values of the two indices of principal diagonal elements in a two-dimensional square array?

8. An array representing a table is dimensioned DIM Table(5,3). This table contains
    (a) how many columns;
    (b) how many rows?

9. What, if anything, is wrong with the following program?

    ```
    DIM Table(1 TO 5, 1 TO 3)
    FOR I = 1 TO 5
       FOR J = 1 TO 3
          Table(I, J) = 0
       NEXT I
    NEXT J
    END
    ```

10. This program is supposed to display the array Mileage as a table with rows and columns.

```
DIM Mileage(1 TO 5, 1 TO 5)
FOR I = 1 TO 5
   FOR J = 1 to 5
      PRINT Mileage(I, J)
   NEXT J
NEXT I
END
```

Will it display the table with five rows and five columns? If not, how would you correct the program to make it work properly?

11. Which statement should be used to write a record containing both strings and numbers on a sequential text file?

12. Which statement is used to read a record from a sequential text file?

13. What types of variables can be used as fields in a record created with the TYPE statement?

14. Can a record be accessed directly in
    (a) a random-access file;
    (b) a sequential text file?

15. Write an expression that calculates the number of records in random-access file #3 containing user-defined type records of type Person and variable identifier Employee?

16. If a random-access file contains records of type integer, how much space is taken by each record?

17. (a) Which statement is used to read a record from a random-access file?
    (b) What arguments are needed with this statement?

18. Is a user-defined record written on a random-access file
    (a) field by field;
    (b) as a whole record?

19. Can you display on the screen the record structure of
    (a) a random-access file;
    (b) a sequential text file?

Practice Programs

1. A matrix is a one-dimensional or two-dimensional array of numbers. Here is a special matrix called an *identity matrix*. It is a square matrix with the same number of rows and columns. The principal diagonal runs from the upper left corner to the lower right corner.

1	0	0	0
0	1	0	0
0	0	1	0
0	0	0	1

The identity matrix is a square matrix with elements along the principal diagonal having a value of 1 and the other elements having a value of 0.

Using FOR statements, create and display an identity matrix with 10 rows and columns (a 10-by-10 matrix).

2. A transposed matrix is a square matrix (see Practice Program 1) whose rows and columns have been interchanged. Thus old row 1 becomes new column 1, old row 2 becomes new column 2, and so forth. Read the elements of a 6-by-6 matrix from DATA statements, trans-pose the matrix, and display the transposed matrix. Test your program using the following DATA statements.

```
DATA 1,5,3,6,7,2
DATA 7,1,4,9,2,3
DATA 9,0,2,1,6,3
DATA 0,1,3,2,7,5
DATA 6,4,7,3,8,9
DATA 4,6,2,2,3,1
```

3. Read eight part names and associated prices from DATA statements and place these values in a two-dimensional array with 100 rows and two columns. Names are placed in column 1 and prices in column 2. Search the array for the name of the highest-priced part and the low-est-priced part. Display these two part names and prices with appropriate labels. Test your program using the following values.

hammer	13.45
pliers	8.60
saw	21.40
wrench	19.95
ruler	1.85
punch	4.50
screwdriver	3.75
crowbar	12.50

4. A primitive way to encode a short message is to substitute a number for each word. Write a function to do the encoding. The value of the function will be the code number when a word is passed to it as a string parameter. The function is also passed an array parameter contain-ing code table values that have been read from the sequential text file CODE.DAT. Each line of the file is a record containing a word and a code number for that word. You should exam-ine the contents of this file. Use this function in a program designed to display a sequence of code numbers for a sentence entered from the keyboard. Your message is limited to one sentence and to the words contained in the file. Do not include any punctuation marks in the sentence. Test your program by encoding the following message.

SEND MONEY STOP FAMILY SENT HOME STOP DANGER TO EAST END

5. Using the same data file as in Practice Program 4, write another function that returns a word when a number parameter is passed to it. The function should return a question mark if the parameter is not a valid number. Use this function in a program to display an English sen-tence for a sequence of code numbers entered from the keyboard. Enter the code numbers as a string of numbers separated by spaces. Test your program by decoding the following coded message.

```
        4 22 17 10 6 18
```

6.   Information on common stocks is contained in a random-access file named STOCKS.DAT.
      Each record contains four fields, designating stock symbol, highest price for the year, lowest
      price for the year, and current price. Here is the record type structure.

```
TYPE StockRec
    StockSymbol AS STRING * 4
    HighPrice AS SINGLE
    LowPrice AS SINGLE
    CurrentPrice AS SINGLE
END TYPE
```

Calculate the relative position of the current price of each stock within the range between its
lowest and highest price for the year. The term relative position is best explained by an
example. Consider the two stocks shown in Fig. 9.5.

StockSymbol	HighPrice	LowPrice	CurrentPrice
A	100	10	15
B	20	10	15

Figure 9.5   Comparison of two stocks.

Each stock has a current price that is $5.00 higher than its low price. For stock A, this repre-
sents a relative position of (5/(100-10)) or .055. Expressed in percentage, stock A has risen
5.5% from its low. For stock B, the relative position is (5/(20-10)) or .5, representing a 50%
rise from its low. Display, with appropriate labels, the symbol of the stock with the highest
relative position and that with the lowest relative position. Show the percentage rise or fall of
each stock.

7.   A salesman maintains a list of prospects in a random-access file named PROSPECT.DAT.
      Each component in the file is a user-defined record type with the following structure.

```
TYPE Person
    Name AS STRING * 30
    Address AS STRING * 30
    City AS STRING * 20
    State AS STRING * 2
    Zip AS STRING * 5
END TYPE
```

Add five records to the file from the keyboard. Print the entire file on your printer with
appropriate labels for each record and field. If a printer is not available, display the file on
the screen.

10

SORTING ALGORITHMS AND RECURSION

10.1 INTRODUCTION

In this chapter we introduce the technique of sorting lists on computers, one of the most important computer applications, and examine two algorithms for implementing this technique. We first discuss a simple algorithm that is easy to understand, the bubble-sort algorithm. A more sophisticated and much faster algorithm is the quicksort algorithm. In order to understand this algorithm, we must first explain recursive procedures. We also discuss how to measure the sorting times for different sorting algorithms.

10.2 SORTING: THE BUBBLE-SORT ALGORITHM

Sorting lists of names or numbers is a frequent and important application of computers. If the list is large, sorting can take a long time. Many algorithms for sorting have been investigated and some of these algorithms can sort very rapidly. Unfortunately, many of the efficient and fast algorithms are also difficult to understand. **We introduce first a relatively simple, but not very efficient sorting algorithm called the *bubble-sort algorithm.*** We then use it in a program that sorts a list of real numbers.

A computer program using the bubble-sort algorithm goes through the list of numbers to be sorted, from one end of the list to the other, comparing numbers in pairs. The

252

first pair consists of the first and second numbers in the list, the second pair consists of the second and third numbers, and so forth. We call this process *scanning the list.*

If a pair is in the wrong numerical order, we swap or interchange the two numbers. If a pair is in the correct numerical order, we move on to the next pair. We repeat this scanning process until we can scan the list without having to swap any names. We know then that the list is in sorted order.

Fig. 10.1 shows the bubble-sort process in detail as a list of five numbers is sorted. Each scan through the list is labeled, and interchanged numbers are shown in bold face. Note how large numbers move or "bubble up" to the top (in our case, the right end) of the list. No interchange is made during the last scan, indicating that the list is sorted.

First scan	1	7	3	2	5
	1	**3**	**7**	2	5
	1	3	**2**	**7**	5
	1	3	2	**5**	**7**
Second scan	1	3	2	5	7
	1	**2**	**3**	5	7
Third scan	1	2	3	5	7

Figure 10.1   Sorting a list with bubble sort.

In most languages, **a third temporary variable must be used when interchanging two numbers.** To interchange the numeric values stored in variables A and B, assign the value of A to the variable Temp, next assign the value of B to A, and finally assign the value of Temp to B. The program statements might look like this.

```
Temp = A   ' assign value of A to Temp
A = B      ' assign value of B to A
B = Temp   ' assign value of Temp to B
```

In QuickBASIC, however, we can use the statement

```
SWAP A, B
```

for the same purpose and do so in our example program.

We use an integer variable as a flag and define two constants TRUE and FALSE. Each time we start to scan the list, we set the value of the flag variable to TRUE. If we make an interchange during this scan of the list, the flag value is changed to FALSE. We examine the flag value at the end of each scan, and if it is TRUE, we know that no interchanges were made during the last scan through the list and that the list is in sorted order.

Our example program consists of three tasks.

- Read values from a file and assign them to an array.
- Sort the array in memory.
- Write the sorted array back on a file.

This program assumes that we have enough memory to allow the entire file to be placed in an array variable in memory. It is much easier and quicker to sort a list in memory than it is to sort a list on a disk file.

The BubbleSort Subroutine

Our program uses a subroutine for the actual sorting. A dynamic, one-dimensional array named SortList contains N% numeric values. Each element in the array is a number. We can change the size of the array by changing the variable N%.

```
SUB BubbleSort (SortList(), N%)
   ' Use the bubble-sort algorithm to sort
   ' an array containing N numeric elements.
   DO
      Sorted% = TRUE
      FOR I% := 1 TO (N% - 1)
         IF SortList(I%) > SortList(I% + 1) THEN
            SWAP SortList(I%), SortList(I% + 1)
            Sorted% = FALSE
         END IF
      NEXT I%
   LOOP UNTIL Sorted% = TRUE
END SUB   ' BubbleSort
```

Pairs of list values, denoted by SortList(I%) and SortList(I% + 1), are compared and interchanged if not in sorted order. Note that I%, the FOR loop control variable, has a final value of only N% - 1. If I% were assigned a value of N%, the program would try to compare array elements SortList(N%) and SortList(N% + 1) and would produce unpredictable results because no number has been assigned to SortList(N% + 1).

Referring to Fig. 10.1, the DO loop performs a single scan of the list. The IF statement performs a swap if two elements in the list must be interchanged.

This subroutine sorts a list of items in ascending order. To sort in descending order, reverse the logical sense of the comparison statement, changing it to the following statement.

```
SortList(I%) < SortList(I% + 1)
```

Testing the BubbleSort Subroutine

The next example program is designed to sort a list of single-precision real numbers. It assumes that the numbers are stored in a text file, one number per record. The length of the list is limited by the amount of available memory, but there should be no difficulty sorting a list of several hundred numbers. Here is the program outline.

> Ask user for file name and open input file.
> Ask user for file name and open output file.
> Calculate length of list and size an array.
>> Read data from input file into the array.
> Sort the array.
> Write the sorted array to the output file.
> Close output file and report results.

Here is the program itself.

```
' Example Program 10-1
' Read a list of numbers from a text file,
' use the bubble-sort algorithm to sort this list,
' and write the sorted list to a text file.
' This program uses the FILES module.

CONST FALSE = 0, TRUE = NOT FALSE
N% = 1
DIM SortList(1 TO N%)
CALL OpenInFile ("Name of input file", 1)
CALL OpenOutFile ("Name of output file", 2)
CALL FillArray (SortList(), N%)
PRINT
CALL DisplayArray (SortList(), N%, "Unsorted List")
CALL BubbleSort (SortList(), N%)
PRINT
CALL DisplayArray (SortList(), N%, "Sorted List")
CALL WriteArray (SortList(), N%)
PRINT
PRINT "Sorted list is in the output file."
END   ' Main Program

ErrorHandler1:
    ' Set NameOK to false if file does not exist.
    IF ERR = 53 THEN
       PRINT "File does not exist - try again"
       NameOK = FALSE
       RESUME NEXT
    ELSE    ' unexpected error, halt the program
       ON ERROR GOTO 0
    END IF
```

```
ErrorHandler2:
    ' Set OverWrite to true if file does not exist.
    IF ERR = 53 THEN  ' no existing file
       OverWrite = TRUE
       RESUME NEXT
    ELSE  ' unexpected error, halt the program
       ON ERROR GOTO 0
    END IF

SUB CheckAnswer (Prompt$, Flag)
    ' Display prompt, get answer, and set flag
    ' to TRUE or FALSE if answer is YES or NO.
    ' Otherwise, prompt for answer again.
    ' Module defines constants TRUE and FALSE.
    DO
        PRINT Prompt$;
        INPUT Ans$
        Ans$ = UCASE$(LEFT$(Ans$, 1))
        SELECT CASE Ans$
        CASE "Y"
           Flag = TRUE
        CASE "N"
           Flag = FALSE
        CASE ELSE
           PRINT "Please answer Y or N"
        END SELECT
    LOOP UNTIL Ans$ = "Y" OR Ans$ = "N"
END SUB   ' CheckAnswer

SUB OpenInFile (Prompt$, N)
    ' Open an existing file for reading.
    ' If file does not exist, ask user
    ' to enter name again.
    SHARED NameOK
    ON ERROR GOTO ErrorHandler1
    DO
        NameOK = TRUE
        PRINT Prompt$;
        INPUT FileName$
        OPEN FileName$ FOR INPUT AS #N
    LOOP UNTIL NameOK = TRUE
END SUB   ' OpenInFile

SUB OpenOutFile (Prompt$, N)
    ' Open a file for writing.
```

```
    ' If file already exists, ask user
    ' if it is OK to overwrite it.
    SHARED OverWrite
    ON ERROR GOTO ErrorHandler2
    DO
        NameOK = FALSE
        OverWrite = FALSE
        PRINT Prompt$;
        INPUT FileName$
        ' Open for input to see if file exists
        OPEN FileName$ FOR INPUT AS #N
        ' ErrorHandler2 is called if file does not exist
        ' and returns flag OverWrite as TRUE
        CLOSE #N
        IF OverWrite = TRUE THEN
            OPEN FileName$ FOR OUTPUT AS #N
            NameOK = TRUE
        ELSE
            CheckAnswer "Overwrite this file", OverWrite
            IF OverWrite = TRUE THEN
                OPEN FileName$ FOR OUTPUT AS #N
                NameOK = TRUE
            END IF
        END IF
    LOOP UNTIL NameOK = TRUE
END SUB   ' OpenOutFile

SUB BubbleSort (SortList(), N%)
    ' Use the bubble-sort algorithm to sort
    ' an array containing N numeric elements.
    DO
        Sorted% = TRUE
        FOR I% = 1 TO (N% - 1)
            IF SortList(I%) > SortList(I% + 1) THEN
                SWAP SortList(I%), SortList(I% + 1)
                Sorted% = FALSE
            END IF
        NEXT I%
    LOOP UNTIL Sorted% = TRUE
END SUB   ' BubbleSort

SUB DisplayArray (SortList(), N%, Title$)
    ' Display a short, single-line array of N real
    ' numbers on the screen, with an appropriate title.
    PRINT Title$
```

```
    FOR I% = 1 TO N%
        PRINT USING "#####"; SortList(I%);
    NEXT I%
    PRINT
END SUB  ' DisplayArray

SUB FillArray (SortList(), Count%)
    ' Read a list of numbers from a text file
    ' and assign them to an array.
    ' First count the items.
    Count% = 0
    DO WHILE NOT EOF(1)
        LINE INPUT #1, Dummy$
        Count% = Count% + 1
    LOOP
    ' Then redimension and fill array.
    REDIM SortList(Count%)
    SEEK #1, 1  ' move to start of file
    FOR I% = 1 TO Count%
        INPUT #1, SortList(I%)
    NEXT I%
END SUB  ' FillArray

SUB WriteArray (SortList(), N%)
    ' Write an array of N numbers to a text file.
    FOR I% = 1 TO N%
        PRINT #2, SortList(I%)
    NEXT I%
    CLOSE #2
END SUB  ' WriteArray
```

The following output is produced by this program.

```
Name of input file? UNSORTED.NUM
Name of output file? SORTED.NUM

Unsorted List
  123   65  887    3   45  110    7   -6 1050    0

Sorted List
   -6    0    3    7   45   65  110  123  887 1050
Sorted list is in the output file.
```

We have inserted a call to the subroutine DisplayArray in the program before and after the BubbleSort subroutine is called. These procedure calls display the list before and after sorting, but can be deleted in a production version of the program. Note that subroutine FillArray must read through the file twice: once to count the numbers in the file and redimension the array, then a second time to assign each numeric value to an array element.

We are careful to open the array initially as a dynamic array by using a variable N% for the size. This action allows us to redimension the array when we know how many numbers are in the file. We also use the SEEK #1, 1 statement to move the file pointer to the first byte in file #1 or the beginning of the file, allowing the file to be read a second time.

Our program, as written, is limited only by the amount of memory available for storing the array. In general, small computers do not have enough memory to hold very large arrays in memory. More sophisticated sorting algorithms have been developed that allow large disk files to be sorted quickly and efficiently. Note that **it is not possible to sort a text file directly with the bubble-sort algorithm** because we cannot access individual lines in the file.

You may have noticed that after the first scan through the list, the largest number is moved to the right end of the list. Each successive scan moves the next larger number toward the right end. This phenomenon is discussed in Practice Program 3 where a modified bubble-sort algorithm is suggested that is more efficient than our original algorithm.

10.3 COMPARING TWO STRINGS

In order to sort or search a list of string values, we need to understand how the computer determines if one string is larger than another string. We shall compare two string variables called Name1$ and Name2$.

We want to know if the logical expression

```
Name1$ > Name2$
```

is true or false. **Comparison of two strings is done character by character and is based on the ASCII values of the characters,** as listed in Appendix B. These characters can be letters, digits, or other nonalphabetic characters.

The computer compares the ASCII value of the first character of Name1$ with that of the first character of Name2$. If the character in Name1$ has the greater value, the logical expression (Name1$ > Name2$) is true. Remember that an uppercase letter and the corresponding lowercase letter are different characters and have different ASCII values.

```
"C"  is greater than  "B"
"a"  is greater than  "A"
```

If the character in Name1$ has the lesser value, the logical expression is false. If the first characters in Name1$ and Name2$ are identical, the computer automatically compares the ASCII values of the second character in each string.

This process continues until (1) the value of a character in one string is greater than the value of the corresponding character in the other string, (2) the end of one string is reached while the other string contains more characters, or (3) the ends of both strings are reached because they are equal in length and have the same sequence of characters.

If the ASCII value of a character in Name1$ is greater or less than the ASCII value of the corresponding character in Name2$, the last comparison determines whether the logical expression is true or false.

> `"ABC"` is greater than `"ABB"`

If Name1$ is longer than Name2$ and the two strings have an identical sequence of characters up to the end of Name2$, variable Name1$ is considered the greater and the logical expression is true.

> `"QED"` is greater than `"QE"`

If Name1$ and Name2$ are of equal length and have the same sequence of characters, the two strings are equal and the logical expression is false.

> `"xyz"` is equal to `"xyz"`

Using a logical expression that compares two string variables, the bubble-sort algorithm can be used to alphabetize a list of string values or arrange the list in ascending alphabetic order. As mentioned previously, changing the sense of the logical expression sorts the list into descending alphabetic order.

10.4 RECURSIVE PROCEDURES

Our next example of sorting uses the quicksort algorithm. This algorithm is usually written with a sorting procedure that calls itself repeatedly, known as a *recursive procedure*. Thus, we interrupt our discussion of sorting to examine the general subject of recursion.

Recursive procedures are usually not as fast, as efficient, or as easy to understand as procedures using an *iterative loop*; that is, a loop with a control variable that is incremented each time the body of the loop is executed. We include a short discussion of recursion and an example program because there are some applications where recursion is the most natural way to solve a problem.

As an example, consider the problem of calculating the factorial value of a number, already discussed in Chapter 7. The definition of factorial N (written as N!) is as follows.

$$N! \; = \; 1 \times 2 \times 3 \times ... \times N$$

Remember that the expression 0! is defined as 1. For example, 3! is equal to $1 \times 2 \times 3$ or 6, while 5! is $1 \times 2 \times 3 \times 4 \times 5$ or 120.

An Iterative Solution

Here is a program (similar to Example Program 7-6) that calculates factorials using a DO statement in an ordinary iterative loop. It is so simple that no outline is required.

```
' Example Program 10-2
' Ask the user to enter a nonnegative integer <= 13
' and calculate the factorial value of that number.
' This program uses a function with an iterative loop.

DECLARE FUNCTION Factorial& (N%)
INPUT "Enter a nonnegative integer: ", Number%
IF Number% > 13 THEN
    PRINT "Factorial is too large to calculate."
ELSE
    PRINT "Factorial"; Number%; "is";
    PRINT Factorial&(Number%)
END IF
END

FUNCTION Factorial& (N%)
    ' Calculate the factorial value of N.
    TempResult& = 1
    Index% = 2  ' because 0! and 1! both equal 1
    DO WHILE Index% <= N%
          TempResult& = Index% * TempResult&
       Index% = Index% + 1
       LOOP
       Factorial& = TempResult&
END FUNCTION   ' Factorial&
```

The function Factorial& (a double-precision real function) uses a DO loop with a control variable Index% that is incremented each time the body of the loop is executed. The initial value of the function is set at 1. The values of 0! and 1! are not calculated in the loop because both have a value of 1, the initial value of the function. The loop starts with an initial value of Index% equal to 2.

Index values greater than 13 are not allowed in this program because the value of Factorial& becomes too large. Here is the display that is produced.

```
Enter a nonnegative integer: 5
Factorial 5 is 120
```

A Recursive Solution

The same results can be obtained by writing the function in a recursive form. We show an example program and then discuss the results.

```
' Example Program 10-3
' Ask the user to enter a nonnegative integer <= 13
' and calculate the factorial value of that number.
' This program uses a recursive function.

DECLARE FUNCTION Factorial& (N%)
INPUT "Enter a nonnegative integer: ", Number%
IF Number% > 13 THEN
    PRINT "Factorial is too large to calculate."
ELSE
    PRINT "Factorial"; Number%; "is";
    PRINT Factorial&(Number%)
END IF
END

FUNCTION Factorial& (N%)
    ' Calculate the factorial value of N.
    IF N% <= 1 THEN
       Factorial& = 1
    ELSE
       Factorial& = N% * Factorial&(N% - 1)
    END IF
END FUNCTION   ' Factorial&
```

In this version of the program, the function is somewhat simpler in format but probably more difficult to understand. Assuming that a user enters a value of 5, the function is called first with N% = 5. The ELSE branch of the IF statement is selected at this point, requiring calculation of the expression 5 * Factorial&(4). **This expression cannot be calculated, however, until function Factorial&(4) has been evaluated,** requiring calculation of the expression 4 * Factorial&(3), and so forth.

Whenever a program calls a function, it puts the call statement for that function on the *stack*, a special section of memory. A stack is often called a last-in-first-out (LIFO) structure. It gets its name from the spring-loaded stack of plates, often seen in a cafeteria, where the last plate placed on the stack is the first plate removed. In this case, function calls placed on the stack have not been evaluated, but will be evaluated when the function call is taken off the stack. In the case of a recursive program, all function calls except the last one placed on the stack are not evaluated immediately, but rather, evaluated later when they are removed from the stack.

In our example program, Factorial&(5) is placed first on the stack. After all function calls are placed on the stack, it looks like Fig. 10.2, with the last call on top. None of these functions on the stack (except the top function) can be evaluated, however, until the value of the previous function call is known.

The last item placed on the stack is Factorial&(1). This function can be evaluated immediately using the first IF branch to assign its value of 1, and it is then removed from the stack. The program now returns to the stack, calculates the value of the current top function, Factorial&(2), as 2×1 or 2, and removes it from the stack.

The program returns again to the stack, calculates what is now the top function, Factorial&(3), as $3 \times 2 \times 1$ or 6, and removes it from the stack. The next function calculated and removed is Factorial&(4), whose value is $4 \times 3 \times 2 \times 1$ or 24, while the last function calculated and removed is Factorial&(5), which has a value of $5 \times 4 \times 3 \times 2 \times 1$ or 120, the desired result.

STACK	VALUE
Factorial&(1)	1
Factorial&(2)	2 × Factorial&(1)
Factorial&(3)	3 × Factorial&(2)
Factorial&(4)	4 × Factorial&(3)
Factorial&(5)	5 × Factorial&(4)

Figure 10.2   Diagram of the stack during recursion.

The length of a recursive calculation, and thus the size of the stack, depends only on the amount of memory available for the stack. **There must always be one nonrecursive value** (in our case, the value of Factorial&(1)) **for recursion to work properly.**

When all is said and done, recursion is not often used in programs, but there are some cases (such as the following QuickSort subroutine) where a recursive solution is clearly the best solution. Recursive procedures are often short and elegant, but they tend to be more difficult to understand than common iterative solutions and execute more slowly. **We recommend that you use recursion only if it appears to be the best way to solve a problem.**

10.5 SORTING: THE QUICKSORT ALGORITHM

One of the fastest sorting algorithms is the *quicksort algorithm.* We again consider the problem of sorting an array or list of elements. The quicksort algorithm works by separating the list into two partitions. One element of the list is selected and called the *pivot element.* **It makes little difference which element is chosen,** although it is often the first or last element in the list.

The elements in the list are rearranged in a systematic manner into two partitions. Assuming that we wish to sort the list into ascending order from left to right, all list elements less than the pivot element are moved into the left partition. All elements greater than or equal to the pivot element are moved into the right partition. The pivot element is then placed between the two partitions. **Note that this rearrangement places the pivot element in its proper position in the final, sorted list.**

We now apply the same quicksort algorithm, recursively and separately, to the left partition and the right partition of the original list. Each time we call quicksort, we must define a new pivot element. We work first on the left partition and continue to subdivide it, calling quicksort recursively until the length of each partition is one element. We then do the same thing to the right partition. Our array is now sorted in ascending order.

Fig. 10.3 shows how a list containing six characters forming the word CATTLE is sorted. The vertical line represents the division between left and right partitions. The bold-face letter is the current pivot element.

We choose the first element (C) as the pivot element. After the first partitioning, the list appears as ACTTLE. The left partition contains one element (A), while the right partition contains four elements (TTLE). The pivot element (C) is in its correct position.

Before separation:	**C**	A	T	T	L	E
After test, no swap:	**C**	A|	T	T	L	E
After moving pivot:	A	**C**	T	T	L	E
Before separation:		**T**	T	L	E
After element swap:		**T**	L|	T	E
After element swap:		**T**	L	E|	T
After moving pivot:		E	L	**T**	T
Before separation:		**E**	L
After moving pivot:		**E**	L
Final sorted list:		A	C	E	L	T	T

Figure 10.3   Sorting a list with quicksort.

In our example we note that the left partition is only one element long, so we cannot subdivide it further. The right partition is a new list containing the four characters TTLE. Applying the quicksort algorithm again, we choose the first element (T) as the pivot element and subdivide the list into two partitions. The resulting list after subdivision becomes ELTT. The first T is the pivot element, while the second T is the right partition. The left partition is EL. We know now that the letters A and C (in positions 1 and 2) and letters T and T (in positions 5 and 6) are all in their correct final positions in the sorted list.

Continuing with our example, we note that the list EL is already in sorted order, so it is partitioned into two single-element lists. The quicksort algorithm determines that each partition has only a single element and so no further action is taken. Thus our original list, written in sorted order, becomes ACELTT.

The QuickSort Subroutine

Here is one implementation of the quicksort algorithm using a subroutine named Quick-Sort. It is written to sort a list of numbers but by changing the type of array variable SortList, it can be used to sort a list of strings.

After checking to see if the list is longer than one element, the first statement calls another subroutine, named Separate, that partitions the list. Then QuickSort is called again to sort first the left partition and then the right partition.

```
SUB QuickSort (SortList(), First%, Last%)
   ' Sort the list of numeric values named SortList from
   ' index First% to index Last% using quicksort.
   ' This is a recursive procedure.
   ' Both QuickSort and Separate must be declared.

   IF First% < Last% THEN   ' more than 1 element in list
      Separate SortList(), Pivot%, First%, Last%
      QuickSort SortList(), First%, Pivot% - 1
      QuickSort SortList(), Pivot% + 1, Last%
   END IF
END SUB   ' QuickSort
```

As you can see, most of the work is done by subroutine Separate that is called from QuickSort. We first list subroutine Separate and then discuss how it works.

```
SUB Separate (SortList(), Pivot%, First%, Last%)
   ' Separate the list into two parts, one with
   ' elements less than PivotValue and the other
   ' with elements greater than or equal to PivotValue.
   Pivot% = First%   ' make first element the pivot
   PivotValue = SortList(First%)
   FOR New% = (First% + 1) TO Last%
      IF SortList(New%) < PivotValue THEN
         Pivot% = Pivot% + 1
         IF New% <> Pivot% THEN   ' different elements
            SWAP SortList(Pivot%), SortList(New%)
         END IF
      END IF
   NEXT New%
   ' Move pivot element to point in list that separates
   ' the smaller elements from the larger elements.
   SWAP SortList(First%), SortList(Pivot%)
END SUB   ' Separate
```

The first element in the list is chosen as the pivot element. Starting with the second element, the value of each other element (denoted as element New%) in the list is compared, in turn, with the value of the original pivot element, PivotValue. If the element value is less than PivotValue, the index of the pivot element is incremented. Procedure Swap is called to interchange the values of the current pivot element (SortList(Pivot%)) and the new element (SortList(New%)).

Note the distinction between the original value of the pivot element (PivotValue), which is used for comparisons, and the index of the current pivot element (Pivot%). If a new element is found whose value is less than PivotValue, index Pivot% is incremented, moving the position of the current pivot element to the right. The values of the new element and the current pivot element (whose index is Pivot%) are then interchanged, placing the new element before or to the left of the current pivot element. No swap is made, of course, if the new element and current pivot element have the same index (they are the same element).

After a complete scan through the list, the location of the current pivot element marks the division between the two partitions. All elements to the left of the division, including the current pivot element, have values less than PivotValue. All elements to the right of the division have values greater than or equal to PivotValue. The remaining task is then to swap SortList(Pivot%) and SortList(First%), placing the original pivot element in its proper position in the list. Note that this position is also its proper position when the list is in final sorted order.

This subroutine is not easy to read. We recommend that you trace through the subroutine by hand (play computer) in order to understand exactly what is taking place.

Testing the QuickSort Subroutine

Our implementation of the quicksort algorithm is shown in an example program that demonstrates how the algorithm works. The subroutine QuickSort does the actual sorting. The user is asked to enter a short string of characters, the characters are sorted in ascending order, and the sorted string is displayed. In addition, a table is created and displayed showing several intermediate steps in the sorting process.

```
' Example Program 10-4
' Test an implementation of the quicksort algorithm.
' Ask the user to enter a short string of characters.
' Display intermediate and final results on the screen.

DIM SortList$(100)
PRINT "Enter a string of up to 15 characters: ";
LINE INPUT Entry$
Length% = LEN(Entry$)
PRINT
FOR I% = 1 TO Length%
    SortList$(I%) = MID$(Entry$, I%, 1)
```

```
NEXT I%
CALL QuickSort (SortList$(), 1, Length%)
PRINT "Final sorted list:    ";
FOR I% = 1 TO Length%
   PRINT SortList$(I%); "   ";
NEXT I%
PRINT
END   ' Main Program

SUB Display1 (Title$, SortList$(), A%, B%)
   ' Display part or all of list.
   PRINT (Title$);
   FOR I% = 1 TO (A% - 1)   ' add leading blanks
      PRINT "    ";
   NEXT I%
   FOR I% = A% TO B%
      PRINT SortList$(I%); "   ";
   NEXT I%
   PRINT
END SUB   ' Display1

SUB Display2 (Title$, SortList$(), A%, B%, Pivot%)
   ' Display list during swapping, showing separator
   ' between low and high element values.
   PRINT (Title$);
   FOR I% = 1 TO (A% - 1)   ' add leading blanks
      PRINT "    ";
   NEXT I%
   FOR I% = A% TO (Pivot% - 1)
      PRINT SortList$(I%); "   ";
   NEXT I%
   PRINT SortList$(Pivot%); "| ";
   FOR I% = (Pivot% + 1) TO B%
      PRINT SortList$(I%); "   ";
   NEXT I%
   PRINT
END SUB   ' Display2

SUB QuickSort (SortList$(), First%, Last%)
   ' Sort the list of numeric values named SortList$
   ' from index First% to index Last% using quicksort.
   ' This is a recursive procedure.
   IF First% < Last% THEN   ' more than 1 element in list
      CALL Separate (SortList$(), Pivot%, First%, Last%)
      PRINT   ' added to format the output
```

```
         CALL QuickSort (SortList$(), First%, Pivot% - 1)
         CALL QuickSort (SortList$(), Pivot% + 1, Last%)
      END IF
   END SUB   ' QuickSort

SUB Separate (SortList$(), P%, F%, L%)
   ' Separate the list into two parts, one with
   ' elements less than PivotValue$ and the other
   ' with elements greater than or equal to
   ' PivotValue$. Change several parameter variable
   ' names to shorten some long statement lines:
   ' F% = First%, L% = Last%, and P% = Pivot%.
   P% = F%   ' make first element the pivot
   PivotValue$ = SortList$(F%)
   A$ = "Before separation:   "
   CALL Display1 (A$, SortList$(), F%, L%)
   FOR New% = (F% + 1) TO L%
      IF SortList$(New%) < PivotValue$ THEN
         P% = P% + 1
         IF New% <> P% THEN   ' different elements
            SWAP SortList$(P%), SortList$(New%)
            A$ = "After element swap:   "
            CALL Display2 (A$, SortList$(), F%, L%, P%)
         ELSE
            A$ = "After test, no swap: "
            CALL Display2 (A$, SortList$(), F%, L%, P%)
         END IF
      END IF
   NEXT New%
   ' Move pivot element to point in list that separates
   ' the smaller elements from the larger elements.
   SWAP SortList$(F%), SortList$(P%)
   A$ = "After moving pivot:   "
   CALL Display1 (A$, SortList$(), F%, L%)
END SUB   ' Separate
```

We show the results produced when a user enters the string of characters CATTLE.

```
Enter a string of up to 15 characters: CATTLE

Before separation:   C  A  T  T  L  E
After test, no swap: C  A| T  T  L  E
After moving pivot:  A  C  T  T  L  E

Before separation:         T  T  L  E
```

```
After element swap:        T  L| T  E
After element swap:        T  L  E| T
After moving pivot:        E  L  T  T

Before separation:         E  L
After moving pivot:        E  L

Final sorted list:    A  C  E  L  T  T
```

As in Fig. 10.3, bold-face style has been added to identify the original pivot element in each case, while the vertical line (produced by subroutine Display2) represents the division between the two partitions. Note how the vertical line moves through the list until the elements have been properly divided. The last step is to swap the values of the original pivot element and the current pivot element.

It is interesting to see how the sorting process is affected when one of the characters in the input string is changed. Here is a second example of output with bold-face style again added.

```
Enter a string of up to 15 characters: WATTLE

Before separation:    W  A  T  T  L  E
After test, no swap:  W  A| T  T  L  E
After test, no swap:  W  A  T| T  L  E
After test, no swap:  W  A  T  T| L  E
After test, no swap:  W  A  T  T  L| E
After test, no swap:  W  A  T  T  L  E|
After moving pivot:   E  A  T  T  L  W

Before separation:    E  A  T  T  L
After test, no swap:  E  A| T  T  L
After moving pivot:   A  E  T  T  L

Before separation:    T  T  L
After element swap:   T  L| T
After moving pivot:   L  T  T

Final sorted list:    A  E  L  T  T  W
```

We now insert subroutine QuickSort into Example Program 10-1 in place of subroutine BubbleSort, producing Example Program 10-5.

```
' Example Program 10-5
' Read a list of numbers from a text file,
' use the quicksort algorithm to sort this list,
' and write the sorted list to a text file.
```

```
CONST FALSE = 0, TRUE = NOT FALSE
N% = 1
DIM SortList(1 TO N%)
CALL OpenInFile ("Name of input file", 1)
CALL OpenOutFile ("Name of output file", 2)
CALL FillArray (SortList(), N%)
PRINT
CALL DisplayArray (SortList(), N%, "Unsorted List")
CALL QuickSort (SortList(), 1, N%)
PRINT
CALL DisplayArray (SortList(), N%, "Sorted List")
CALL WriteArray (SortList(), N%)
PRINT
PRINT "Sorted list is in the output file."
END   ' Main Program

ErrorHandler1:
    ' Set NameOK to false if file does not exist.
    IF ERR = 53 THEN
       PRINT "File does not exist - try again"
       NameOK = FALSE
       RESUME NEXT
    ELSE   ' unexpected error, halt the program
       ON ERROR GOTO 0
    END IF

ErrorHandler2:
    ' Set OverWrite to true if file does not exist.
    IF ERR = 53 THEN   ' no existing file
       OverWrite = TRUE
       RESUME NEXT
    ELSE   ' unexpected error, halt the program
       ON ERROR GOTO 0
    END IF

SUB CheckAnswer (Prompt$, Flag)
    ' Display prompt, get answer, and set flag
    ' to TRUE or FALSE if answer is YES or NO.
    ' Otherwise, prompt for answer again.
    ' Module defines constants TRUE and FALSE.
    DO
       PRINT Prompt$;
       INPUT Ans$
       Ans$ = UCASE$(LEFT$(Ans$, 1))
       SELECT CASE Ans$
```

```
         CASE "Y"
            Flag = TRUE
         CASE "N"
            Flag = FALSE
         CASE ELSE
            PRINT "Please answer Y or N"
         END SELECT
      LOOP UNTIL Ans$ = "Y" OR Ans$ = "N"
   END SUB   ' CheckAnswer


   SUB OpenInFile (Prompt$, N)
      ' Open an existing file for reading.
      ' If file does not exist or is empty,
      ' ask user to enter name again.
      SHARED NameOK
      ON ERROR GOTO ErrorHandler1
      DO
      ' Check if the file exists.
         DO
            NameOK = TRUE
            PRINT Prompt$;
            INPUT FileName$
            OPEN FileName$ FOR INPUT AS #N
         LOOP UNTIL NameOK = TRUE
         ' Check if the file contains data.
         IF EOF(N) THEN
            PRINT "This file is empty,";
            PRINT " please try again."
            CLOSE #N
            NameOK = FALSE
         END IF
      LOOP UNTIL NameOK = TRUE
   END SUB   ' OpenInFile
   SUB OpenOutFile (Prompt$, N)
      ' Open a file for writing.
      ' If file already exists, ask user
      ' if it is OK to overwrite it.
      SHARED OverWrite
      ON ERROR GOTO ErrorHandler2
      DO
         NameOK = FALSE
         OverWrite = FALSE
         PRINT Prompt$;
         INPUT FileName$
```

```
      ' Open for input to see if file exists
      OPEN FileName$ FOR INPUT AS #N
      ' ErrorHandler2 is called if file does not exist
      ' and returns flag OverWrite as TRUE
      CLOSE #N
      IF OverWrite = TRUE THEN
         OPEN FileName$ FOR OUTPUT AS #N
         NameOK = TRUE
      ELSE
         CheckAnswer "Overwrite this file", OverWrite
         IF OverWrite = TRUE THEN
            OPEN FileName$ FOR OUTPUT AS #N
            NameOK = TRUE
         END IF
      END IF
   LOOP UNTIL NameOK = TRUE
END SUB   ' OpenOutFile


SUB QuickSort (SortList(), First%, Last%)
   ' Sort the list of numeric values named SortList from
   ' index First% to index Last% using quicksort.
   ' This is a recursive procedure.
   IF First% < Last% THEN   ' more than one element in
list
      CALL Separate (SortList(), Pivot%, First%, Last%)
      CALL QuickSort (SortList(), First%, Pivot% - 1)
      CALL QuickSort (SortList(), Pivot% + 1, Last%)
   END IF
END SUB   ' QuickSort


SUB Separate (SortList(), Pivot%, First%, Last%)
   ' Separate the list into two parts, one with
   ' elements less than PivotValue and the other
   ' with elements greater than or equal to PivotValue.
   Pivot% = First%   ' make first element the pivot
   PivotValue = SortList(First%)
   FOR New% = (First% + 1) TO Last%
      IF SortList(New%) < PivotValue THEN
         Pivot% = Pivot% + 1
         IF New% <> Pivot% THEN   ' different elements
            SWAP SortList(Pivot%), SortList(New%)
         END IF
      END IF
   NEXT New%
   ' Move pivot element to point in list that separates
```

```
     ' the smaller elements from the larger elements.
     SWAP SortList(First%), SortList(Pivot%)
END SUB   ' Separate

SUB DisplayArray (SortList(), N%, Title$)
   ' Display a short, single-line array of N real
   ' numbers on the screen, with an appropriate title.
   PRINT Title$
   FOR I% = 1 TO N%
      PRINT USING "######"; SortList(I%);
   NEXT I%
   PRINT
END SUB   ' DisplayArray


SUB FillArray (SortList(), Count%)
   ' Read a list of numbers from a text file
   ' and assign them to an array.
   ' First count the items.
   Count% = 0
   DO WHILE NOT EOF(1)
      LINE INPUT #1, Dummy$
      Count% = Count% + 1
   LOOP
   ' Then redimension and fill array.
   REDIM SortList(Count%)
   SEEK #1, 1   ' move to start of file
   FOR I% = 1 TO Count%
      INPUT #1, SortList(I%)
   NEXT I%
END SUB   ' FillArray


SUB WriteArray (SortList(), N%)
   ' Write an array of N numbers to a text file.
   FOR I% = 1 TO N%
      PRINT #2, SortList(I%)
   NEXT I%
   CLOSE #2
END SUB   ' WriteArray
```

We have also deleted the calls in subroutine QuickSort that display intermediate results. The program outline is unchanged. Example Program 10-5 produces the same results as Example Program 10-1.

10.6 TIMING PROGRAM SEGMENTS

One of the important properties of sorting algorithms is the speed with which they can sort various kinds of lists. We claim that the quicksort algorithm is a faster sorting technique than the bubble-sort algorithm. To substantiate this claim, we need a method for measuring the execution time of a sorting routine in a program.

We use the standard function TIMER that returns the number of seconds elapsed since midnight. We then insert a statement like

```
StartTime = TIMER
```

at the beginning of the program section to be timed and a statement like

```
StopTime = TIMER
```

at the end of the section. The execution time for that section is given by

```
ExecutionTime = StopTime - StartTime
```

As an example, we made timing measurements while sorting an array of 1000 random integers using different sorting methods. The quicksort algorithm took 0.54 seconds while the bubble-sort algorithm took 51.68 seconds on our particular computer. When sorting long lists, there is a substantial time advantage if the quicksort algorithm is used instead of the bubble-sort algorithm.

Summary of Important Points

- The bubble-sort algorithm is a relatively simple but not very efficient sorting algorithm.
- A third, temporary variable must be declared when using assignment statements to interchange two values.
- It is much easier and quicker to sort a list in memory than to sort a list on a disk file.
- It is not possible to sort a text file directly.
- Comparison of two strings is done character by character, based on the ASCII values of the characters.
- In a recursive function, the value of a one function call often cannot be calculated until the value of another function call is known.
- When using a recursive function, there must always be one nonrecursive value of the function for recursion to work properly.
- Recursion should be used only if it is clearly the best way to solve a problem.
- It makes little difference which element in a list is chosen as the pivot element for quicksort.
- Partitioning a list during quicksort places the pivot element in its proper position in the final, sorted list.

Common Errors

- Modifying the wrong statement when changing the bubble-sort algorithm from an ascending sort to a descending sort.
- Using assignment statements to interchange the values of two variables without using a third variable.
- Attempting to sort a text file directly on the disk.
- Writing a long text file to an array for further sorting when there is insufficient memory to hold the array. One solution is to convert the text file to a random-access file and sort the file directly on the disk.
- Comparing two strings representing numeric values rather than comparing the numeric values themselves. Note that "+12.7" is less than "12.3" but +12.7 is greater than 12.3.
- Writing a recursive function that does not include at least one nonrecursive value of the function, thus overflowing the stack and crashing the program.
- Using a recursive procedure when the problem can be solved just as easily (and probably more quickly) using an iterative procedure.
- Using the bubble-sort algorithm, instead of a faster algorithm like quicksort, to sort a long list.
- Placing statements to start and stop timing at the wrong places in a program so that extraneous statements are included in the timed block.

Self-Test Questions

1. Is the bubble-sort algorithm considered to be a fast sorting algorithm? Explain your answer.
2. What kind of change must be made in the BubbleSort subroutine to produce a descending sort rather than an ascending sort?
3. Can a partially filled array be sorted by
   (a) the bubble-sort algorithm;
   (b) the quicksort algorithm?
4. Is the string "ABCEF" larger or smaller than the string "ABCDF"?
5. Name one or more advantages of the quicksort algorithm.
6. Name one or more advantages of the bubble-sort algorithm.
7. (a) Where does a recursive program store its intermediate results?
   (b) What limitation, if any, does this storage requirement place on a recursive program?
8. (a) What QuickBASIC function can be used to time the execution of a program?
   (b) What value does this function return?

Practice Programs

1. Example Program 10-1 uses the bubble-sort algorithm to sort a list into ascending order. Rewrite subroutine BubbleSort so that it sorts in either ascending or descending order. You

should ask the user which kind of sort to make and pass an appropriate parameter to the sub-routine. This parameter should have a value of "A" for an ascending sort or a value of "D" for a descending sort. Test your program by sorting the file UNSORTED.NUM into a new file ASCEND.NUM for ascending order, and another new file DESCEND.NUM for descending order. Hand in listings of the two new files.

2. Modify the QuickSort subroutine for either ascending or descending sorts, as described in Practice Program 1. Test your modified subroutine in the same manner, using the same input file.

3. The bubble-sort algorithm scans through an entire list, comparing every pair of contiguous elements in the list. The first scan positions the largest element at the right end of the list. This means that the next scan needs to cover only the first (N - 2) pairs of elements, not (N - 1) pairs. Rewrite subroutine BubbleSort to take advantage of this fact. Your FOR statement might look like

```
FOR I = 1 TO ScanLimit
```

where ScanLimit starts at (N - 1) and is decreased by one after each scan. Test your program by sorting the file UNSORTED.NAM into the file SORTED.NAM.

4. Compare the sorting times for the bubble-sort and quicksort algorithms. Use the timing tech-nique discussed in Section 10.6. Use the text file LARGE.NUM for your comparison and display the sorting times with appropriate labels. If the times turn out to be excessively long, reduce the length of the input file. Be sure to write your output to a file other than LARGE.NUM.

5. The text file LARGE.NAM contains about 500 ten-letter strings. Sort this file and create a random-access file named LARGE.DAT, containing the strings in sorted order.

6. Practice Program 7 in Chapter 9 refers to a random-access file named PROSPECT.DAT. Sort this file using the sorting algorithm of your choice. First, sort the file in descending order by zip code and display the sorted results. Second, sort the file in ascending order by last name and display the sorted results.

11

SEARCH ALGORITHMS
AND DATA FILES

11.1 INTRODUCTION

Another important technique in programming is searching, looking for a particular value in a list or a file. We discuss two algorithms, the sequential search algorithm and the binary search algorithm. We give examples of searching a file and searching an array. We distinguish between searching an unsorted list and searching a sorted list.

Storing information in and retrieving information from data files is a major computer application. We introduce the concept of indexed data files and design an example program that shows how these files can be searched.

11.2 SEQUENTIAL SEARCH OF AN UNSORTED LIST

If a list has been created by adding items to it from time to time, it is usually not in sorted order. Probably the best and simplest way to search such a list is to use the *sequential search algorithm.*

As the name implies, a sequential search means to go through the list, examining each item, until the desired item is found or the end of the list is reached. Starting at the beginning of the list, we read each name in sequence and compare it to a target name. If the two names are equal, we report success. If the target name is not equal to any name in the list, we report failure. **A sequential search can take a long time if the list is long and the desired name is near the end.**

Our example program opens a text file containing names and asks the user for a target name. The file is searched sequentially until a match is found or the end of the file is reached. Here is an outline of the program.

> Ask user for input file name.
> Open the text file.
> Start outer loop
> > Ask user for target name.
> > Exit loop if target is Q or null.
> > Do until end-of-file or flag is set
> > > Read name from file.
> > > Set flag if name matches target.
> > Loop back
> > Display results.
> > Reset file to the beginning.
> Loop back

Here is the program itself.

```
' Example Program 11-1
' Ask user for a target name and search
' for that name in a sequential text file.
' Stop when user types Q or presses Enter.

DEFINT A-Z
CONST FALSE = 0, TRUE = NOT FALSE

CALL OpenInFile ("Name of data file", 1)
PRINT
DO
    PRINT "Target name (press Q or Enter to stop)? ";
    LINE INPUT Target$
    IF Target$ = "" OR UCASE$(Target$) = "Q" THEN EXIT DO
    Found = FALSE
    DO UNTIL EOF(1) OR Found = TRUE
        LINE INPUT #1, Name$
        IF UCASE$(Name$) = UCASE$(Target$) THEN
            Found = TRUE
        END IF
    LOOP
    IF Found = TRUE THEN
```

```
            PRINT Target$; " is in the file."
        ELSE
            PRINT Target$; " is not in the file."
        END IF
        PRINT
        SEEK #1, 1
    LOOP
END   ' Main Program


ErrorHandler1:
    ' Set NameOK to false if file does not exist.
    IF ERR = 53 THEN
        PRINT "File does not exist, please try again"
        NameOK = FALSE
        RESUME NEXT
    ELSE   ' unexpected error, halt the program
        ON ERROR GOTO 0
    END IF


SUB OpenInFile (Prompt$, N)
    ' Open an existing file for reading.
    ' If file does not exist or is empty,
    ' ask user to enter name again.
    SHARED NameOK
    ON ERROR GOTO ErrorHandler1
    DO
    ' Check if the file exists.
        DO
            NameOK = TRUE
            PRINT Prompt$;
            INPUT FileName$
            OPEN FileName$ FOR INPUT AS #N
        LOOP UNTIL NameOK = TRUE
        ' Check if the file contains data.
        IF EOF(N) THEN
            PRINT "This file is empty,";
            PRINT " please try again."
            CLOSE #N
            NameOK = FALSE
        END IF
    LOOP UNTIL NameOK = TRUE
END SUB   ' OpenInFile
```

As before, we make use of the OpenInFile procedure written for a previous
program. By now you should have started to develop your own library or collection of

procedures or modules. Whenever possible, use an already-developed procedure in new programs that you write. This technique not only reduces the time required to write a program, but also reduces debugging time because previously developed library units tend to have fewer errors than does newly written code.

This program produces the following output.

```
Name of input file? unsorted.nam

Target name (press Q or Enter to stop)? JOHN
JOHN is in the list.

Target name (press Q or Enter to stop)? Bart
Bart is in the list.

Target name (press Q or Enter to stop)? Bill
Bill is not in the list.

Target name (press Q or Enter to stop)? q
```

Note that the program, as written, is insensitive to case. All letter characters in names are changed to uppercase before comparisons are made.

11.3 BINARY SEARCH OF A SORTED LIST

When the items in a list are in sorted order, we can use another, faster searching technique called the *binary search algorithm*. This method works by repeatedly dividing the list in half and discarding one half, resulting in successively shorter lists to search.

We assume that the list is sorted with the highest-valued item at the bottom of the list. This would be true of a list of names in alphabetic order. If the list is an array, the top of the list has the smallest index and the bottom has the largest index. The user is asked to specify a target name.

We define three index values: a top index, a midpoint index, and a bottom index. When we start, the top index is the index of the first name in the list. This index value is usually one. The bottom index is the index of the last name in the list. The midpoint index (an integer value) is approximately halfway between the top and bottom indices.

We designate the name with the midpoint index as the midpoint name. We compare the target name to the midpoint name. If the target name equals the midpoint name, we have completed a successful search. The function is assigned the value of the midpoint index.

If the target name is less than the midpoint name, we know that any further search can be confined to the top half of the list. We leave the top index unchanged but designate a new bottom index equal to the midpoint index minus one. In effect, the length of the list to be searched has been cut in half, as shown in Fig. 11.1.

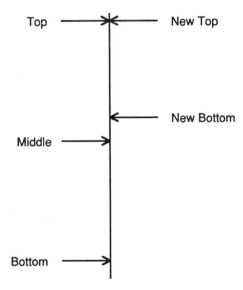

Figure 11.1   Target name is in top half of list.

Conversely, if the target name is greater than the midpoint name, we know that any further search can be confined to the bottom half of the list. We leave the bottom index unchanged and designate a new top index equal to the midpoint index plus one. Fig. 11.2 shows the result.

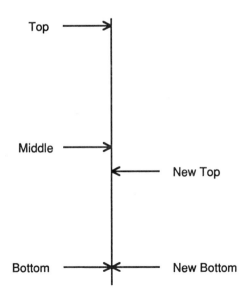

Figure 11.2   Target name is in bottom half of list.

The search is considered unsuccessful when the top and bottom indices cross; that is, when the top index value is greater than the bottom index value. This result (an unsuccessful search) is denoted by assigning a value of zero to the function. Note that the use of a zero value to denote an unsuccessful search means that the range of index values cannot include zero. Here is our binary search function.

```
FUNCTION Search (List$(), N, Target
    ' Search an array List$ containing N names,
    ' using the binary search algorithm.
    ' Variable Target$ contains the target name.

    Top = 1
    Bottom = N
    Found = FALSE
    DO
        Mid = (Top + Bottom) \ 2   ' integer division
        IF UCASE$(Target$) = UCASE$(List$(Mid)) THEN
            Found = TRUE
        ELSEIF UCASE$(Target$) > UCASE$(List$(Mid)) THEN
            Top = Mid + 1
        ELSE   ' Target$ < UCASE$(List$(Mid))
            Bottom = Mid - 1
        END IF
    LOOP UNTIL Found = TRUE OR Bottom < Top
    IF Found = TRUE THEN
        Search = Mid
    ELSE
        Search = 0
    END IF
END FUNCTION   ' Search
```

We now incorporate this function into an example program, using the following outline.

Ask user for input file name.

Open the text file.

Count number of names in the file.

Redimension and fill the array.

Start loop

    Ask user for target name.

    Exit loop if target is Q or null.

    Use binary search to look for target name

    in array, return zero if target not found.

Display results of the search.

Loop back

A list of names in the specified text file is counted and array List$ is redimensioned to the proper size. Names are then read from the file and assigned to the array.

The user is asked to specify a target name. If the letter Q or a null string is entered, the program stops. A binary search of the list is made and the search results are displayed.

```
' Example Program 11-2
' Read a list of names from a text file and
' write them to an array. Use the binary search
' algorithm to find a target name in the array.

DEFINT A-Z
CONST FALSE = 0, TRUE = NOT FALSE
DECLARE FUNCTION Search (NameList$(), N, Target$)

CALL OpenInFile ("Name of input file", 1)
PRINT
N = 1   ' dummy value
DIM NameList$(1 TO N)   ' dynamic array
CALL FillArray (List$(), N)
' N returns with size of redimensioned array
DO
    PRINT "Target name (press Q or Enter to stop)? ";
    LINE INPUT Target$
    IF Target$ = "" OR UCASE$(Target$) = "Q" THEN EXIT DO
    Result = Search(NameList$(), N, Target$)
    IF Result > 0 THEN
       PRINT Target$; " is in the list."
    ELSE
       PRINT Target$; " is not in the list."
    END IF
    PRINT
LOOP
END   ' Main Program


ErrorHandler1:
    ' Set NameOK to false if file does not exist.
    IF ERR = 53 THEN
       PRINT "File does not exist, please try again"
       NameOK = FALSE
       RESUME NEXT
```

```
      ELSE   ' unexpected error, halt the program
         ON ERROR GOTO 0
      END IF

SUB FillArray (List$(), Count)
   ' Read a list of names from a text file
   ' and assign them to an array.
   ' First count the items.
   Count = 0
   DO WHILE NOT EOF(1)
      LINE INPUT #1, Dummy$
      Count = Count + 1
   LOOP
   ' Then redimension and fill array.
   REDIM List$(Count)
   SEEK #1, 1  ' move to start of file
   FOR I = 1 TO Count
      INPUT #1, List$(I)
   NEXT I
END SUB   ' FillArray

SUB OpenInFile (Prompt$, N)
   ' Open an existing file for reading.
   ' If file does not exist or is empty,
   ' ask user to enter name again.
   SHARED NameOK
   ON ERROR GOTO ErrorHandler1
   DO
   ' Check if the file exists.
      DO
         NameOK = TRUE
         PRINT Prompt$;
         INPUT FileName$
         OPEN FileName$ FOR INPUT AS #N
      LOOP UNTIL NameOK = TRUE
      ' Check if the file contains data.
      IF EOF(N) THEN
         PRINT "This file is empty,";
         PRINT " please try again."
         CLOSE #N
         NameOK = FALSE
      END IF
   LOOP UNTIL NameOK = TRUE
END SUB   ' OpenInFile
```

```
FUNCTION Search (List$(), N, Target$)
   ' Search an array List$ containing N names,
   ' using the binary search algorithm.
   ' Variable Target$ contains the target name.
   Top = 1
   Bottom = N
   Found = FALSE
   DO
      Mid = (Top + Bottom) \ 2   ' integer division
      IF UCASE$(Target$) = UCASE$(List$(Mid)) THEN
         Found = TRUE
      ELSEIF UCASE$(Target$) > UCASE$(List$(Mid)) THEN
         Top = Mid + 1
      ELSE   ' Target$ < UCASE$(List$(Mid))
         Bottom = Mid - 1
      END IF
   LOOP UNTIL Found = TRUE OR Bottom < Top
   IF Found = TRUE THEN
      Search = Mid
   ELSE
      Search = 0
   END IF
END FUNCTION   ' Search
```

The following output is produced by this program.

```
Name of input file? sorted.nam

Target name (press Q or Enter to stop)? JOHN
JOHN is in the list.

Target name (press Q or Enter to stop)? Bart
Bart is in the list.

Target name (press Q or Enter to stop)? Bill
Bill is not in the list.

Target name (press Q or Enter to stop)? q
```

A random-access file can be searched directly using the binary search algorithm, provided that the components of the file are in sorted order. The method is essentially the same as that used for searching an array, except that the component or file record number is used instead of the array element index. We ask you to use this technique in Practice Program 1 at the end of the chapter.

A binary search has the advantage of being much faster than a sequential search, especially for a long list. It has the disadvantage of requiring a sorted list. In the problems at the end of the chapter, we suggest that you compare the times required for these two searching methods.

11.4 FILE CONVERSIONS

Many professionals who know BASIC do not write large programs. They use their computers for running application programs such as electronic spreadsheets and database managers. They sometimes find that the file produced by one application cannot be read by another application.

One solution to that problem is to write your own QuickBASIC program to convert the format of a file. **If the file is a text file containing only ASCII characters, such a conversion is easy to accomplish.**

Converting Text Files

Our first example program demonstrates the conversion of a file of information, commonly called a *data file*. This file consists of names (data items) separated from each other by blank spaces. The names themselves do not contain any spaces. Thus the only role of spaces is to serve as data item delimiters or separators. The data items are contained in text lines that end with the usual end-of-line marker (a pair of characters, the carriage return and the line feed).

This data file will be read by an application program requiring that every data item be enclosed in quotation marks and that the items be separated from each other by commas. Spaces are not allowed. An end-of-line marker is expected at the end of each line. Here is a line from the original data file.

```
JOHN WILLIAM MARY PETER SUSAN JENNIFER
```

Here is how the line must look for the application program.

```
"JOHN","WILLIAM","MARY","PETER","SUSAN","JENNIFER"
```

As you can imagine, it would be a time-consuming job to convert such a data file by hand. We will write a QuickBASIC program to make the conversion.

Both an input file and an output file are opened. A line of text is read from the input file, its format is changed, and it is written on the output file. The process continues until the end of the input file is reached.

The conversion is accomplished by scanning a line of text, using the INSTR function to find the location of the first space. The characters to the left of the space are enclosed in quotation marks. Note the use of the string variable Quote$ to hold a double quotation mark. The characters to the right of the space are the remainder of the old line of text, and this remainder line is analyzed again as the program searches for the next space. A new line of text is gradually constructed and when finished, is written on the output file. The process continues until the entire input file has been read. Here is the conversion program.

```
' Example Program 11-3
' Convert the format of a text data file.
' Input file strings are separated by spaces.
' Output strings are in quotes and separated by commas.

CONST FALSE = 0, TRUE = NOT FALSE
Quote$ = CHR$(34)
CALL OpenInFile ("Input file", 1)
CALL OpenOutFile ("Output file", 2)
DO UNTIL EOF(1)                    ' read a line
   LINE INPUT #1, Old$
   New$ = ""
   DO                              ' scan old line
      X = INSTR(Old$, " ")   ' look for a space
      IF X = 0 THEN
         New$ = New$ + Quote$ + Old$ + Quote$
      ELSE
         Temp$ = LEFT$(Old$, X - 1)
         Old$ = RIGHT$(Old$, LEN(Old$) - X)
         New$ = New$ + Quote$ + Temp$ + Quote$ + ","
      END IF
   LOOP UNTIL X = 0
   PRINT #2, New$                 ' write modified line
LOOP
CLOSE #1, #2
PRINT "The output file has been written."
END   ' Main Program


ErrorHandler1:
   ' Set NameOK to false if file does not exist.
   IF ERR = 53 THEN
      PRINT "File does not exist, please try again"
      NameOK = FALSE
      RESUME NEXT
   ELSE   ' unexpected error
      ON ERROR GOTO 0
   END IF
```

```
ErrorHandler2:
   ' Set OverWrite to true if file does not exist.
   IF ERR = 53 THEN  ' no existing file
      OverWrite = TRUE
      RESUME NEXT
   ELSE  ' unexpected error
      ON ERROR GOTO 0
   END IF

SUB CheckAnswer (Prompt$, Flag)
   ' Display prompt, get answer, and set flag
   ' to TRUE or FALSE if answer is YES or NO.
   ' Otherwise, prompt for answer again.
   ' Module defines constants TRUE and FALSE.
   PRINT Prompt$;
   INPUT Ans$
   DO
      Ans$ = UCASE$(LEFT$(Ans$, 1))
      SELECT CASE Ans$
         CASE "Y"
            Flag = TRUE
         CASE "N"
            Flag = FALSE
         CASE ELSE
            PRINT "Please answer Y or N"
      END SELECT
   LOOP UNTIL Ans$ = "Y" OR Ans$ = "N"
END SUB   ' CheckAnswer

SUB OpenInFile (Prompt$, N)
   ' Open an existing file for reading.
   ' If file does not exist, ask user
   ' to enter name again.
   SHARED NameOK
   ON ERROR GOTO ErrorHandler1
   DO
      ' Check if the file exists.
      DO
         NameOK = TRUE
         PRINT Prompt$;
         INPUT FileName$
         OPEN FileName$ FOR INPUT AS #N
      LOOP UNTIL NameOK = TRUE
```

```
            ' Check if the file contains data.
          IF EOF(N) THEN
             PRINT "File is empty,";
             PRINT " please try again."
             CLOSE #N
             NameOK = FALSE
          END IF
       LOOP UNTIL NameOK = TRUE
    END SUB   ' OpenInFile


    SUB OpenOutFile (Prompt$, N)
       ' Open a file for writing.
       ' If file already exists, ask user
       ' if it is OK to overwrite it.
       SHARED OverWrite
       ON ERROR GOTO ErrorHandler2
       DO
          NameOK = FALSE
          OverWrite = FALSE
          PRINT Prompt$;
          INPUT FileName$
          ' Open for input to see if file exists
          OPEN FileName$ FOR INPUT AS #N
          ' ErrorHandler2 is called if file does not exist
          ' and returns flag OverWrite as TRUE
          CLOSE #N
          IF OverWrite = TRUE THEN
             OPEN FileName$ FOR OUTPUT AS #N
             NameOK = TRUE
          ELSE
             CALL CheckAnswer ("Overwrite file", OverWrite)
             IF OverWrite = TRUE THEN
                OPEN FileName$ FOR OUTPUT AS #N
                NameOK = TRUE
             END IF
          END IF
       LOOP UNTIL NameOK = TRUE
    END SUB    ' OpenOutFile
```

Try running this program using the input file NAMES.DAT in directory CH11 on the example program disk. Examine the output file and note that each line is converted according to specifications.

Converting to Random-Access Format

Another example program converts a text file to a random-access file. This is a good example of a custom program that has to be written for a specific random-access file structure. Once again, a QuickBASIC program is often the simplest way to accomplish the conversion task.

The input text file, named EMPLOYEE.TXT, is in directory CH11 of the example program disk. It contains three lines of information on company employees: name, age, and salary. We wish to write an output file that is a random-access file with the following record structure.

```
TYPE Person
    FullName AS STRING * 80
    Age AS INTEGER
    Salary AS SINGLE
END TYPE
```

As we mentioned before, the program is designed for this specific task and the preceding record structure is an integral part of the program.

```
' Example Program 11-4
' Convert a text data file to a random-access
' file. Each record in the text file consists
' of three separate lines.

CONST FALSE = 0, TRUE = NOT FALSE
TYPE Person
    FullName AS STRING * 80
    Age AS INTEGER
    Salary AS SINGLE
END TYPE
DIM Employee AS Person

CALL OpenInFile ("Input text file", 1)
PRINT "Output random-access file";
INPUT FileName$
OPEN FileName$ FOR RANDOM AS #2 LEN = LEN(Employee)
RecNum = 1
DO UNTIL EOF(1)
    LINE INPUT #1, InName$
    INPUT #1, InAge
    INPUT #1, InSalary
    Employee.FullName = InName$
    Employee.Age = InAge
    Employee.Salary = InSalary
```

```
      PUT #2, RecNum, Employee
      RecNum = RecNum + 1
   LOOP
   CLOSE #1, #2
   PRINT "File "; FileName$; " written and closed."
   END  '  Main Program


ErrorHandler1:
      ' Set NameOK to false if file does not exist.
      IF ERR = 53 THEN
         PRINT "File does not exist, please try again"
         NameOK = FALSE
         RESUME NEXT
      ELSE  ' unexpected error
         ON ERROR GOTO 0
      END IF


SUB OpenInFile (Prompt$, N)
      ' Open an existing file for reading.
      ' If file does not exist, ask user
      ' to enter name again.
      SHARED NameOK
      ON ERROR GOTO ErrorHandler1
      DO
         ' Check if the file exists.
         DO
            NameOK = TRUE
            PRINT Prompt$;
            INPUT FileName$
            OPEN FileName$ FOR INPUT AS #N
         LOOP UNTIL NameOK = TRUE
         ' Check if the file contains data.
         IF EOF(N) THEN
            PRINT "File is empty,";
            PRINT " please try again."
            CLOSE #N
            NameOK = FALSE
         END IF
      LOOP UNTIL NameOK = TRUE
   END SUB   ' OpenInFile
```

The conversion process is straightforward. Three lines are read from the input file, assigned to the proper fields of the record structure, and a record is written on the output file. Once again, we do not show program output but urge you to run the program yourself. A utility program named READ4.BAS on the example program disk can be used to read the output file and verify that a successful conversion has been accomplished.

11.5 INDEXED DATA FILES

If a random-access data file is long and has large file records, it can take an appreciable amount of time to sort the file each time a record is added or deleted. In addition, the file can be sorted on only one of the fields in the file record. For example, a data file might contain both a part name and a part number in each record. If it is sorted by part name, a binary search cannot be used to find a specific part number.

As an example, we consider a system designed to search for information on parts used by a small business. The computer program written to meet this need must access a file of inventory information. The inventory file is a random-access file of user-defined records with each record having the following structure.

```
TYPE Part
    PartNumber AS STRING * 6
    Description AS STRING * 50
    Quantity AS INTEGER
    UnitPrice AS SINGLE
    BinNumber AS STRING * 4
    OrderLevel AS INTEGER
    OrderQuant AS INTEGER
    VendorName AS STRING * 30
    VendorPhone AS STRING * 12
END TYPE
```

The part number is used as the primary identifier of a particular part. It is stored in a variable of type string because it is never used in arithmetic operations. To find a specified part, we need to create an *index file* that shows which record contains the information on a particular part. In this application, the part number field is called the *key field*.

Using an Index File

To understand the concept and use of an index file, remember that one of the fastest ways to search a file is a binary search but that type of search only works if the file is in sorted order. We could sort our inventory file on any field (for example, part number) but each time we added a new part, we would have to sort the file again. This can be a slow process if the file is long and the record size is large.

As an alternative, we can create another file called an index file that has small records containing only the part number and the record number for that part. This file can be sorted more quickly than the inventory file. When we search the index file for a part number, we find the inventory file record number for that particular part. The index file gets its name because it is similar to an index in a book: It tells us which record in the inventory file contains the desired information.

The index file is also a random-access file of records, with each record having the following structure.

```
TYPE Index1
    PartNumber AS STRING * 6
    RecNum AS INTEGER
END TYPE
```

An index record contains the record number of an inventory file record that has information on a particular part, identified by part number. The part numbers are in sorted order but not the record numbers. An advantage of this design is that there can be more than one index file, each sorted on a different field, for a given inventory file. In addition to an index file that is sorted by part number, we can have another index file containing the part description and record number, sorted by part description. We can search this second index file for a particular part description and find the corresponding record number in the inventory file. In fact, we can have as many index files as there are fields in the inventory file record.

A Program Outline

We design our program as a menu-driven program. We have the usual main program and several procedures. We have included only four commands in our menu and execute each command (except the Quit command) from a separate subroutine. Other commands can be added and will be discussed in the practice programs at the end of the chapter. Here is an outline of the main program.

> Open the inventory file.
> Open the index file.
> Start loop
> > Display the command menu.
> > Select a command: Quit, Edit, List, or Search.
> > Branch to appropriate subprogram.
> Loop until selected command is Quit.
> Close all files.

The Edit command allows a user to change any field (except the part number) in a record specified by its record number. If you do not know the record number, you can use the Search command to find the record number corresponding to a given part number. We do not allow the part number field to be edited because a part number change would require resorting the index file, a procedure we wish to avoid in our simple program. We do include a practice program at the end of the chapter that requires resorting the index file. Here is an outline of the Edit command.

> Get record number.
>
> Read record from inventory file.
>
> Start loop
>
>> Display old field value.
>>
>> Ask if new field value is wanted.
>
> Loop until all record fields have been displayed.
>
> Write new record to inventory file.
>
> Return to menu.

The List command displays the contents of the entire inventory file. Each record is read and displayed on the screen.

> While not at end of inventory file
>
>> Read record from inventory file.
>>
>> Display record number and record fields.
>
> Loop back.
>
> Return to menu.

The Search command uses a binary search function to search in the index file for the record number corresponding to a specified part number. If the record exists, it is read and displayed.

> Get part number.
>
> Search index file for record number.
>
> If record exists
>
>> Read record from inventory file.
>>
>> Display record number and record fields.
>
> Else
>
>> Display failure message.
>
> Return to menu.

The Main Program

In addition to the command procedures, we call three other subroutines from the main program. One subroutine opens the inventory file and the index file. Another displays the command menu and prompts the user to select a command number. The third subroutine calls the appropriate command procedure for the selected command number.

Error-trapping routines are used when opening files. This program assumes that both files have already been created and loaded with information. If either the inventory file or index file does not exist, the user is given an opportunity to try again because the entered file name may have been misspelled.

After opening both files, the subroutine DisplayMenu is called and the menu is displayed. The subroutine SelectCommand is used to call the selected command procedure. If an invalid command is entered, an error message is printed and the menu is displayed again.

This program is so long that it is more understandable if presented in sections. We now show the main program and the subroutines that it calls directly.

```
' Example Program 11-5
' Inventory record file with index.

DEFINT A-Z
CONST FALSE = 0, TRUE = NOT FALSE
CONST INDENT$ = "

TYPE PartType
    PartNumber AS STRING * 6
    Description AS STRING * 50
    Quantity AS INTEGER
    UnitPrice AS SINGLE
    BinNumber AS STRING * 4
    OrderLevel AS INTEGER
    OrderQuant AS INTEGER
    VendorName AS STRING * 30
    VendorPhone AS STRING * 12
END TYPE


TYPE Index1Type
    PartNumber AS STRING * 6
    RecNum AS INTEGER
END TYPE


DECLARE FUNCTION Found (Target$)
DIM SHARED Part AS PartType
DIM SHARED Index1 AS Index1Type
CLS
CALL (OpenRndFile "Name of data file", 1, LEN(Part))
CALL OpenRndFile ("Name of index file", 2, LEN(Index1))
DO
    CALL DisplayMenu (Command)
    CALL SelectCommand (Command)
LOOP UNTIL Command = 0
CLOSE #1, #2
END   ' Main Program
```

```
SUB DisplayMenu (Command)
   ' Display the command menu.
   CLS
   LOCATE 10, 1
   PRINT INDENT$; " Command Menu"
   PRINT
   PRINT INDENT$; "0.....stop the program"
   PRINT INDENT$; "1.....edit a record"
   PRINT INDENT$; "2.....list all records"
   PRINT INDENT$; "3.....search for a part number"
   PRINT
   PRINT INDENT$; "   Your selection";
   INPUT Command
END SUB   ' DisplayMenu

SUB OpenRndFile (Prompt$, N, Length)
   ' Ask user for file name and open a random-access
   ' file with number N and of record length Length.
   ' Ask user to verify if an empty file is opened.
   DO
      NameOK = TRUE
      PRINT Prompt$;
      INPUT FileName$
      OPEN FileName$ FOR RANDOM AS #N LEN = Length
      IF LOF(N) = 0 THEN
         PRINT "Empty file, is the name correct";
         INPUT Reply$
         IF LEFT$(UCASE$(Reply$), 1) <> "Y" THEN
            PRINT "Please enter the file name again."
            NameOK = FALSE
         END IF
      END IF
   LOOP UNTIL NameOK = TRUE
END SUB   ' OpenRndFile

SUB SelectCommand (Command)
   ' Select the command procedure
   ' for an entered command.
   SELECT CASE Command
   CASE 0
      ' Exit command
   CASE 1
      CALL EditFile
   CASE 2
```

```
           CALL ListFile
      CASE 3
           CALL SearchFile
      CASE ELSE
           PRINT
           PRINT INDENT$; "Enter number between 0 and 3."
           PRINT INDENT$; "Press any key to continue.";
           DO
           LOOP WHILE INKEY$ = ""
      END SELECT
END SUB   ' SelectCommand
```

The statement DEFINT A-Z defines all unspecified variables as integers. Constant declarations are global with constants TRUE, FALSE, and INDENT$ defined throughout the program. The inventory file is designated file #1 while the index file is file #2. Record types are defined for both these files using TYPE statements.

We use the SELECT CASE statement to select a command procedure in subroutine SelectCommand. This design choice allows the subroutine to be expanded easily if more commands are added. Note our use of a dummy loop with INKEY$ to make the program pause so comments can be read. When the user presses any key, the program continues.

Shared Global Variables

You may remember that we discussed shared variables in Chapter 8 and explained that the simple SHARED statement could appear only in a procedure. There is another variation of the SHARED statement, however, that can be used in the main program.

The statement

```
COMMON SHARED Variable1, Variable2,...
```

can be placed anywhere in the module-level code of a program, including the main program. This statement changes all simple variables listed in the statement to *global variables*, which are known throughout the program file or module. The similar statements

```
DIM SHARED Variable AS Type
DIM SHARED Array(Size)
```

are used with record and indexed variables in place of the COMMON SHARED statement.

In this program, the record variables Part and Index1 are declared as shared global variables, thus making them available to all procedures. This program design avoids the necessity of passing these two variables as arguments to all command procedures, but does introduce a greater risk of their values being changed by mistake.

The Edit Command

The Edit command allows the contents of any record to be modified. The user is asked to enter a record number that is checked to make sure it is within the allowed range. Note that the local variable RecNum is specified as a long integer. If a user enters a part number instead of a record number (as we did once while testing the program), the use of a long integer ensures that the program error message is displayed rather than a cryptic system error message. The specified inventory file record is then read.

As mentioned earlier, we do not allow the part number field to be edited because if this field value is changed, the index file must be sorted again. Each of the other fields in the record is displayed and the user is asked either to enter a new value or to press the Enter key to keep the same value. After the entire record has been edited, it is written back on the inventory file.

Note that all new values are entered as string values. If a particular value is to be assigned to a numeric field variable, the VAL function is used to convert the string value to a numeric value. Here is the EditFile subroutine.

```
SUB EditFile
    ' Edit a specified record in the inventory file.
    CLS
    Size = LOF(1) \ LEN(Part)
    DO
        INPUT "Record Number"; RecNum&
        IF RecNum& < 1 OR RecNum& > Size THEN
            PRINT
            PRINT "Record numbers are from 1 to"; Size
            PRINT
        END IF
    LOOP UNTIL RecNum& >= 1 AND RecNum& <= Size
    GET #1, RecNum&, Part
    PRINT
    PRINT "Press Enter to keep current field value."
    PRINT
    PRINT "Part Number: "; Part.PartNumber
    PRINT "The part number cannot be changed."
    PRINT "Description: "; Part.Description
    LINE INPUT "New value? "; Field$
    IF Field$ <> "" THEN Part.Description = Field$
    PRINT "Quantity: "; Part.Quantity
    LINE INPUT "New value? "; Field$
    IF Field$ <> "" THEN Part.Quantity = VAL(Field$)
    PRINT "Unit Price: "; Part.UnitPrice
    LINE INPUT "New value? "; Field$
    IF Field$ <> "" THEN Part.UnitPrice = VAL(Field$)
    PRINT "Bin Number: "; Part.BinNumber
```

```
      LINE INPUT "New value? "; Field$
      IF Field$ <> "" THEN Part.BinNumber = Field$
      PRINT "Reorder Level: "; Part.OrderLevel
      LINE INPUT "New value? "; Field$
      IF Field$ <> "" THEN Part.OrderLevel = VAL(Field$)
      PRINT "Reorder Quantity: "; Part.OrderQuant
      LINE INPUT "New value? "; Field$
      IF Field$ <> "" THEN Part.OrderQuant = VAL(Field$)
      PRINT "Vendor Name: "; Part.VendorName
      LINE INPUT "New value? "; Field$
      IF Field$ <> "" THEN Part.VendorName = Field$
      PRINT "Vendor Phone: "; Part.VendorPhone
      LINE INPUT "New value? "; Field$
      IF Field$ <> "" THEN Part.VendorPhone = Field$
      PUT #1, RecNum&, Part
      PRINT
      PRINT "Press any key to continue...";
      DO
      LOOP WHILE INKEY$ = ""
   END SUB   ' EditFile
```

The number of records is determined by dividing the file length LOF(1) by the record length LEN(Part). The division is integer division. Knowing the number of the last record allows the program to check for an error when the user enters a record number.

This subroutine contains a sequence of almost-identical statement blocks and at first glance looks as though it should be written as a loop. There is enough variation in the statements, however, to make this a difficult task. We believe that the subroutine as written is easier to read and understand.

The List Command

The List command simply reads each record from the inventory file and displays the record number and record fields on the screen. It pauses after displaying each record and continues when any key is pressed. It calls a subroutine named PrintRec to display a record, showing the name of each field and the field value. Here are the PrintRec and ListFile subroutines.

```
   SUB ListFile
      ' Display the entire inventory file.
      CLS
      Size = LOF(2) \ LEN(Index1)
      FOR I = 1 TO Size
         GET #2, I, Index1
         PrintRec Index1.RecNum
         PRINT "Press any key to continue..."
```

```
            DO
            LOOP WHILE INKEY$ = " "
            PRINT
            PRINT
        NEXT I
    END SUB   ' ListFile

    SUB PrintRec (RecNum AS INTEGER)
        ' Display a specified record in the inventory file.
        GET #1, RecNum, Part
        PRINT "Record Number"; RecNum
        PRINT
        PRINT "Part Number:      "; Part.PartNumber
        PRINT "Description:      "; Part.Description
        PRINT "Quantity:        "; Part.Quantity
        PRINT "Unit Price:      ";
        PRINT USING "##.##"; Part.UnitPrice
        PRINT "Bin Number:      "; Part.BinNumber
        PRINT "Reorder Level:   "; Part.OrderLevel
        PRINT "Reorder Quantity:"; Part.OrderQuant
        PRINT "Vendor Name:     "; Part.VendorName
        PRINT "Vendor Phone:    "; Part.VendorPhone
        PRINT
    END SUB   ' PrintRec
```

The number of records in the inventory file is calculated as before. A FOR loop can then be used by the ListFile subroutine to read and display the contents of each record. **Note that the EOF function in QuickBASIC can only be used reliably with sequential text files, so loops that check this function should not be used to read random-access files.**

The PrintRec subroutine uses a PRINT USING statement for displaying the unit price. This statement ensures that the price value is always displayed with two digits after the decimal point.

The Search Command

A major purpose of our program is to provide a fast way to search for a specific inventory record. For this reason, the index file is kept in sorted order and the Search command uses a binary search algorithm to search the file for a specified part number.

The user enters a part number that must contain six digits. The Found function performs a binary search for that number. If the part number is found, the function returns the record number; otherwise, it returns a value of zero. Once a record has been found, it is displayed by the PrintRec subroutine. Here are the Found function and the SearchFile subroutine.

```
FUNCTION Found (Target$)
   ' Search a random-access file for a target name.
   ' Returns record number if name is found;
   ' if not, returns a value of zero.
   Size = LOF(2) \ LEN(Index1)
   Top = 1
   Bottom = Size
   Success = FALSE
   DO
      Mid = (Top + Bottom) \ 2
      IF Mid >= Size THEN
         Success = FALSE
         EXIT DO
      END IF
      GET #2, Mid, Index1
      IF Target$ = Index1.PartNumber THEN
         Success = TRUE
         RecNum = Index1.RecNum
      ELSEIF Target$ > Index1.PartNumber THEN
         Top = Mid + 1
      ELSE  ' Target < Index1.PartNumber
         Bottom = Mid - 1
      END IF
   LOOP UNTIL Success = TRUE OR Bottom < Top
   IF Success = TRUE THEN
      Found = RecNum
   ELSE
      Found = 0
   END IF
END FUNCTION  ' Found


SUB SearchFile
   ' Search the inventory file for a record with
   ' a specified part number and display the record.
   CLS
   DO
      INPUT "Part number to find"; Target$
      IF LEN(Target$) <> 6 THEN
         PRINT
         PRINT "Part number must have six digits."
         PRINT
      END IF
   LOOP UNTIL LEN(Target$) = 6
   RecNum = Found(Target$)
```

```
    IF RecNum = 0 THEN
        PRINT
        PRINT "Part number is not in the file."
        PRINT
    ELSE
        PRINT
        PrintRec (RecNum)
    END IF
    PRINT "Press any key to continue...";
    DO
    LOOP WHILE INKEY$ = ""
END SUB   ' SearchFile
```

The disk of example programs provided with this book includes both an inventory file and an index file that are designed to be used with this program. The inventory file is named PARTS.DAT and the index file is named XPARTS.DAT. We recommend that you run the program with these files. In several of the practice programs, we suggest ways to expand this example program.

As mentioned previously, this program is listed in sections to make it easier to read. It is available in its entirety, however, on the example program disk. You can display it on the screen or print out a listing on a printer.

Summary of Important Points

- A sequential search can take a long time if the list is long and the desired name is near the end.
- A binary search has the advantage of being much faster than a sequential search, especially for a long list. It has the disadvantage of requiring a sorted list.
- It is easy to write a QuickBASIC program that converts a text file into a different format.
- An advantage of the indexed file structure is that there can be more than one index file, each for a different field.
- The EOF function in QuickBASIC can only be used reliably with sequential text files, so loops that check this function should not be used to read random-access files.

Common Errors

- Searching an unsorted list with the binary search algorithm.
- Failing to compensate for differences between uppercase and lowercase characters during a search.
- Using the EOF function to detect the end of a random-access file.

- Adding records to or deleting records from an indexed database file without modifying the index file.

Self-Test Questions

1. Describe a method for searching an unsorted list.

2. Describe a method for searching a sorted list.

3. Is it faster to search a text file by searching the file directly, or by copying the file to an array and then searching the array? Explain your answer.

4. Two files, one a text file and the other a random-access file, contain 100 real numbers. Both files are in numeric order. Each file is to be searched for a particular number. Which searching method would you select to search each file, and why?

5. Given the two files described in Question 4, is it always true that one file can be searched more quickly than the other? Explain your answer.

6. Can the binary search algorithm be used to search a disk file directly? Explain your answer.

7. What is the advantage of using an index file to find a particular item in a data file?

8. What is the reason for sometimes having more than one index file for a given data file?

Practice Programs

1. Ten-letter character strings are used as proprietary code names for different versions of a program being developed by a software firm. Ask the user to specify a code name string and then search for that string in the random-access file LARGE.DAT. The components of this file are 10-character strings and are in sorted order. Report whether the specified string is found, and if so, its record number. Test your program with the strings TEUMSEJSQR and KUICHPWNZX.

2. The text file LARGE.TXT has 10 characters on each line and is in sorted order. Compare the time required to search this file with the time required to search the random-access file LARGE.DAT, described in Practice Program 1. Test your program with the code name strings FLAFNBTKRO and ZSJHYWGVKW. One of these strings is near the beginning of file LARGE.TXT and the other is near the end, so you should get quite different times for your two sequential searches.

3. A text file contains information stored as one string per line. A logical record consists of six lines containing the following information.

  last name
  first name
  department
  current salary
  date of last hire
  date of last pay increase

Write a new random-access file containing the same information. Test your program using the input file PAYROLL.DAT and write the output file NEWPAY.DAT.

The following practice programs consist of enhancements or modifications to the example database program in this chapter.

4. Write a Delete command procedure to delete a record from the inventory file. Write null strings and zero numeric values in the specified inventory record. This empty record in the inventory file will do no harm, although it wastes space. Remove the corresponding entry from the index file and adjust that file so there is no empty record. Do you need to sort the index file again?

5. Modify the Delete command procedure to allow a specified range of records to be deleted.

6. Write an Add command procedure to add additional records to the inventory file. You should prompt the user with the field name for each field. As minimum error checking, make sure that numeric fields are valid numbers, that the part number contains exactly six digits, and that the telephone number contains exactly 10 digits. Ask the user to confirm the accuracy of a complete record before writing it on the file. Add an appropriate entry to the index file for each new inventory record. After you have finished adding records, be sure to sort the index file.

7. Write a Create command procedure to create a new inventory file. After the inventory file and index file have been opened, call the Add subroutine to start adding new inventory records.

8. Modify the PrintRec procedure to allow optional printed reports on an attached printer. Add another parameter to specify whether the report should be displayed or printed. If you use networked printers, send your report to a text file for later printing.

9. Write a command procedure to display or print the records of all parts supplied by a specified vendor.

10. Write a command procedure to display or print all records of parts whose quantity is less than or equal to the reorder level. For each item, include the reorder quantity in a separate column. The resulting report might be used as the basis for ordering new stock.

11. Write a Purge command procedure to purge all empty records from the inventory file. Do you have to create and sort a new index file?

12. Modify the Edit command procedure to allow any specified field in a specified record to be changed. Your program must check to see if a field being changed is a key field and if so, resort its index file.

A

RESERVED WORDS

ABSOLUTE	ACCESS	ALIAS	AND	ANY	APPEND
AS	BASE	BEEP	BINARY	BLOAD	BSAVE
BYVAL	CALL	CASE	CDECL	CHAIN	CHDIR
CIRCLE	CLEAR	CLOSE	CLS	COLOR	COM
COMMON	CONST	DATA	DATE$	DECLARE	DEF
DEFDBL	DEFINT	DEFLNG	DEFSNG	DEFSTR	DIM
DO	DOUBLE	DRAW	ELSE	ELSEIF	END
ENVIRON	EQU	ERASE	ERROR	EXIT	FIELD
FILES	FOR	FUNCTION	GET	GOSUB	GOTO
IF	IMP	INPUT	INTEGER	IOCTL	IS
KEY	KILL	LET	LINE	LIST	LOCAL
LOCATE	LOCK	LONG	LPRINT	LSET	MID$
MKDIR	MOD	NAME	NEXT	NOT	OFF
ON	OPEN	OPTION	OR	OUT	OUTPUT

PAINT	PALETTE	PCOPY	PEN	PLAY	POKE
PRESET	PRINT	PSET	PUT	RANDOMIZE	READ
REDIM	RESET	RESTORE	RESUME	RETURN	RMDIR
RSET	RUN	SCREEN	SEEK	SEG	SELECT
SHARED	SHELL	SIGNAL	SLEEP	SOUND	STATIC
STEP	STOP	STRIG	STRING	SUB	SWAP
SYSTEM	THEN	TIME$	TIMER	TO	TROFF
TRON	TYPE	UEVENT	UNLOCK	UNTIL	USING
VIEW	WAIT	WEND	WHILE	WIDTH	WINDOW
WRITE	XOR				

B

THE ASCII SET
OF CHARACTERS

NAME		DEC	HEX	NAME		DEC	HEX
^@	(null)	0	0	^P		16	10
^A		1	1	^Q		17	11
^B		2	2	^R		18	12
^C	(break)	3	3	^S		19	13
^D		4	4	^T		20	14
^E		5	5	^U		21	15
^F		6	6	^V		22	16
^G	(bell)	7	7	^W		23	17
^H	(backspace)	8	8	^X		24	18
^I	(tab)	9	9	^Y		25	19
^J	(line feed)	10	A	^Z	(end of file)	26	1A
^K		11	B	^[	(escape)	27	1B
^L	(form feed)	12	C	^\		28	1C
^M	(return)	13	D	^]		29	1D
^N		14	E	^^		30	1E
^O		15	F	^_		31	1F

Note: The caret prefix (^) means a control character, for example, ^A means Ctrl-A.

NAME	DEC	HEX	NAME	DEC	HEX
sp (space)	32	20	@	64	40
!	33	21	A (uppercase)	65	41
"	34	22	B	66	42
#	35	23	C	67	43
$	36	24	D	68	44
%	37	25	E	69	45
&	38	26	F	70	46
' (acute accent)	39	27	G	71	47
(	40	28	H	72	48
)	41	29	I	73	49
*	42	2A	J	74	4A
+	43	2B	K	75	4B
, (comma)	44	2C	L	76	4C
− (minus)	45	2D	M	77	4D
. (period)	46	2E	N	78	4E
/ (forward slash)	47	2F	O	79	4F
0 (zero)	48	30	P	80	50
1	49	31	Q	81	51
2	50	32	R	82	52
3	51	33	S	83	53
4	52	34	T	84	54
5	53	35	U	85	55
6	54	36	V	86	56
7	55	37	W	87	57
8	56	38	X	88	58
9	57	39	Y	89	59
:	58	3A	Z	90	5A
;	59	3B	[(bracket)	91	5B
<	60	3C	\ (reverse slash)	92	5C
=	61	3D	] (bracket)	93	5D
>	62	3E	^ (caret)	94	5E
?	63	3F	_ (underline)	95	5F

NAME	DEC	HEX	NAME	DEC	HEX
' (grave accent)	96	60	p	112	70
a (lowercase)	97	61	q	113	71
b	98	62	r	114	72
c	99	63	s	115	73
d	100	64	t	116	74
e	101	65	u	117	75
f	102	66	v	118	76
g	103	67	w	119	77
h	104	68	x	120	78
i	105	69	y	121	79
j	106	6A	z	122	7A
k	107	6B	{ (brace)	123	7B
l	108	6C	| (vertical bar)	124	7C
m	109	6D	} (brace)	125	7D
n	110	6E	~ (tilde)	126	7E
o	111	6F	del (delete)	127	7F

C

QUICKBASIC COMMANDS

All but two of these commands are available in QuickBASIC 4.5. An asterisk (*) denotes a command that is also available in the QuickBASIC Interpreter. A plus sign (+) indicates a command or special command name available only in the QuickBASIC Interpreter.

FILE Command Menu

New Program (New +)

Erases the current program so that a new program can be written

Open Program (Open +)

Opens an existing program as the current program

Merge

Merges the specified file into the current program at the cursor position

Save

Saves the current program using its current file name

Save As *

Saves the current program using a name specified by the user

Create File

Creates a new file for a multiple-module program

Load File

Loads files from disk to build a multiple-module program

Unload File

Deletes an unwanted module from a multiple-module file

Print *

Prints the current program on an attached printer

DOS Shell

Exits temporarily to DOS so that system commands can be executed

Exit *

Exits the QuickBASIC system

EDIT Command Menu

Undo

Reverses the most recent edit action as long as the cursor is still on the edited line

Cut *

Deletes selected text from the current document and places it in the Clipboard

Copy *

Copies selected text from the current document and places it in the Clipboard

Paste *

Copies text from the Clipboard and pastes it into the current document at the cursor location

Clear

Deletes a block of selected text from the current document

New SUB *

Creates an outline for a new subroutine

New FUNCTION *

Creates an outline for a new function

VIEW Command Menu

SUBs *

Displays a list of all procedures in the current program

Next SUB

Displays another procedure in the active window

Split *

Divides the View window into two separate windows

Next Statement

Moves the cursor to the next executable program statement

Output Screen *

Toggles between the normal View window screen and the program output screen

Included File

Loads an include file into the View window for editing

Included Lines

Toggles the display of include file text between on and off

SEARCH Command Menu

Find *

Searches in the current program for a specified string of characters

Selected Text

Searches in the active window for a string that matches the selected string of one line or less

Repeat Last Find *

Repeats the most recent Find or Change command

Change *

Searches in the current program for a specified string of characters and allows the user to replace it with another string

Label

Searches in the current program for the specified line label

RUN Command Menu

Start *

Clears memory and starts execution of the current program at the first executable statement

Restart *

Clears memory and highlights the first executable statement of the current program

Continue *

Continues program execution after a running program has stopped

Modify COMMAND$

Tests a program's response to new command lines without switching from QuickBASIC to DOS

Make EXE File

Builds an executable version of a QuickBASIC program

Make Library

Combines a set of program modules into a Quick library file

Set Main Module

Selects the main module of a multiple-module program

DEBUG Command Menu

Add Watch

Adds a variable name to the Watch window at the top of the screen

Instant Watch

Displays the value of a selected variable or expression

Watch Point

Suspends program execution when a specified logical expression becomes true

Delete Watch

Removes a single item from the Watch window

Delete All Watch

Removes all items from the Watch window and closes that window

Trace On *

Toggles between regular program execution and slow motion execution

History On

Saves the last 20 lines of executed code for examination while program execution is suspended (see Toggle Breakpoint)

Toggle Breakpoint *

Sets a breakpoint at the current line

Clear All Breakpoints *

Removes all breakpoints from the program

Break on Errors

Stops a program at the first statement in the most recently executed error-handling routine

Set Next Statement *

Changes the program executing sequence so that the next statement executed is the one the cursor is on

Step +

Executes the next program statement and then stops execution

Procedure Step +

Moves through program execution one step at a time, tracing around any procedure calls (not executing any procedure statements)

CALLS Command Menu

Shows the last eight procedure calls executed prior to an untrapped error, a breakpoint or watchpoint, or a user-initiated break (pressing the interrupt key)

OPTIONS Command Menu

Display *

Controls display unit options such as screen colors, scroll bars, and spaces in a tab

Set Paths (Help Path +)

Specifies the default DOS paths for executable, include, library, and help files

Right Mouse

Changes the effect of single-clicking the right mouse button

Syntax Checking *

Toggles checking for program syntax errors between on and off

Easy Menus

Toggles between full menus and easy (simplified) menus

HELP Command Menu

Index *

Displays an alphabetical list of help topics

Contents *

Displays an outline of QuickBASIC's on-line help capabilities

Topic: *

Displays information on a selected topic identified by the cursor's current position

Help on Help

Describes how to get help on an item displayed on the screen

D

QUICKBASIC PROGRAM STATEMENTS

BEEP

Sounds the speaker

BLOAD

Reads a memory-image file, created by BSAVE, into memory

BSAVE

Writes the contents of an area of memory on an output file or device

CALL

Transfers control to a QuickBASIC SUB procedure

CALL ABSOLUTE

Transfers control to a machine-language procedure

CALL INTERRUPT

Allows BASIC programs to perform DOS system calls

CHAIN

Transfers control from the current program to another program

CHDIR

Changes the current default directory for the specified drive

CIRCLE

Draws an ellipse or circle with a specified center and radius

CLEAR

Reinitializes all program variables, closes all files, and sets the stack size

CLOSE

Closes a file or device for I/O so that it is no longer associated with a file number

CLS

Clears the screen

COLOR

Selects the display unit foreground and background colors

COM

Enables, disables, or inhibits event trapping of communications activity on a specified port

COMMON

Defines global variables for sharing between modules or for chaining to another program

CONST

Declares symbolic constants for use in place of numeric or string values

DATA

Creates a file of values in memory that can be read by a program's READ statements

DATE$

Sets the current date

DECLARE

Declares references to BASIC procedures and invokes argument type checking

DEF FN

Defines and names a function (use the FUNCTION procedure instead)

DEF SEG

Sets the current segment address for a subsequent function or statement that addresses memory

DEFDBL, DEFINT, DEFLNG, DEFSNG, DEFSTR

Sets the default data type for variables and FUNCTION procedures

DIM

Declares a variable and allocates storage space

DO...LOOP

Repeats a block of statements while a condition is true or until a condition becomes true

DRAW

Draws an object defined by a string expression

END

Ends a BASIC program, procedure or block

ENVIRON

Modifies a parameter in the DOS environment-string table

ERASE

Reinitializes the elements of static arrays; deallocates dynamic arrays

ERROR

Simulates the occurrence of a BASIC error or allows the user to define error codes

EXIT

Exits a procedure or a program loop

FIELD

Allocates space for variables in a random-access file buffer

FILES

Displays the names of files in a specified directory

FOR...NEXT

Repeats a block of statements a specified number of times

FUNCTION

Declares the name and parameters of a FUNCTION procedure

GET

Reads information from a disk file into a random-access buffer or variable

GOSUB...RETURN

Branches to, and returns from, a subroutine (use the SUB procedure instead)

GOTO

Branches unconditionally to the specified line (do not use unless absolutely necessary)

IF...THEN...ELSE

Allows conditional execution of one or more statements, based on the value of a logical expression

INPUT

Reads input from the keyboard and assigns it to variables

INPUT #

Reads data items from a sequential file and assigns them to variables

IOCTL

Transmits a control data string to a device driver

KEY

Assigns soft-key string values to the function keys

KILL

Deletes a file from disk

LET

Assigns the value of an expression to a variable

LINE

Draws a line or box on the screen

LINE INPUT

Accepts an entire line of input from the keyboard and assigns it to a string variable

LINE INPUT

Reads an entire line from a sequential file and assigns it to a string variable

LOCATE

Moves the cursor to the specified position

LOCK...UNLOCK

Controls access by other processes to all or part of an opened file

LPRINT

Prints data on an attached printer

LPRINT USING

Prints data on an attached printer using a specified format string

LSET

Moves data from memory to a random-access file buffer

MID$

Replaces a portion of a string variable with another string

MKDIR

Creates a new directory

NAME

Changes the name of a disk file or directory

ON ERROR

Enables error handling and specifies the first line of the error-handling routine

ON...GOSUB, ON...GOTO

Branches to one of several specified lines (do not use unless absolutely necessary)

OPEN

Opens a file or device for I/O and associates it with a specified file number

OPTION BASE

Declares the default lower bound for array subscripts

OUT

Sends a byte to a machine I/O port

PAINT

Fills a graphics area with the color or pattern specified

PALETTE, PALETTE USING

Changes one or more of the colors in the palette

PCOPY

Copies one screen page to another

PEN ON, PEN OFF, PEN STOP

Enables, disables, or suspends lightpen-event trapping

PLAY

Plays music as specified by a string

POKE

Writes a byte into a specified memory location

PRESET

Draws a specified point on the screen

PRINT

Displays data on the screen

PRINT #

Writes data on a sequential file

PRINT USING

Displays data using a specified format string

PRINT # USING

Writes data on a sequential file using a specified format

PSET

Draws a point on the screen

PUT

Writes from a variable or a random-access buffer to a file

RANDOMIZE

Initializes the random-number generator

READ

Reads values from DATA statements and assigns the values to variables

REDIM

Changes the space allocated to a dynamic array

RESET

Closes all disk files

RESTORE

Moves the data pointer to the beginning of the specified DATA statement

RESUME

Continues program execution after an error-trapping routine has been invoked

RMDIR

Removes an existing directory

RSET

Moves data from memory to a random-access file buffer

RUN

Executes the program currently in memory or executes a specified program

SCREEN

Sets the specifications for the display screen

SEEK

Sets the position of the file pointer for the next read or write

SELECT CASE

Executes one of several statement blocks depending on the value of an expression

SHARED

Gives a procedure access to variables declared at the module level without passing them as parameters

SHELL

Exits the BASIC program to execute a DOS command or another program

SLEEP

Suspends execution of a running program for the specified time

SOUND

Generates sound through the speaker

STATIC

Makes simple variables or arrays local to a procedure and preserves values between calls

STOP

Terminates the currently-running program

STRIG...ON, STRIG...OFF, STRIG...STOP

Enables, disables, or inhibits trapping of joystick activity

SUB

Declares the name and parameters of a SUB procedure

SWAP

Exchanges the values of two variables

SYSTEM

Closes all open files and returns control to the operating system

TIME$

Sets the time

TIMER ON, TIMER OFF, TIMER STOP

Enables, disables, or inhibits timer event trapping

TROFF

Turns off program tracing (not needed if debugger is used)

TRON

Turns on program tracing (not needed if debugger is used)

TYPE

Defines a data type containing one or more variables that may be of different types

UEVENT ON, UEVENT OFF, UEVENT STOP

Enables, disables, or suspends trapping for a user-defined event

UNLOCK

See the LOCK statement

VIEW

Defines screen limits for graphics output

VIEW PRINT

Sets the boundaries of the screen text viewport

WAIT

Suspends program execution while monitoring the status of an input port

WHILE...WEND

Executes a block of statements in a loop as long as a given condition is true (use the DO...LOOP structure instead of the WHILE...WEND structure)

WIDTH

Changes the number of columns and lines displayed on the screen or written on a file

WINDOW

Defines the dimensions of the current viewport

WRITE

Writes data on a sequential file

E

QUICKBASIC STANDARD FUNCTIONS

In the following definitions, Nmbr denotes a numeric expression and Strg denotes a string expression.

ABS(Nmbr)

Returns the absolute value of Nmbr

ASC(Strg)

Returns the numeric ASCII code for the first character in Strg

ATN(Nmbr)

Returns the arctangent of Nmbr (the angle whose tangent is equal to Nmbr)

CDBL(Nmbr)

Converts Nmbr to a double-precision value

CHR$(Nmbr)

Returns a one-character string whose ASCII code is Nmbr

CINT(Nmbr)

Returns an integer by rounding the fractional part of Nmbr

CLNG(Nmbr)

Returns a long integer by rounding the fractional part of Nmbr

COMMAND$

Returns a string containing the command line used to invoke the program

COS(Nmbr)

Returns the cosine of an angle Nmbr given in radians

CSNG(Nmbr)

Converts Nmbr to a single-precision value

CSRLIN

Returns the current line position (row number) of the cursor

CVI(Strg), CVS(Strg), CVL(Strg), CVD(Strg)

Converts string containing numeric values to an integer, single-precision, long integer, or double-precision number

CVSMBF(Strg), CVDMBF(Strg)

Converts string containing Microsoft binary format number to a standard IEEE-format single or double-precision number

DATE$

Returns a string containing the current date

ENVIRON$(N)

Returns the Nth environment string from the MS-DOS environment-string table

EOF(FileNmbr)

Returns a value of true if the end of the file denoted by FileNmbr has been reached; otherwise returns a value of false

ERDEV, ERDEV$

Returns device-specific status information, error code and name of device creating the error after an error occurs

ERR, ERL

Returns error code and error line number after an error occurs

EXP(Nmbr)

Returns the exponential function of Nmbr

FILEATTR(FileNmbr, Attribute)

Returns information about the mode of an opened file denoted by FileNmbr

FIX(Nmbr)

Returns the truncated integer part of Nmbr

FRE(Nmbr or Strg)

Returns the amount of available memory

FREEFILE

Returns the next free BASIC file number

HEX$(Nmbr)

Returns a string representing the hexadecimal value of the decimal number Nmbr

INKEY$

Returns a one or two-byte string representing a character key that is pressed, or a null string if no key is pressed

INP(PortNmbr)

Returns the byte read from the I/O port denoted by PortNmbr

INPUT$(N, FileNmbr)

Returns a string of N characters read from the file denoted by FileNmbr

INSTR(N, Strg1, Strg2)

Returns the character position of the occurrence of Strg2 in Strg1, starting at character position N

INT(Nmbr)

Returns the largest integer less than or equal to Nmbr

IOCTL$(FileNmbr)

Returns a control data string from a device driver

LBOUND(Array, Dimension)

Returns the lower bound value of the specified Dimension of Array

LCASE$(Strg)

Returns a copy of Strg with all lowercase letters

LEFT$(Strg, N)

Returns a string consisting of the leftmost N characters of Strg

LEN(Strg)

Returns the number of characters in Strg

LOC(FileNmbr)

Returns the current position of the file pointer in file FileNmbr

LOF(FileNmbr)

Returns the length in bytes of file FileNmbr

LOG(Nmbr)

Returns the natural logarithm of Nmbr

LPOS(PrinterNmbr)

Returns the current position of the printer head denoted by PrinterNmbr

LTRIM$(Strg)

Returns a copy of Strg with leading spaces removed

MID$(Strg, P, N)

Returns a substring of Strg, starting at position P and of length N

MKI$(Nmbr), MKS$(Nmbr), MKL$(Nmbr), MKD$(Nmbr)

Converts an integer, single-precision, long integer, or double-precision number to a fixed-length string

MKSMBF$(Nmbr), MKDMBF$(Nmbr)

Converts an IEEE-format single or double-precision number to a string containing a Microsoft binary-format number

OCT$(Nmbr)

Returns a string representing the octal value of Nmbr

PEEK(Address)

Returns the byte stored at the specified memory address

PEN(N)

Returns lightpen coordinate values as specified by code N

PLAY(N)

Returns the number of notes in the background-music queue; N is a dummy argument

PMAP(Expression, Function)

Maps view-coordinate expressions to physical locations, or vice versa

POINT(X, Y)

Returns the color number of the pixel at coordinates X,Y

POS(0)

Returns the current horizontal (column) position of the cursor

RIGHT$(Strg, N)

Returns a string consisting of the rightmost N characters of Strg

RND(N)

Returns a single-precision number between 0 and 1, with the value of N determining the sequence

RTRIM$(Strg)

Returns a copy of Strg with trailing spaces removed

SADD(Strg)

Returns the memory address of Strg

SCREEN(Row, Column, ColorFlag)

Returns atributes of character at screen location Row, Column, as specified by ColorFlag

SEEK(FileNmbr)

Returns the current position of the file pointer in file FileNmbr

SETMEM(Nmbr)

Changes the amount of memory used by the far heap

SGN(Nmbr)

Returns value denoting the algebraic sign of Nmbr

SIN(Nmbr)

Returns the sine of an angle Nmbr given in radians

SPACE$(N)

Returns a string of N spaces

SPC(N)

Skips N spaces in a PRINT statement

SQR(Nmbr)

Returns the square root of Nmbr

STICK(N)

Returns the X and Y coordinates of the joystick, as specified by N

STR$(Nmbr)

Returns a string representation of the value of Nmbr

STRIG(N)

Returns the status of a specified joystick trigger

STRING$(N, Code)

Returns a string of N identical characters whose ASCII code is Code

TAB(Column)

Moves to specified column position in a PRINT statement

TAN(Nmbr)

Returns the tangent of an angle Nmbr given in radians

TIME$

Returns a string containing the current time

TIMER

Returns the number of seconds elapsed since midnight

UBOUND(Array, Dimension)

Returns the upper bound value of the specified Dimension of Array

UCASE$(Strg)

Returns a copy of Strg with all uppercase letters

VAL(Strg)

Returns the numeric value of Strg

VARPTR(Variable), VARSEG(Variable)

Returns the offset and segment parts of the memory address of Variable

VARPTR$(Variable)

Returns a string representation of a variable's address for use in DRAW and PLAY statements

F

QUICKBASIC
RUN-TIME ERROR CODES

CODE	DESCRIPTION	CODE	DESCRIPTION
2	Syntax error	25	Device fault
3	RETURN without GOSUB	27	Out of paper
4	Out of data	39	CASE ELSE expected
5	Illegal function call	40	Variable required
6	Overflow	50	FIELD overflow
7	Out of memory	51	Internal error
9	Subscript out of range	52	Bad file name or number
10	Duplicate definition	53	File not found
11	Division by zero	54	Bad file mode
13	Type mismatch	55	File already open
14	Out of string space	56	FIELD statement active
16	String formula too complex	57	Device I/O error
19	No RESUME	58	File already exists
20	RESUME without error	59	Bad record length
24	Device timeout		

CODE	DESCRIPTION	CODE	DESCRIPTION
61	Disk full	70	Permission denied
62	Input past end of file	71	Disk-not ready
63	Bad record number	72	Disk-media error
64	Bad file name	73	Advanced feature unavailable
67	Too many files	74	Rename across disks
68	Device unavailable	75	Path/file access error
69	Comm. buffer overflow	76	Path not found

G

INITIAL SETTINGS FOR QUICKBASIC

The QuickBASIC compiler system must be set to the appropriate initial conditions.

Adjustment for Different Monitors

Fig. G.1 shows how to adjust screen output for different monitors.

MONITOR DISPLAY	COMMAND
16 colors (CGA, EGA, or VGA)	QB
4-color monochrome (MDA)	QB
8 colors (CGA, EGA or VGA)	QB /NOHI
4-color black-and-white composite (CGA, EGA, or VGA)	QB /B
2-color black-and-white composite (CGA, EGA, or VGA)	QB /B /NOHI

Figure G.1   Command parameters for various screen displays.

When you type the initial command QB at the DOS level, QuickBASIC determines what kind of monitor you are using and adjusts screen output accordingly. It assumes that your monitor can display high intensity. If this is not the case, or if you are operating your monitor in black-and-white mode, you must add one or more parameters to the QB command. The parameter /NOHI means that the monitor has no highlighting capability. The parameter /B designates a black-and-white monitor.

Laptop computers usually use liquid crystal or plasma displays, and these displays should be treated as 2-color black-and-white composite displays.

Selecting the Initial System State

The Options command in the main menu allows you to customize certain parts of the QuickBASIC system. Selecting this command displays the Options menu. Beginning programmers are urged to set the Full Menus command in this menu to off. Note that the Full Menus command is a toggle command. When you select it with the up and down arrow keys and press Enter, it switches between on and off. In the off condition, the displayed menus are called Easy Menus, displaying a subset of the full or complete menus.

The Display command in the Options menu allows you to make limited changes in the appearance of your screen display. If you have a color monitor, you can change both foreground and background colors. You can change the Tab setting, and we recommend a setting of 3 to 5, rather than the default setting of 8. The Tab key is used to indent program lines, and if the indentation is too large, program lines tend to be pushed off the right edge of the screen.

You can also specify whether or not you want scroll bars displayed. Scroll bars are used with a mouse for scrolling a program. If you are using a mouse with QuickBASIC, you will probably want to have scroll bars. If you are not using a mouse, scroll bars are of no use and should be eliminated. An X in the Scroll Bars check box means that you have chosen to display scroll bars.

When you have finished customizing your display, select the OK command button and press the Enter key. Until you make other choices, the selections you have made will be in effect each time you enter the QuickBASIC system.

H

HOW TO USE THE
EXAMPLE PROGRAM DISK

We suggest you use the DISKCOPY command of DOS to make a working copy of the example program disk.

Instructions for Reading Program Files

Example programs are stored in separate directories on the example program disk. For instance, programs for Chapter 2 are stored in a directory named CH02.

To examine these programs on a computer with two floppy disk drives, put the DOS disk in drive A and the example program disk in drive B. Change the current disk drive to B by entering the B: command. At the B> prompt, change directories by entering

```
CD \CH02
```

where the command CD means to change the current directory. If you now enter the command DIR, the names of all files in directory CH02 will be displayed. For example, the file containing Example Program 2-1 is named EX02-01.BAS.

We recommend that you start QuickBASIC from the directory containing the programs and files you wish to use. For example, to access program file EX02-01.BAS in directory \CH02 on the disk in drive B, use the appropriate DOS commands to make that the current directory. Assuming that the QuickBASIC system is in the root directory of disk A, enter the command A:\QB (or A:\QBI for the interpreter) to start. You can then select the Open command from the File command menu, and enter or select the file name EX02-01.BAS to open the desired program.

Instructions for Reading Test Files

The practice programs in this book often use test files, especially for reading information. These files are stored on the example program disk in the same directories as the example programs. For example, the test files for practice programs in Chapter 5 are stored in the directory named CH05.

If you start QuickBASIC from the directory containing these files, as we recommend, then that is your current directory. If not, you should make it your current directory using the appropriate QuickBASIC commands. For example, if the directory containing the test file FIRST.TXT is B:\CH05 and it is your current directory, you can use the statement

```
OPEN "FIRST.TXT" FOR INPUT AS #1
```

in your program to access the file. This method allows you to specify a test file by a simple file name instead of the complete path name.

INDEX

PROGRAMS

Chapter 4

FIGURES